ANDRÉ GIDE

THE MAKERS OF MODERN LITERATURE SERIES

James Joyce by Harry Levin

Virginia Woolf by David Daiches

E. M. Forster by Lionel Trilling

García Lorca by Edwin Honig

Nikolai Gogol by Vladimir Nabokov

G. M. Hopkins by The Kenyon Critics

Edwin Arlington Robinson by Yvor Winters

André Gide by Van Meter Ames

Thomas Wolfe by H. J. Muller

Bernard Shaw by Eric Bentley

Oscar Wilde by Edouard Roditi

Robert Louis Stevenson by David Daiches

Others in preparation

ANDRÉ GIDE

André Gide

BY VAN METER AMES

THE MAKERS OF MODERN LITERATURE

New Directions Books · Norfolk, Connecticut

KRAUS REPRINT CO.
New York
1971

L.C. 47-11811*

Reprinted with the permission of the original publisher
KRAUS REPRINT CO.
A U.S. Division of Kraus-Thomson Organization Limited

Printed in U.S.A.

New Directions Books are published by James Laughlin

NEW YORK OFFICE—500 FIFTH AVENUE—18

TO CALOUB

NOTE

Most of the references to Gide's works are to his *Oeuvres Complètes* in 15 volumes, edited by Louis Martin-Chauffier and published by the *Nouvelle Revue Française*, Paris, 1932–1939: designated as *OC*. In the case of books not included in this collection, or consulted because more accessible, the edition used is indicated. Gide's *Journal, 1889–1939*, as published in Paris in 1939 by the Bibliothèque de la Pléiade for the N.R.F., is referred to as Pléiade ed. of *Journal*. Where simply the date of a *Journal* entry is given, the Pléiade edition was used as reprinted by Americ-Edit. at Rio de Janeiro in 1943. By permission of the publishers a dozen passages have been quoted from *Pages de Journal, 1939–1942*, edited by Jacques Schiffrin for Pantheon Books, Inc., New York, 1944. All the translating from Gide is my own.

V. M. A.

CONTENTS

1. MARRIED TO A SAINT

THE CAREER OF ANDRÉ GIDE EPITOMIZES THE TENSIONS OF our time: between tradition and science, culture and progress, bourgeoisie and proletariat, past and future. He is worth reading for his masterful expression, imagination, subtlety, erudition, and unremitting search for values. He is also worth studying because some of his weaknesses illuminate the modern dilemma as strength alone might not do. His vacillation records the impulses and reluctances of the intellectual; his ceaseless exploration of alternatives leaves no spiritual niche unpried. The crux of his writing is the conflict between faith in men's capacity to build a better life through science, and fear of letting go the consolations that once compensated for inability to change the world. He has shown the promise of guiding life by a conception of scientific method that cannot be consistent without becoming democratic.

Perhaps no way to this consummation will be found which does not lead through the kind of introspective data he presents. For while the hope is general it has the pressure of private concern. Gide reveals how momentously unsettled the whole human situation is. He shows what there is to win, how far from won; what there is to lose, and how much may already be lost. Such a revelation might seem superfluous. If one needed to be reminded, there is all that is being said about political, economic and social problems. But there are insights which perhaps can be well presented only by a man with no professional interest or authority beyond that of really reading literature and contributing to it an altogether honest sense of the modern predicament, felt to be his own.

Gide was born in Paris on the twenty-second of November, 1869, to a heritage so divided that he could ascribe to it his habit of entertaining the other side of any question. His father's family were Huguenots in the south of France. Most of his mother's people in Normandy were Catholics, but she and her mother were not, and he was brought up in austere Protestantism, although later much attracted by the other faith. His father, dying when the boy was eleven, had little direct influence upon him; but left a library to evoke the studious example of a law professor, which was reinforced by contact with André's famous uncle, Charles Gide the economist. The father had introduced the son to the *Arabian Nights* he loved, as a boy, next to the Bible. The Oriental inventiveness and imagery of both were his delight, and he was no less susceptible to the indulgence of sense in one than to the sense of sin in the other, as he found elaborated in print the conflict that obsessed him almost from infancy. His passion for these two books was prophetic of his long struggle to re-

2

think the Hebraic-Christian tradition and accommodate it to the sunny naturalism confirmed in him by the Arabs of North Africa. This accommodation was not merely a revolt from the generous but over-anxious mother and the often-present punctilious Aunt Claire who dominated her and restricted his childhood. He pursued the effort of these tense women to select and filter out what was worth while from all the waste, although he was critical where they were conventional: trying to assess value in the light of learning and experience.

He found schools unbearable, and the private tutors to whom his mother often turned were, with a few exceptions, not very satisfactory. He became so accomplished at the piano that his teacher foresaw a career on the concert stage. Madame Gide decided against it without letting her son know that such a decision had been made, until it seemed too late for him to follow the rejected path. But he kept up his music on the side throughout his life, with such loving diligence that the playing of a virtuoso would usually annoy him as showy. His mastery of the piano is established indirectly for the most part, since he would stop playing when he realized he was not alone. But even if he had never been overheard, there is evidence of his achievement in his *Notes Sur Chopin;* and in all that he said in the *Journal* about the delicate difficulty and joy of doing justice to his favorite composer, in many hours stolen from literature (cf. *Journal,* 8 Feb., 1934). Meanwhile his mother's circumstances were such that there was no question of how he would make a living. He said in his autobiography that if it had been necessary for him to support himself he would have become a piano

3

ANDRÉ GIDE

teacher (*Si le Grain ne Meurt,* Part One, Ch. IX). He
retained for his music master, Marc de la Nux, a veneration that he had for only one person later: Mallarmé.

Perhaps his most crucial instruction was received early
from Anna Shackleton of Scotland, who had long been
with his mother, almost a sister. Anna was dependent
economically, at a time when this made it hard for a lone
and gentle woman to get married or make her way in
the world. But she generously gave her life to the family
that was "lent" to her, adopting the little André as she
had his older cousins; joining in his father's laughter, and
standing by to cheer the severe widowed mother. Anna
was a blithe dispenser of joy amid the encircling gloom.
She loved to translate literature from various languages
into French; she sketched and did water colors. She was
also passionately fond of botany, so that the child had no
feeling of alienation between art and science as they
emanated from her warm person. For him there was never
a conflict here. Nor was there actually much tension for
him between his maternal northerners and paternal south-
erners, but a picturesque contrast; except as he must have
felt a lack of harmony between his humorous father and
anxious mother. Even the debate he was repeatedly
tempted to renew between Protestantism and Catholicism,
with their practically identical theologies, was not vital
compared with the choice he had to make between Anna
and his cousin Emmanuèle, his muse and his angel: one
guiding him toward a trinity of science, art and sense; the
other guarding him for God.

Anna died while he was still young, and he married
Emmanuèle. But their rivalry went on. It goes on through

4

all Gide's work. How it comes out is the secret shared with those who read him through. If this were only his secret, curiosity about it might seem idle and gossipy. But since many a reader is sure to have the same problem, it is instructive to see Gide at grips with it; more so than to be told simply which woman won, if one did. Much as men influenced him, the adage holds: *Cherchez la femme.*

One must find out who she was, what she was, and guess at his relation with her. At first it may not appear very substantial, may seem rarefied to little more than idealizing desire, as in the blurred love of Joyce's Stephen as a young man wanting to write more than to live. "I write because I have to write, and that is all," says Gide's image of his youthful self, André Walter, who in Gide's maiden work *Les Cahiers d'André Walter* (published when he was twenty-two) keeps a journal which records the effort to write a novel about a youngster who is a further dim reflection of both André author and André narrator (*Oeuvres Complètes,* hereafter designated as *OC* I, 31). Folded in this involution there is the experience of adolescence, somewhat as it must be inside anyone whose self-consciousness is heightened by a Puritan training taken seriously. A youth is growing here and the pains of it are real. There is impetus toward what is suddenly felt to be in store, and nostalgia for things past. Gide like Walter was eased from childhood by the beloved cousin. In the focus of aspiration she was the ideal, unattainable ahead, while holding in her heart the past of author and hero. Each André wanted to live in the spirit, attached to images fortuitous for all but his soul-mate. "Oh! you remember, Emmanuèle! you remember, and

5

you love me. A thing is not quite dead which is not yet forgotten; you cannot forget our love" (*Cahiers d'André Walter, OC* I, 97).

Yet neither André was disembodied, and spring made it hard to live in fancy. Deliverance could never be final as long as the flesh was solid. Purity was beautiful, its splendor alluring. "But if I burn completely and if the vision consumes me?" André Walter wondered (*OC* I, 100). Gide himself did not burn too much to ask how it would be if he burned away humanity to holiness. Projecting André Walter along an "if" course, Gide heard him asserting that intuitive knowledge alone was necessary, that reason was useless and science dangerous in exalting reason. Eager for spirituality, Walter shunned science, which he regarded in nineteenth-century fashion as an abstract scheme inimical to inner worth. On paper Emmanuèle was winning.

For the young Gide, however, science did not reduce the world to dull categories. He knew botany was not antithetical to value, for his intimacy with plants was no less information than love. He speaks in his autobiography of Anna's reverence for plant-names and their consequent aureole for him; of the central place held in the house by her collection, his pleasure in helping with it and in beginning one of his own (*Si le Grain ne Meurt,* Part One, Ch. I). Uniqueness and particularity were cherished here as much as in any heart or heaven. No scalpel could have lifted the boy's emotion from what he saw under the magnifying glass, or the man's pang of remembering Anna from the singularities of form and label associated with her. But field trips and work in the garden do not figure

6

in the notebooks of André Walter whose fictive life was reduced to contemplation in the grip of concupiscence. The André lost to Anna was not the author.

Walter hesitated even to read, except the Bible "and some sage classics," adding Schopenhauer to help escape reality. Walter's aim was "to love with the soul alone a soul who loves you the same, so that the two, having become alike by a slow education, should know each other to the point of identity. For talking together they will need at the outset only a tacit language; the body will bother them, having other desires" (*OC* I, 124). Contrary to this pure and pious character, at the time of projecting him, Gide confessed in his *Journal:* "My thought becomes voluptuously impious and pagan," and he felt the need of exaggerating this tendency by reading, to wring out his religion, Stendhal, the *Encyclopedia,* Swift, Condillac, vigorous authors, "especially the male ones: Aristophanes, Shakespeare, Rabelais. . . . I have enough tears in my soul to irrigate thirty books." Then on the next page he became like Walter again, saying: ". . . and so much the better. Decidedly nothing is as beautiful as the nobility of the soul; no, not beautiful; it should only be called sublime" (*OC* I, 476–477). Traveling in Belgium he was sad to be robbing Emmanuèle of what he saw without her, and would sleep each afternoon to dream of her a little. Feeling close to her he prayed, as if with her: "Lord, I come back to Thee, for I believe that all is vanity aside from knowing Thee. Guide me in Thy paths of light. . . One is not uneasy except far from God; only in Him can one rest, for He is that which does not change" (*OC* I, 485).

7

Thus Gide had spells when he did not want to acknowledge change, or when he wanted to be steadfast in spite
of it, as when he wrote in the *Journal:* "I thank Thee,
Lord, that the only influence of a woman on my ravished
soul, which craves no other influence than that of Em.,
has always guided my soul toward the highest truths. . . .
It is a joyful thought that, if she came back to me, I'd
have nothing to hide from her" (*OC* I, 488–489). But
while this was true, it was to be less true as he became
less dependent upon the medicine of Em.'s influence and
the truths that were highest for her. "Troubles of the
flesh and anxieties of the soul may last a while yet, but
they are interesting only as long as one thinks these things
are important," he said when he was twenty-three (*OC* I,
492–493). André Walter's only way out was to die of
brain-fever; André Gide could objectify what troubled
him, enough to have some respite, and take a new
tack.

Whereas young André Walter fervently exclaimed: "O
Lord! I am pure! I am pure! I am pure!" (*OC* I, 133) the
surviving André wrote: "And now my prayer (for it is
still a prayer): O my God, let this too tight morality
burst that I may live, oh! fully; and give me the strength
to do it, oh! without fear, and without always thinking I
am going to sin. . . . Now it takes as much effort for me
to let go as holding back used to" (*OC* I, 500–501). In
the entry for October, 1893, the momentous month in
which he embarked for North Africa, are these words:
"Christianity, above all consoles; but there are naturally
happy spirits who have no need of being consoled. And
so Christianity must begin by making these unhappy,

having otherwise no hold on them" (*OC* I, 516). He left his Bible at home.

He left Emmanuèle, who was not ready to marry him after the publication of his *Cahiers* as he had hoped; and he sought to break from puritanism which had been their bond. If he continued to feel indefinitely engaged to her, apparently he thought the ghost of Walter in him would be enough for her, now that the living André wanted to wander. Wandering from her, leaving her with only a wraith of former devotion and repudiating puritanism, may be interpreted less as forsaking her than as reaction to feeling forsaken by her: a feeling that spread to doubt about the religion and morality she represented. Having sought throughout a prolonged adolescence to subject flesh to spirit, according to what he had accepted as Christian morality, he doubted now whether God required this, and decided to find a harmony. Still it was in line with Christian dualism that he came to think pleasure would be more pure and love more perfect if kept apart (cf. *Si le Grain ne Meurt*, Part Two, Ch. I). At any rate this idea, which he later thought the devil must have inspired, enabled him to go on loving his cousin in her fashion while setting forth, a virgin with a virgin friend Paul Laurens, to try carnal delights. They hoped to find a wholesome classical ideal.

The irony of this hope is clear. Edouard Martinet argues quite plausibly, from *Les Cahiers d'André Walter,* from the fact that passages of Gide's *Journal* were inserted into it as well as parts of other early works—and finally, from what is said in *Si le Grain ne Meurt*—that he wanted to love a woman not only with all his heart but with his body, in the most complete fashion. The wholeness of his devotion, and puritanism, had kept him from touching any woman but the one he loved, and he had counted on marrying her after publishing his first book. Then his fierce struggle with the flesh would be resolved. The blow of being turned down at this point was catastrophic for him. Emmanuèle thought she ought not to get married ahead of her sisters, and she may have had a complex about marriage if, as Martinet states, she had been shocked by her mother's marital infidelity, as Alissa was by that of her mother in *La Porte Étroite*. Gide waited two years in vain, and he was almost twenty-four when he went to Africa. Only then did he think he discovered that he was homosexual, or declare that love and pleasure should be kept apart. Love for him still meant woman, and only one woman. The pleasure he found in desperation could not have anything to do with his love for her, especially after that love had to be sublimated. The "classical" ideal he sought was only a substitute for the integral happiness put off so indefinitely that he began to believe its two halves did not belong together (cf. Martinet, *André Gide: L'Amour et la Divinité*, 120–124).

He inauspiciously caught cold in Toulon before sailing with Paul Laurens. They landed at Tunis and started on a roundabout carriage trip to Biskra. At Zaghouan, after an exhausting day, they spent a miserable night in an army camp. They reached Enfida the next day, then Kairouan. At Sousse a doctor found Gide gravely ill; they went back after a week to Tunis and took the train prosaically to Biskra. But one day at Sousse, when left alone, he had climbed a dune and been surprised by the advances of an Arab boy. Most surprising to Gide was the discovery in himself of what seemed to be a natural proclivity. At sunny Biskra in Algeria he fought tuberculosis and watched the children playing on terraces about the apartment, or in the public garden. Thinking he should not give in to his bent, he endeavored through sympathy with Paul's desires to normalize his own. They shared the favors of Mériem, complaisant daughter of the Oulad Naïl, who came to their rooms alternately. Gide found his relation with her purely hygienic. Health returned but the cure was interrupted by the coming of his mother who thought she ought to relieve Paul of responsibility. One dawn she happened to glance out the window and see Mériem leaving Paul's door. That the girl would also come to André he hastened to tell his mother, lest she think worse of his friend than of him. She went home.

In Paris in the summer of 1894 he suffocated in the salons, and could not be happy until on his way back to the sun. His mother commenced to approve of his marrying Emmanuèle as a way of disciplining his course. In Algiers in January he was dismayed not to find spring. Blidah also was dismal. Ready to leave, regretting Biskra, he saw chalked among arriving guests the name of Oscar Wilde. The man had reached the point where his company was compromising; Gide hesitated between escaping and shame at avoiding an old friend. The devil had intervened, as it would seem in retrospect, though the youth did not realize it. This was at the beginning of Gide's long belief that nothing unhappy could happen to him, and what was suddenly to make him doubt it he cherished as one of the most important events of his life. He went with

11

his obese crony to be shown the night spots of Algiers, and was left with Mohammed the little flute-player. "Ever since, each time I have sought pleasure, it was to run after the memory of that night," Gide wrote a quarter of a century later (*Si le Grain ne Meurt,* Part Two, Ch. II). He had struggled against the revelation of Sousse and was getting desperate. Now his joy was without reservation or remorse, though without love.

At Biskra again, he lingered with his servant Athman of the previous year, and broached the idea of bringing him to Paris. The opposition of his mother and family was successfully backed by her faithful maid's threat to leave if the sashed and turbaned infidel appeared. The mother, unable to erase the muffled image of Mériem, feared a liaison and urged the son to return. He might have broken off an affair but he could not give up himself, now that he had discovered "the tables of my new law." For it was not enough to reject the old code. He must make clear that in his apparent madness was a method right and reasonable. Because he sincerely tried, over many years, to establish this, his African experience proved important. If he had simply sowed his wild oats it would have had no more to do with Anna than with Emmanuèle. The exciting thing was that it had as much to do with science and religion as with sex.

He maintained he had not become an immoralist, had not acquiesced in a facile hedonism. He was vindicating experimental living against submission to authority, tradition, taboos. He was daring, like Descartes, to doubt all he had taken for granted, and setting out to accept only what he found indubitable. Descartes had the assurance

12

that God would not let clear and distinct ideas be deceptive. Thus the devil was disarmed. Gide became sure that
God would not let natural pleasure be wrong, and the
devil was given his due. He was more real than people
thought, while the good depended much upon what they
thought was bad. Descartes trusted ideas and reason. Gide
put faith more in feeling and the senses. Yet both writers
were methodical in relying on man's ability to find his
way, no matter how it deviated from the past; while God
did not interfere, either for the one who was a founder of
scientific method or for him who used it in questions
Descartes would have considered beyond its range.

When Gide was in danger he was saved by the hand
of Anna. That is to say, he was not left without moral
orientation when he gave up orthodox Christianity, because through appreciation of science he would arrive
at a humanistic morality and religion. He could not formulate this position until later, but he was on the way to it
in Africa in 1895. It may be fanciful to see the hand of
Anna here, but she gave him the love of science which
was the basis for his slowly developing generalization of
scientific method as the guide of life. If Anna continued
to influence him, however, he did not cease to hear the
voice of Emmanuèle. Loyal to each, he could not rest
without trying to reconcile them. With "transports of
love" he found this possible in the Gospel, as opened eyes
recovered its human empirical teaching from "what the
churches had made of it" (*Si le Grain ne Meurt,* Part Two,
Ch. II). For him to actualize the possibility of this recon-
ciliation was not going to be easy. His cousin would read
the New Testament for herself, however much they might

still read it together. But faithful to it and to her, convinced that his new morality was divinely sanctioned, and that pleasure had nothing to do with love (though this might be the devil's idea), he did not think it inconsistent to plan marriage.

The urgent step was to leave Algeria in response to his mother's objurgation. He and she were able to make up in two weeks together in Paris, despite what he speaks of as their difference in nearly everything. When he saw her again she was dying at her old home of La Roque in Normandy. To the last "she kept wearing herself out with that uneasy need of meddling, giving advice, persuading" (*ibid.*, Part Two, Ch. II). But it was comforting to have her say she wanted nothing now so much as for him to marry Emmanuèle. It was in July, 1895, that the end overcame him with filial love and a frightening sense of liberty. He went back to his cousin who now seemed the only orientation of his life. She would be his heaven. They were married in the fall.

The autobiography breaks off at this point, and the *Journal* reveals only glimpses of the wife who is designated simply as "Em." The editor of the *Oeuvres Complètes* does not say how much of the *Journal* was suppressed but makes plain that some of it involved another person too much for publication (*OC* X, ix). Yet it may not be indiscreet, at this remove, to piece together what Gide has released about his ménage, or bearing on it. In 1926 he said in the preface to a new edition of *Les Nourritures Terrestres:* "I wrote this book at the moment when, through marriage, I had just tied up my life; when I was voluntarily giving up a freedom which my book

14

as a work of art vehemently demanded back. And, it goes without saying, I was perfectly sincere in writing it; but quite as sincere in my heart's denial" (*OC* II, 228). Although his wedded heart could not be in the book, his unyoked mind was on it—with the emotion generated by the conflict which was to thwart him and drive him forward.

Husband and wife did have good times. In 1902, in the seventh year of marriage, he mentioned their enjoying friends together, and evenings at home when she read and he played the piano, then read to himself or to her. After seeing sculpture at the Louvre one day he remarked how much he would have liked to bring Em. at once (*OC* III, 525–526). And she must have managed the household with tact for him to say: "I'm getting along fine. My mornings, my days, my evenings, are almost empty: that is to say, full as I could wish of meditation, working, reading" (*OC* III, 527). Again he wrote: "A quiet day, with César Franck, Balzac . . . Retz. Read aloud to Em. the *Salomé* of Laforgue" (*OC* III, 540). He would mark passages for reading to her, looking ahead to more sharing. There is the impression of a calmly elevated life oscillating between Paris and her old home, which they had taken over, at Cuverville in Normandy, where he spent much time in the garden.

But he worried about his work, and when it was not going well he worried about himself. Even when he could finish a book it did not seem worth while. His joyous *Nourritures Terrestres* had not been a success, and he was going to allow only 300 copies of *L'Immoraliste* to be printed, so that its failure would be less apparent.

15

More serious was the fact that none of his books really represented him. Yet he had to write, if only to make up for not being able to talk. Whatever he amounted to in solitude he felt utterly stupid in company, and there was very little of it that he enjoyed. "As soon as I begin to tell something my only concern is to finish as fast as possible" (*OC* III, 532). After not accomplishing much during the day he would come home from a "social evening" exasperated, and soothe himself by confiding in his *Journal* (*OC* III, 533). He said of one of his best friends, "If he were deaf and dumb I couldn't ask for a better one"; and he would hesitate to call on a sick friend for fear that when sick himself the visit would be returned (*OC* III, 537). At the end of his rope he would run off to Africa again or just run wild. Then he worried because he was not up to his former wildness. One evening, when he had thought he would have to go out, he stayed in and slept well. Wistfully he observed: "Two years ago I couldn't have gone to bed before three in the morning, after having roamed the boulevards from ten o'clock. I seem wiser; I am older" (*OC* III, 517). As if it gave vicarious relief from a regular and peaceful life he was glad of a chance to listen in a Montmartre café to the boasting of a shady character. He said how instructive it would have been if he could have believed it (*OC* III, 518). He was still fascinated by the underworld, though at thirty he could look back upon his campaign to shake puritan pride, now given fictional form in *L'Immoraliste*. It seemed so far behind him that he could hardly bring himself to read the proofs. He said: "I have spent four years not writing it but living it. I wrote it to get over it; I have suffered this

16

book as one does a disease. . . . The only books I care for now are those in which the author almost cracked up" (*OC* III, 562).

In March, 1902, the author of the *Immoraliste* seemed to have recovered at Cuverville where he was busy and eager to use the precious early hours. "At the latest I get up at six o'clock; nearly every day I am at work at five-thirty, and sometimes even by five. The day takes its course according to the weather, somewhat haphazardly, in gardening, reading, and piano practice. Since the living room is not in order yet, Em. is established in the dining room, I in my study. We have fire in these two rooms, and the big stove heats the rest of the house. Dinner comes round, and in the evening we reunite our lamps" (*OC* III, 553). They read all kinds of things, often aloud. But Gide could not keep going. For years he was unable to work seriously, after finishing the *Immoraliste* on the 25th of October, 1901. Its apparent failure, after that of the *Nourritures Terrestres,* disheartened him, affected his health.

In the fall of 1904 he made his sixth trip to Africa, much upset that he could not persuade Em. it was necessary. According to his *Journal* her "well of indifference" demoralized him further (*OC* IV, 495). He was projecting a book on Africa which he had not managed to develop from notes on a previous trip with Em. "I had to see this land again. I went resolved just to jot down day by day. Considerations, reflections, and the like, could be added afterward; what cannot be found or invented later is sensation" (*OC* IV, 496). Haunting sketches, mingling fresh impressions with lingering ones of the convalescence ten

17

years before, were to renew and remove his youth. "I put my feet back in my tracks. Here are the charming borders of the path I followed that first day when, still weak, just escaped from the horror of death, I sobbed, drunk with the bare astonishment of being, the ravishment of existing. Ah! but the shade of palms was calming to my tired eyes! The sweetness of clear shadows, the murmur of gardens, I recognize it all, trees, things—the only strange thing is myself" (*Le Renoncement au Voyage*). When a month alone had composed him, Em. joined him at Algiers. "Then we led a tranquil life that left me only pleasant memories" (*OC* IV, 496). Again they read much together, this time largely in German. But once more at home he feared he was losing his grip, that at thirty-five he was old. The ordered appearance of his life oppressed him as hypocritical, because he felt himself to be a mass of complications and contradictions (*OC* IV, 547–548).

He was struggling to write *La Porte Étroite*, the first ambitious work after the *Immoraliste*. People who would apply the latter title to the author, simply accusing him of what they suppose he practiced, have been disconcerted or annoyed by his taking for his next subject a Puritan girl. If he was frank before, how could he be sincere now? Yet he had been a Puritan and he had married one. It was natural to guess that he was writing about Em. Perhaps he had been tempted to, when he noted in his *Journal:* "I am reading over my old letters to Em. . . . In vain I seek some sustenance for my novel. Instead I see bared all the faults of my spirit. There isn't one of them that doesn't irritate me" (*OC* IV, 595). It was easy for him to feel that he was not good enough for her, and he might

18

have considered that neither of them was suited for normal marriage. That they were missing something in not having children, he would recognize now and then. "What *profound* pleasure I had yesterday in going out with the four little children of A. . . . On the whole walk the little Jean and the tiny André were hanging on to me. From time to time, suddenly one or the other would squeeze my hand with a sort of transport. The breath of their affection was like perfume. Jean held my right hand, the wee André my left. The day was splendid. We watched a balloon take off" (*OC* IV, 602).

The gate to a life of prayer must be very narrow if one cannot take children through, and things that go with them. Such a life must be very high, gauged by what is sacrificed, or barren. Here was enough for a story, regardless of Gide's own past or that of his wife. A story needs a setting. As his mother's La Roque had provided the scene for much of the *Immoraliste*, so his wife's property at Cuverville would locate *La Porte Étroite*. But the editor of the *Oeuvres Complètes* is careful to say that "reality furnished only the point of departure for a narration wherein all is invention, and where the character Alissa is so much a fictitious creation that the author, to develop her inner life and make it apparent . . . undertook to compose out of whole cloth her letters and diary" (*OC* V, ix).

It was discouraging work, and must have weighed on Em. as well as upon her husband. His *Journal* of May, 1906, speaks of reading to her with difficulty, because both were filled "with a kind of anguish almost intolerable." The same page continues: "Never a man, I'll be only an old child. I live with the inconsequence of a lyric poet, but two or three ideas, fixed like bars through my brain, crucify all joy; everything which would wing freely crashes there" (*OC* V, 326). Things brighten on the next page, thanks evidently to the effort of Em. "Excellent reading of Darwin aloud. The moments passed by the side of Em. (especially in the garden) are of an extraordinary sweetness. Her tenderness, her charm, her poetry make a kind of radiance around her in which I thaw and let my bad humor melt" (*OC* V, 327). Then, unable to concentrate, he forces himself to keep up his *Journal,* hoping that writing it will help him toward his work. Abruptly in 1907 his *Retour de l'Enfant Prodigue* burst from him in a couple of weeks, to relieve him from the uphill tussle with *La Porte Étroite.* He became sanguine enough to have a house built in Paris, at Auteuil; though the expense worried him, and he seemed to have given up the idea of being happy—he who had taught the beauty and duty of it in *Les Nourritures Terrestres.*

It does not seem to be only married happiness that he was deriding when he scolded against Léon Blum's *Du Mariage* for its preoccupation with happiness, or what might pass for such: "It is not at all proved to me that in the easiest and most economical interpretation of his satisfactions man becomes most worthy of my love and admiration. And what about woman! The most lovely women's faces I have known are resigned; and I cannot imagine one whose contentment would please me . . . if not qualified by some resignation" (*OC* V, 374). Em. had cause to be resigned, with a husband who said: "I am only a little boy amusing himself—doubled by a

Protestant pastor who bores him" (*OC* V, 377). If in spite of this combination, or on account of it, he could do his unique work, he would not have it otherwise. Loving Em. as he did, prizing what they had together, though not on the same footing, he thought it monstrous for Blum's book to imply "that only *naturally* does a tree ever produce the most or the finest fruit" (*OC* V, 377). Nothing Gide wanted to do seemed easy or natural.

When Gide was forty, *La Porte Étroite* was finally published. Frightened friends discouraged him from working on *Corydon,* and he turned to *Isabelle* just to keep his hand in. He was still trying to get hold of himself and overcome his indecision. In all his writing he felt he had put off his best work—waiting to be worthy of it—now to be afraid he had waited too long (*OC* VII, 530). But *L'Immoraliste* and *La Porte Étroite* were gaining recognition. They seemed like twins to be proud of: "the excess of one finding in the other's excess a secret permission while the two balanced each other" (*OC* VII, 530). At home his ups and downs continued. Something upset him and he put in his *Journal* that he was sorry to have been complaining—no doubt to Em., for he added that he had "one of the best conversations I have ever had with Em. But I forbid myself to speak here of anything touching Em." (*OC* VII, 533). There follows a comment on the importance of patience, the value of waiting and not forcing things. But that was easier said than lived up to. Annoyed at the theater by a man who sat in her way and would not budge: "I feel that I can't control myself any longer; I am on the point of striking, shouting, weeping. All in a tremble I leave the box and go home alone to

21

Auteuil" (*OC* VII, 542). Friends with her would escort her. On the next page of the *Journal* Gide wrote: "The Augean stables are *in us*—the hydras, the marshes to clean up. It is in us that Hercules must go to work."

Lest one get from such moody statements the idea that he was entirely enmeshed in himself and his work at home, or his trips abroad, unable to be interested in other people or to appear well in company, the testimony of his friends should be consulted. Léon Pierre-Quint tells what a warm friend and genial host he was; how fully and effectively he gave himself in conversation; though he might just slip away when he got tired, or play some disconcerting trick to liven things up (cf. Jacques Copeau, *Remarques Intimes,* in *Hommage à André Gide* by Henry Bernstein et al.). Gide and his wife did a great deal of entertaining in the country, keeping friends for days or weeks, and several at once. People came to him for advice, unburdening themselves as to a confessor, before they loaded his mail with gratitude for his books. Bands of children played with him. His gaiety was the delight of young and old: on walks or fishing parties, or when he talked and read aloud in the evening. Around him grew a group, catching his enthusiasm for Whitman, Nietzsche, Dostoyevsky (Pierre-Quint, *André Gide: Sa Vie, Son Oeuvre*). But Gide's intellectual friendships were for the most part with equals whom he treated as such. He said: "Nothing is more inhibiting than disciples. I have done what I could to discourage them. I have never tried to do anything but encourage each in his own path and would draw no one to me" (*Un Esprit Non Prévenu,* 45–46).

22

Pierre-Quint also tells how in 1896 the new editor of the dying Symbolist magazine *L'Ermitage* asked Gide to collaborate to save it, and how he did this with the help of his friends: Jammes, Ghéon, Copeau, Signoret, Claudel, Valéry. It became "the best poetic review of the time." In 1908 it went under, largely because the editor could not maintain harmony between his original advisers and the new ones. Gide and his friends, after an abortive effort to join with the staff of still another magazine, decided to strike out for themselves, and founded the *Nouvelle Revue Française* in 1909—the year his *Porte Étroite* was published. He and Schlumberger contributed financially to the new enterprise, and the latter gave all his time as well as the use of his apartment. Gide was clearly the prime mover, although avoiding any title. But he did not simply dictate with his personal authority. He worked intimately and continuously with his friends, in a democratic cooperation that would be incredible if one thought of him only as wrapped up in himself, as some passages of the *Journal* would suggest. Other pages of it are studded with the names of his co-workers, and show the joy of going ahead with them, or the strain of dealing with their differences. They accepted a discipline in which standards came before feelings, and for years reviews of their own books were forbidden, to prevent favors. Their critical dedication to the best, their disregard of official opinion and commercial or conventional norms, commanded respect. The rare phenomenon of such gifted writers controlling their egos enough to function as a team enabled them to develop the literary magazine with the greatest prestige in the world (cf. Jean Schlumberger,

Gide et les Débuts de la N.R.F., in *Hommage à André Gide).*

In 1911, with the help of Gallimard, they set up a publishing house to get out their own books with the imprint of *N.R.F.* After the first successes the manuscripts flowed in and a select number of the best authors appeared on their list. Proust wanted to be one of them but was turned down, not only to his disappointment but to the subsequent chagrin of Gide, for it had been his decision. Eventually realizing and handsomely admitting his error, he was glad to have the *Revue* take over the work that only his own has rivaled in contemporary France.

In 1913, Jacques Copeau wanted what the *Revue* was doing for literature to be extended to the stage, and brought this about through the *Vieux-Colombier,* where he attracted such actors as Dullin and Jouvet. Gide was joyfully surprised by the success of this theater, which in its new way was soon hailed as sharing honors with the *Théâtre Français (Journal,* 18 June, 1914). The connection with the *Revue* was made known by Copeau, and Pierre-Quint goes so far as to say: "the living theater of today comes more or less directly from the group of the *N.R.F.*" (*André Gide: Sa Vie, Son Oeuvre).*

After 1914, Gide had less to do with the *Revue.* It had taken a great deal of energy. It was established and expanding. He could trust his friends to carry on, while devoting himself more to his own art and thought, and so much to the complications of his private life that the reader of his *Journal* might almost forget the influence he had already exerted upon his time.

In July, 1914, he had published *Les Caves du Vati-*

can and was bearing the attacks upon it. He was forty-five. An evening was spoiled because he had replied roughly to Em. when she interrupted his reading. A few *Journal*-pages further he was leaving her at Cuverville to take the last train out for civilians. He kneeled beside her, as he had not done for a long time, and asked her to say the Lord's Prayer. "I did this for her, and my pride gave way without difficulty to love. Moreover my heart joined in her prayer" (*OC* VIII, 65). In Paris, where he did what he could to help in the war, his letters to her took the place of his *Journal* for the most part. He did record that, suffocating in horror, he wished he could be with her (*OC* VIII, 165). Back with her at Cuverville in September, 1916, he noted that at her request he had torn out pages about a crisis caused by her. Deprived of the support he found in keeping the *Journal*, he said he wallowed in appalling disorder of mind (*OC* VIII, 243). Somewhat later he was reading with Em. as usual. Then he was upset because she was to meet him in her room before breakfast, and instead she was busy about the house, as ever. When he thought she was finally coming he heard her stop to wind and strike a clock. He calculated he would have to wait 54 strokes. But she did not excuse herself. She remained so calm, he so beside himself, that he felt it had been a mistake to wait for her, that she was right not to have come. Silent he thought: "My poor friend, you will always find clocks to wind on your path, whenever you are to rejoin me" (*OC* VIII, 270–272).

Whether the reader's sympathy is with husband or wife, it is obvious that such tensions in their duration and accumulation, should not be regarded lightly, even if Gide

25

had not confessed the painful effect upon himself. One may think that this would have been less severe if there had been a happy sexual adjustment. His venturing to read his autobiography to Em., albeit with palpitations, would suggest a fair amount of rapport (*OC* VIII, 286). Significantly his memoirs break off on the brink of marriage. Whether it was consummated or not is kept a secret. More important is the fact, showing through his reticence, that their relations were unsatisfactory, and that he sought healing away from her. Thus he says that health and happiness came back when he was with a young man M.: "near him even chastity is easy for me, and the smiling repose of the flesh." This joy lingered through a headache that he had while helping Em. serve soup to seventeen children, as she did each noon to compensate for the excessive war-rationing of bread (*OC* IX, 427). After going off, even a long distance, he would hurry home, and always for her birthday. It hurt him to hurt her, as when he announced the plan of going off again and she said: "*I owe you at least that.*" He says she said it "with an effort of her whole being which immediately rendered her face so sad, so grave, that at once I can't dream of anything but giving up this project like so many others, since it costs her so much that I'd have to pay with her happiness for mine—which then can no longer be my happiness" (*Journal,* 7 October, 1916).

He remained sincere in loving her and persisted in maintaining that "love cannot pretend to last, once it is tinged with desire" (*OC* IX, 482). But his lasting love was incomplete, while amorous affairs gave only flashes of the whole and sustained body-and-person relationship that was impossible for him, for all his emancipation from orthodox Christianity, because he failed to reject its prejudice against the flesh. He went only far enough to find the pleasures of sense good in themselves. He did not discover how they could blend with the complex social structure of what he considered the finer feelings; did not learn how love could be fed by the senses and suffuse them—except in situations where his disembodied idea of love was out of place, and where there was not much to lift affection over the lapse of desire. The habits and associations he had developed around desire made it incongruous with the New Testament conception of love that he had cultivated and fixed for life, partly in his adolescent devotion to his cousin, and then in his African convalescence. After that the *eros* of sex could never come near the *agape* or communion mood of love he cherished for her. She was forced into the corresponding role of the ideal he imagined. Meanwhile he made his divided nature plain enough on paper for her to have no illusions. That his relationship with her was thereby arrested, so that they could not grow together, would seem to follow. If it was strange for him to marry her, it must have been hard for her to put up with him. His realization of what it cost her, with his guilty feeling about it, Martinet seems right in assuming as the key to the love-suffering of Gide's heroines, Marceline, Alissa, Gertrude, Eveline: each one sacrificed to a man whose incompatibility with her blocks her natural development (Martinet, *André Gide: L'Amour et la Divinité*, 138).

The hardest thing for Emmanuèle to tolerate was her husband's ideas. If they had married before he went to

Africa they might have evolved together intellectually. But what his ideas would have been if he had not been rejected by her and at the same time alienated from her religion, is beyond conjecture. As it was, the rock on which they split was religion, the foundation of their union. Her unyielding stand on what they once had shared made discussion painfully the same as between pious mother and wandering boy. At fifty-three he wrote in his *Journal:* "Hardly a day passes when I do not again throw everything into question" (*OC* XI, 359). If Christianity had coalesced with the hypocrisy, the subjectivity and hidden feelings it had set out to cure, he thought the problem was how to be cured of the remedy (*OC* XI, 364). He strove to hold his tongue, as Em. must have striven, but things were said. They got into an altercation about a young woman whose life Em. considered necessarily a failure because she had been brought up without religion. He observed (to his *Journal*) that he suffered intolerably "from such false ideas felt to flow from such false premises" (*OC* XI, 371).

Les Faux-Monnayeurs, which was occupying him at the time, kept bogging down. But it got finished with the help of the demon who figures in it. This enabled him to guess that Racine's wife had ignored his work through Christian horror of what proceeded from the demon (*OC* XIV, 386–387); and the *Journal* of 9 June, 1928, reveals that *Les Faux-Monnayeurs* was not written for Em. like its predecessors, but for Marc Allégret who went with Gide on his Congo trip to take pictures. The earlier books were written "under the influence of Em. or in the vain hope of convincing her. . . . I must grant that my path removes me from those toward whom my heart yearns; and even recognize my path by the fact that it isolates me" (*OC* XV, 136). Such a confession is the more poignant in view of his having said that he felt his effort useless if he did not carry along the reader "with all his load of reticences and objections. . . . This is the same thing as those mountain hikes when the little Gerard was surprised that I wanted Em. to come too. 'You could go so much farther if you were willing to go alone,' he said to me in front of her. *Parbleu,* I know it well; yet the important thing for me is not to go far myself but to take others along" (*OC* IX, 449). He still took Em. to art museums, and read to her "as I did when we were children" (*OC* XV, 181); but she was trying to hold back her Theseus and not letting go the string of her past (*OC* XIV, 357).

In 1930, when Gide was sixty-one, he reflected that love of Em. had not simply held back his thought but had forced him to consider what was left behind, so that his thinking "gained in depth and breadth what it lost in pointedness and dash." Even *Corydon* and *Si le Grain ne Meurt,* which had been tempered to spare her feelings, he might not have felt sufficient urge to write "if not goaded by such painful thwarting" (*OC* XV, 300). Later he said of his other important books, including *Les Faux-Monnayeurs,* that they could not have been written without Em., for they were all done in protest (*OC* XV, 396) His thirst for sincerity, ever present in his writing, had to be controlled where he most wanted to be open. "Complete frankness with you, how could it have been possible, from the moment it involved admission that I knew you

29

considered abominable what I did not? from the moment you found abominable a part of me which I neither would nor could put away?" (*OC* XV, 329). But he could not face separation from her, "nor dissociate my head from my heart." Better to go on with passionate reserve, condemned to indecision. Impossible to serve two masters— nor could he deny either, and not because they were mistresses but because one was religion and attachment to the past, the other his scientific bent and hope of the future. Em. he loved for herself but also for his mother and Bible: home port in all his roving—what he wanted to get away from, and come back to.

Anna Shackleton, lonely and laughing, foreign and given to excursions, belonged also in his heart and family. He was true to her in refusing to feel that thinking was a betrayal of feeling, or that an entente was impossible between her spirit and that of Emmanuèle; for if Em. was uncompromising, Anna could make allowances. Her feelings apparently had never been a problem to anyone but herself, and her pupil need not consider them now. How often she was in his thoughts may be wondered, and how much she would have approved them. But he remembered her as all sympathy for him. And while it may be that her influence was neither as explicit nor as powerful as Em.'s, he gave up Em.'s religion except as he could reinterpret it in keeping with science that in his life was personified first by Anna. He was nearly fifty when he wrote his apostrophe to her: "Anna Shackelton! I see your calm face again, your pure brow, your somewhat severe mouth, your smiling looks which shed so much kindness on my childhood. To speak of you I would invent words more vibrant, more respectful and more tender." (*Si le Grain ne Meurt*, Part One, Ch. I). The real tribute to her is that, although he became a man of letters and married Em., his thinking was experimental, eager for outdoor discoveries, and disappointed when they could no longer collect in the house.

Renunciation was what he admired in love, however, so that his own would have been less exalted if sacrifice had not been necessary; while it would have been awkward if Em. had not been worthy of it (*OC* XV, 446). But his love for her and the sense of her incomparable worth were one; as in what he wrote about her hands, after a doctor she consulted had remarked that they must have been very fine. "She had the most exquisite hands that could be imagined. I loved them, not only as parts of her person, but for themselves, and especially. She persuades herself and wants to persuade me that her hands are naturally deformed. But there is more to it: she has deformed them in misusing them, subjecting them to gross chores for which they were not made and which Em. took over through modesty, through abnegation, through maceration, and for a heap of virtuous reasons enough to give me a horrror of the spirit of sacrifice. And she has done the same thing with her mind, which was endowed with the most exquisite and rare qualities, apt for the most delicate attentions. Her natural humility would not admit that she could be superior in anything, and that is why she condemned herself to the most ordinary occupations, where in spite of everything her superiority shone out. In watching this progressive despoliation, which she refused even to recognize, I suffered unspeakably. Had I complained of it she would have said that all these superiorities, which I saw her renouncing, existed only in my loving imagination. She truly believed this, and thereby showed herself to be above these superiorities themselves, of which her virtue made so little" (*OC* XV, 404–405).

Looking up to her so much, while obliged to look down and back upon her position, made his quandary. At last he would say: "it is because of removing me from her that I find so painful each step ahead. I can no longer think without cruelty" (*Journal*, 6 Jan., 1933). He was tempted to give up his thinking and go back to her faith; wondering whether, unwittingly, he had ever left it. But in August, 1938, when he was sixty-eight, mourning her death, he stated plainly that he could not share her belief in a survival which would let him feel her eyes still upon him. "As during her life I did not allow her love to bend my thought her way, I must not, now that she is no more, permit to weigh upon my thought more than her love itself the memory of that love." Gratefully he remembered how miraculously, while living at his side, she had known how to surround him with the harmonious silence that his thinking needed. Gradually he adjusted to her absence, less saddened by it as he reflected that she could not have borne the anguish spreading over Europe. Though it did not seem possible at first, his life surprisingly went on as if nothing had changed; for all that she represented was still there, unaffected by her death. "She was one direction of my heart; and even during her lifetime her voice, at times, seemed to reach me from very far" (Pléiade ed. of *Journal*, 1309–1325).

His relation with Em. when she had gone appears the same as before: ambivalent; though the *Journal* asserts that throughout their "perpetual mute dialogue" they had been in agreement (*ibid.*, 1329). He warns that systematic suppressions, at least up to her death, have "blinded" the *Journal*. "The few allusions to the secret drama of my life become incomprehensible there, through the absence of what would have illuminated them; incomprehensible or inadmissible the image of the mutilated self I leave there, which in the heart's ardent place offers only a hole" (*ibid.*, 1331, 26 Jan. 1939). In September, 1940, he put down that if his former self could have been advised by his present one: "I'd have made four tours of the world . . . and not have got married." But he does not let this confession constitute a definite reversal, for he adds: "In writing these words I tremble as from an impiety. It is that I have remained, in spite of everything, very much in love with what has troubled me most, and that I cannot swear that this painful situation has not brought out the best in me" (*Pages de Journal 1939–1942*, 75).

2. FROM PURITAN TO PAGAN

ON HIS HONEYMOON GIDE WENT BY WAY OF ITALY BACK TO Africa, where he began his "manual of escape, of deliverance," *Les Nourritures Terrestres*. The previous book, *Paludes,* had left a young man looking out on life from a tower, hesitating to venture forth. Now he was making the plunge: into frightening freedom, where the road must be his own discovery in an unknown country. "The springs will be where our desires make them well up; for the country exists only as our approach shapes it. . . And you will be, Nathanaël, like one who would follow for guidance a light held in his own hand" (*Les Nourritures Terrestres, in OC* II, 62–63). Thus in prophetic tone a disciple, a young man perhaps unborn, addressed by a name meaning "Gift of God," is urged to trust his own initiative as if it were divine. Anticipating advice the aging Gide would like to have given his youthful self, to roam freely over the earth, untrammeled by marriage— the tie that symbolized for him the Jewish-Christian prohibitions and taboos—the young Gide tried to travel with his bride as he would have done without her, and seemed to declare an independence he could only imagine.

Personal and impetuous as the expression is, it is not as rash and egoistic as might appear. At least it cannot be dismissed as such, though it may have literary kinship with the so-called satanic school of Byron and Shelley. They also offered something more constructive than pride and impiety: a revolutionary zeal for the rights of man. This zeal is what the enemies of man, or his fearful friends who do not think he could or should stand on his own feet, would like to discredit. One who becomes lyrical about liberty and the pursuit of happiness is for them an anti-social character. To want more life than a narrow church encourages, they consider dangerously loose. But Gide was too good a Protestant to stop with protesting against the authority of the Catholic Church. He went on to question all authority that kept men from testing their desires by their own light. If he was wilfully speaking for himself, merely demanding license to do as he pleased and inviting young people to be irresponsible, that is one thing. But in his *Nourritures Terrestres* he first and last begs the reader to throw the book away. No book is sufficient. To warn against taking this one as such, to warn especially against interpreting it as legitimizing any desire and the path of mere temptation, he went on to write *Saül*.

But *Les Nourritures Terrestres* should be read first; one should learn to love life before putting on blinkers. At least when one has been brought up a Puritan it is well to go to grass a while and forget that some kind of harness will have to be worn later. Perhaps the provincialism of

35

the landed gentry might explain some of Gide's egocentricity here, his apparent unawareness of several previous movements to emancipate the spirit in France, as well as in England and America. But he seemed under compulsion to exhaust every stage of experience for himself, regardless of his information. And it may be said parenthetically that the American reaction against Puritanism in the 1920's was superficial compared to that of Gide a generation earlier—more content with breaking blue laws for sense-indulgence than bent upon fulfilling human possibilities. It may be that in any age some letting down has to precede a new keying up. And westerners in general are still puritanical in being trained to believe in the depravity of their nature, to assume that their true values do not spring up in their own experience but drop from heaven by a special grace, on condition that they repent and accept commands laid upon them by institutions and individuals supposed to represent an eternal and superhuman order. People may be more or less sensitive and obedient to this scheme, it may still have uses and beauties; but Gide would have Nathanaël see how high and narrow it is, would have him get down to earth and find God. "Wherever you go you cannot help meeting God; God . . . is what is in front of us" (*OC* II, 61). Becoming aware of what life offers, one should live in the immediate present so intensely as to die completely satisfied, with no hope or wish left for anything but the sleep of death (*ibid.*, 65).

It is not just the imposition of a supernatural scheme that weighs upon men. All habit, order, virtue, does that. But men are entitled to fervor. When life becomes stale and unprofitable they should take a moral holiday and burn for a while with Pater's gemlike flame: act without thinking, love without judging whether it is good or bad. This admittedly is risky, though it is guarded by what is called "the good formula" of "assuming as much humanity as possible" (*ibid.*, 67). If, as suggested, the formula calls for acquaintance with all passions and vices, one may wonder. Gide cannot pause here to explore that problem, but does raise it for the reader to ponder when he throws the book away. Then he will presumably be well again, equal to thinking things through. But he will not be well until his vision has become as fresh as sensation. To recover he must convalesce with the medicine of immediacy. "Do not distinguish God from happiness, and place all happiness in the moment. . . . The sage is he who is astonished at everything" (*ibid.*, 73–74). This is not so much wisdom as love, and love is not the same as possession. "I have called God all that I love. . . . I have wanted to love everything" (*ibid.*, 87). Only a few lovely things can be named: a road opening out, rest in the shade, swimming in deep water, bare feet in sand, spring, gardens, temperatures, tastes, light; the natural existence of earth and man and self, the bitter-sweet brevity of life. Scenes of childhood, vignettes of travel, windows leaned from, places slept in, joys of sunrise, come flooding so vividly that the question is: "Do you think I am only a rendezvous of sensations?" (*ibid.*, 182).

Strictly, these are not sensations—not just present stimulations of sense-organs, but perceptions; that is, clusters of sensations coming in combinations that form recognizable objects, reviving the past and shading into generalizations of thought. Instead of impinging with utter novelty and wholly at random, the images of *Les Nourritures Terrestres* are highly selected for their associations: refreshing naturalistic ones. By the very fact of appearing in print they must be familiar enough to have conventional tags. But however lacking the book may be in actual sensations, there is no doubt of its suggesting the relatively sensuous features of experience as they would appeal to a person suddenly finding much good fruit forbidden or neglected in his diet.

Gide felt obliged to explain years later in the 1927 preface that here is "the excess of one who embraces life as something he had almost lost (*ibid.*, 227–229). Also the book was written at a time when literature, become glassed in, needed to be freshly grounded. He wanted it understood that this book was not intended to be final, that its traits were plucked from him in the writing, that he was the first to drop the book and leave the one who wrote it, as he advised the reader to do; for in the 1927 preface Gide had come to feel that fidelity rather than inconstancy was the keynote of his life. Yet the same preface maintained that the book itself, though glorifying desire and impulse, went on to celebrate denudation, divestment. The term used here (*dénuement*) is evidently to be translated as the complete shedding of things supposed to be necessary but only impedimenta. And the lesson of divestment is not merely what he kept as the kernel of this book but that to which he thought he remained faithful—what he learned to reconcile with the Gospel teaching: "to find in self-forgetfulness the most perfect self-realization, the highest requirement, and the most

38

unqualified permission of happiness" (*ibid.*, 229; cf. also *Un Esprit Non Prévenu*, 98–100).

He rejected his book so far as it advocated inconstancy, but even in this negative aspect he found something positive to take up into his ideal. Indulgence in sense, as a reversion to sub-normal existence, could not constitute a good life; but would help to wash away personal concern, undue commitment, and release attention for surprising departures. Thus everyone should be "capable of nudity"—unafraid to strip off ideas, beliefs, possessions, and each layer of self that comes to bind the free being. In time new interests form another ego, jealous and fearful of being superseded but needing in turn to be sloughed. No shyness should prevent the growth waiting beyond each divestment. Morning: "If you knew how to give yourself to it wholly . . . but the best of your nature is cloistered; your wife and your children, your books and your study hold it back and rob it of God" (*OC* II, 121). Old notions must be laid aside for new; and the new must be thrown off not only when they fail to pioneer but when they cannot match values valid from yesterday. To be alert to worth, wherever it appears, requires men free and flexible, not letting their energy be assigned entirely to fixed uses, but keeping some of it ready for new occasions. That is why Gide loves youth. It is *disposable*, with the poet's "gift of perpetual adventure" (*ibid.*, 115).

In Gide's case this "gift" was not given with youth but had to be won. He was like Schiller in presenting a "sentimental" or romantic poet yearning for the at-homeness in nature supposedly characteristic of the "naive" poet of antiquity. Also like Schiller, Gide believed that initial

39

alienation from nature enabled him to appreciate its variety more fully. "No indirect method could, so well as my puritan education, have saved for my enjoyment such multiple virginities" (*Le Renoncement au Voyage*). How he had hovered on the verge of life was told in the book just before *Les Nourritures Terrestres*. That was *Paludes*, conceived on the way home from the author's first trip to North Africa, and completed when he was heading south again after finding his former existence in Paris too stuffy. *Paludes* is about a celibate youth trying to write about such a youth looking out on the marshes around his tower; his mind open to possibilities while his will holds back. Gide himself, having got beyond this stage, found it onerous to go on writing about it. For the writer in the story, finishing his book was made synonymous with the happiness of finally daring to act. As for Gide himself, the completion of this book within a book freed him to abandon himself in *Les Nourritures Terrestres*.

If the rashness of living according to that "manual" is not sufficiently exhibited in *L'Immoraliste*, *Saül* makes dramatic the torments of conscience a puritan might have in trying to turn pagan. Vivid again in *Bethsabé* is the evil lurking in uncurbed desire. Yet so strongly did Gide resent the strictness of his early training that he remained willing to take the risk of breaking from it. After all his searching of motives and weighing of consequences he wanted to be through with foreboding and repenting. He wanted the happiness, announced in *Paludes*, of daring to act. One may observe with Ramon Fernandez, however, that there is little action in *Les Nourritures*. Its daring consists in leaving the tower of *Paludes* and coming down to earth; in tasting and lingering over the delights of a dreamy traveler. His pleasures are largely those of contemplation. There is some talk of wild things but they wait to be done. The sick and vacillating spirit of *Paludes* is convalescing in *Les Nourritures*. Not until *Le Prométhée Mal Enchaîné* is he up and doing enough to run the risk of sinning like King Saul and King David.

Contemplation may be exciting but is passive and innocuous compared to setting off a train of events. Gide is fascinated by the potentiality of an act. It is wonderfully unpredictable. It releases novelty that cannot be controlled or kept within established law. Codes are exploded by action. Each genuine deed is a departure, an adventure, not just revealing a world unexpectedly there but leaving it to launch a new one. There is no blueprint of the future. Anything can happen. It is reckless to act, really to act, freely, impulsively, without authority or sanction. To have a good reason for acting, to have any reason, justification, purpose or excuse, other than the delight of doing something for its own sake, is not to act but to conform, submit, accept. The true act is pure bravura, uncalled for, unmotivated, inexplicable. It is gratuitous.

This is the fascination of the Greek myths for Gide: the great unreflective initiative of the demi-gods and heroes. He admires in Theseus "the defiance of rule, nature, morality, laws." Hercules is unique as the first virtuous hero. He is the only one who hesitates. Ulysses has so much caution as to be almost anti-heroic. In this vein Gide is carried to the point of saying: "Instinct is usually a better guide than reason." (*Un Esprit Non Prévenu,* 72–87).

41

Perhaps so, if the idea is to act irrationally. On the other hand, reason itself can be used creatively, to do things that would not seem reasonable or feasible. It takes thinking as well as daring to break significantly from what is thought and done. In Gide's *Thésée,* Dedalus hopes through science to make man the rival of the gods, and remarks that the stupid strength of Hercules was capable only of the heroic. Why Theseus should be destined for greater things is not made clear. Joyousness is said to distinguish him from Hercules. Theseus is certainly not more conscientious and he is equally unreflective. "I shall praise you for not being embarrassed by thought," says Dedalus (*Thésée, Pantheon Books,* 1946, pp. 56–57). It seems quite improbable that a hero in whom imperious desire silences "the voices of gratitude and decency" (*ibid.,* 96), should found Athens except by accident or fate; much less plan it for the public welfare, and "for the good of future generations," on the basis of respect for law and popular government (*ibid.,* 105–109, 123). For Theseus to depart so completely from the limitations of his previous role and character is indeed to act gratuitously.

Thus Gide returns in *Thésée,* which he had long in mind, to his early concern with the need of breaking from established ways as the one condition of progress. This calls for a divine indifference toward the sense of safety in attachment to the past.

Perhaps men are incapable of it. Hard pressed, needy, fearful of loss and punishment, with others dependent on them, they must be eager for recompense, they must count the cost and look before they leap. At best they can play at doing what they please, but it becomes serious unless they play safe. There is, however, a vicarious way of making the sky the limit without ceasing to be playful. That is to imagine gods. This is the fun Gide has in *Le Prométhée Mal Enchaîné*. Stepping from a taxi in Paris, to find without choosing someone, a person drops a handkerchief. The passerby happening to pick it up is asked to write someone's address on an envelope containing a 500-franc note, and is thanked with a slap in the face by the stranger, who disappears. The person who receives the money through the mail dies from the embarrassment of not being able to return it. But the slapped one loses an eye and yet profits from the experience. Is there a point in the episode except to foil the effort to make sense of it? The reader learns that the practical joker is Zeus in the guise of a millionaire who boasts that he alone can act with absolute disinterestedness, because his fortune is infinite. But the power of Zeus had not kept Prometheus from defying it to bring men fire; and this deed, though intended to help them, turned out to be gratuitous. Lecturing about that in the Hall of the New Moons, Prometheus promises to pass around obscene photographs and shoot off rockets if the crowd gets bored. But for sure-fire entertainment he opens his vest "with an atrocious gesture," baring his liver to the eagle's beak.

Declaring that he had loved men at first, Prometheus says he now loves that which devours them. He confesses he feels responsible for marring their happiness, and that when he thinks about it the eagle comes to feed like a remorse. Along with all the arts which the fire-bringer had given men went the egg of an eagle like his own, for

43

each—the eagle being the belief in progress, the *raison d'être* of human life. Prometheus on the platform tries to get the eagle to say where he came from and where he is going. Silence. "Yet isn't it enough that he is beautiful?" Prometheus appeals to the audience. "Or will you deny that? . . . As for me, I lived for him—but he, why does he live?"

At last, at a café, Prometheus has killed the eagle and is having him for dinner, laughing. "In his time could I dare to laugh? And wasn't I frightfully thin? . . . He was eating me long enough; I decided it was my turn." The eagle is delicious. "Then he was good for something after all?" someone asked. "His flesh has nourished us. When I questioned him he wouldn't answer. But I eat him without rancor: if he had made me suffer less he would have been less fat; less fat he would have been less delectable."

Progress is what Gide believes in, if one may judge by his work as a whole. Yet he knows progress is not straightforward, that something is always given for something gained. Not wanting to be naive and gullible about it he makes a farce of his own credo, leaving nothing for a scoffer to add. What could be added when Prometheus, the father of progress, has satirized it? He says men have exchanged the good for a "morbid hope of the better," though for Gide nothing is sounder than this hope. When Prometheus had first occupied himself with men their condition did not seem a happy one—without arts and culture. He was moved to pity by their lack of light. If they had *the good* it was an abstraction in the realm of contemplation, ruling out the idea of improvement;

44

whereas "the better" he brought was increasingly available in tangible ways. If still it may be asked why it is better to have progress, what it is good for, what its goal, such asking is ironical, for it pretends ignorance of the unanswerable answer already given. Since the better is a matter of comparison it is decisive that men have found progress better than the unprogressive good. That they have found this may be said to beg the question whether they should have; but begging the question is simply affirmation of temperament, says Prometheus. In making men become like him he made them such that they should be devoted to progress. Is it worth the suffering involved? Perhaps not to a non-Promethean. But as Protheans men should not be daunted by suffering. As men they are for progress. To ask them what progress is for is absurd—as if it were not for them. It is theirs, for them to enjoy, if they are Promethean enough.

That human beings can become so godlike is the conviction for which Gide is ever seeking evidence and argument. He is excited when they do something out of the way, no matter how insignificant or obnoxious, because progress begins in doing what is not done—what is thought improper, impossible, or simply not thought of. Progress is the success of the unthinkable. It is the gratuitous act on the grand scale. The waiter, in the café where Prometheus brought the eagle, said: "Man is the animal capable of the gratuitous act."

This capacity, as it threatens a pattern of behavior patiently acquired and jealously guarded, may seem to derive from the animal in man rather than from the divine. If accepted as human, the venturesome streak will

45

be called too human and will be blamed on the natural man of the earth, who needs to be reborn in keeping with a higher ideal. The puritan will brand as unregenerate all unauthorized experience, frowning upon it as survival of pagan beliefs and ways. But a person wanting to relinquish puritanism is likely to find his reasons more in the present than in the past. Though he may become fond of old gods in whom the natural was divine, his budding paganism will depend less on knowledge of its ancient patrons than upon the fresh delight and awe from which belief in them arose. Fervor over the possibilities of the earth, as contemplated in *Les Nourritures Terrestres,* is the same as that once giving life to Dionysus. With gathering verve Gide craved, beyond a passionate receiving and undergoing, a creative doing and daring, such as brought to mind the myth of Prometheus defying Zeus, the god of moral law and order. Zeus himself exercised power to do as he pleased, but sporadically; whereas Prometheus, in fathering the arts, launched the gratuitous act on a long career.

Men were to carry it on so collectively that any one man, considering himself, might feel helpless, too dependent on authority and tradition to strike out—especially a puritan. Yet Gide, after enjoying the freedom of the immortals, hunted for its eagle egg in the conduct of a human being—one ceasing to be a puritan—not in cooperative enterprise where the initiative of the individual would be hard to isolate, but in very personal, identifiable doings. Since the most private behavior, if it conformed to conventional morality and religion, might be motivated and controlled thereby instead of being spontaneous, then immoral and irreligious actions might presumably be more independent. How childish, selfish or perverse they happened to be would not matter for the purpose of this investigation, if they were unmistakably gratuitous. On the first page of *L'Immoraliste* the question, "What are you going to think of our friend?" is answered by another question: "Shall we simply damn him, denying that faculties manifested as cruel could be turned to good?"

The first part of *L'Immoraliste* goes over the crisis of the author's initial trip to Africa, and the sensuous convalescence already celebrated in *Les Nourritures Terrestres*. It seems that, to get momentum for a jump, he went back for a run. While back in that stretch of his life he was moved to relate an incident he would record again in his autobiography. Michel, like Gide before him, was standing at the mantel, apparently absorbed in a book while watching in the glass a young Arab friend purloin a pair of scissors. The theft did not surprise Michel so much as the joy it filled him with. What delighted him was that he could not understand such an action. It struck him as unpremeditated, unmotivated, a sheer act. This impression was confirmed when it turned out that the boy had no use for the scissors but to break and ruin them. Here was an authentic outburst of the Old Adam opposed by the Gospel: "the one whom everything around me—books, teachers, parents and myself—had tried to suppress" (*L'Immoraliste*, 1923 ed., 83). Michel's suppressed self, as he freshly discovered it, seemed to be only physical, sensuous, with nothing to do. The "astonishing acts" he expected of it would have to come later. But they would hatch from feigning not to see the snatching of the scissors.

In developing the power to act, Michel simply wanted to live: to have "a more spacious and airy existence," which he felt to be one not constrained by thought of past or future, and certainly not by concern for other people. To the reader's disgust he sought this expansion at the expense of his bride, when she had nursed him back to health and lost her own. As Gide says in the preface, it was not in vain that he had endowed her with the moral and religious virtues Michel was to spurn: he could not be forgiven for treating her as the scissors were. And he was not forgiven by Gide who was to point out, in defending *L'Immoraliste,* that he had led his hero to moral bankruptcy as a result of letting him make his desire his law, and asked: "What can you say or think against him that I have not already suggested to you?" (1927 letter to Poucel, *OC* XIV, 410).

He had to be bad for the book to be good. If Marceline had been less lovely or less wronged, if there had been no affront in Michel's behavior, the grievous conflict between ingrained convictions and sharp departure from them might not have been sufficiently etched. Just because Michel has no justification, but is flagrantly egoistic and heartless, he throws into relief the trait he shares with the reformer, the radical, the artist, the scientist: the capacity to disregard the ties holding back ordinary men. If creative action is sure to hurt those who cannot go along, because they are not strong or independent enough, the noblest advance will have a dismaying aspect. There is the problem. Gide demonstrates with all his art what a problem it is. He does not pretend to solve it. But since it is increasingly unavoidable in our society, it is well to have his help in seeing what is involved. The story of Marceline and Michel deepens the tragic sense of life in a changing world, unless Michel can be dismissed as satanic. One who simply blames him or blots him out as unrepresentative will not see much point in writing about him. The author himself is denounced or excused according as he is supposed to be Michel, at least to approve him, or not. Resentment is the usual response to the book. But gratitude is more in order for a work which brings to focus possibilities, however ugly, in the gratuitous act, if it is the egg of progress.

The value of such an act may be as hard to believe as to admit that it can occur. That Michel, on his own place, would buy wire for poachers' snares while rewarding the guards for finding them, is incredible to his overseer. In his mind people do only what makes sense. Stealing and getting drunk are understandable—the reasons for them are plain as for honest work. But who would spend money to cheat himself? and also pay to have the cheating discovered? A man could much more plausibly abuse his wife and reproach himself for it. But to be as inconsiderate of Marceline as Michel is, when she is in need of the very care she had given him in the same case, letting her die after she had pulled him through, would seem inexcusable. There is not the excuse that he hates her, or even that he does not love her passionately—for a while. "That he had egotistically accepted all she did for him when he was sick, was no excuse for neglecting her when he was strong, even while she was still well. So

49

he told himself" (1923 ed., 102). He plunged away from her because "her too calm joy would have tempered mine, as her pace would have slowed my own" (*ibid.*, 98). When she became seriously ill he was outraged. "I have a horror of sympathy; it hides all contagions; one should not sympathize except with the strong" (*ibid.*, 219).

Gide was in the midst of hinging his book on this Nietzschean sentiment when he came upon Nietzsche for the first time, and felt there was no use going on. It had all been said. Then he decided that it was an advantage to have the similarity with Nietzsche's work. This enabled Gide "to expurgate from his a whole theoretic section which would have burdened it," as Louis Martin-Chauffier explains in a note. "Thus disencumbered the depiction of life gained in intensity without losing any of its substance" (*OC* IV, viii). But Gide, looking back after twenty years, spoke regretfully of things he might have said if he had not found them in Nietzsche while writing *L'Immoraliste*. "Who knows how much he hampered me . . . how much my book is impoverished on account of all that I did not want to repeat" (*OC* XI, 351). Yet what appealed to Gide in Nietzsche he found more acceptable in the Gospel, saying that the teaching of Christ was "more emancipating . . . more concerned about individual value, abnegation and joy, and more calm, secret, assured" (*Journal 1889–1939*, Pléiade ed., 1282). Also, when defending himself from attack, Gide could believe that he was against Nietzsche while with Christ in writing *L'Immoraliste;* and was astonished that a careful reader should be unable to see how in this book "the very process of abandon *to* self . . . is precisely opposite to the abandon *of* self which the Gospel teaches us" (*OC* XV, 532).

Certainly Michel is more Nietzsche-like than Christ-like in these terms. But Sybrandi Braak has pointed out that in letting himself go, to the neglect of all his obligations, Michel would have been censured by Nietzsche. To be free and masterful, for Nietzsche, did not mean a proud self-exemption from responsibility. "Quite the contrary: the stronger one is, the more one has duties toward oneself and others." (Braak, *André Gide et l'Ame Moderne*, 131. The same point is made in Schreiber, *Leben und Denken im Werk von André Gide*, 31. See also Drain, *Nietzsche et Gide*, 180, ff.). Yet Michel is like Nietzsche in the thing Gide is characteristically eager about: the thing he wanted so much to say that he resented finding much of it said in German: that men should face forward. Nietzsche's own doctrine of eternal return was incompatible with this, though Gide thought the explanation lay in the need to wipe out regret (*OC* XV, 524). He would rather overcome it with optimism about the future.

There was this positive value in the insouciance of Michel: that he asked what was still possible for man, and looked ahead for the answer, not toward the past. "What man had already said, was that all he could say? . . . And each day increased in me the confused sense of untouched riches, covered, hidden, choked by cultures, decencies, moralities." Michel continues: "It seemed to me then that I was born for an unknown kind of discovery; and I was strangely passionate in my dark research, wherein I know the investigator must give up and push from him culture, decency, and morality." (*L'Im-*

51

moraliste, 1927 ed., 222–223). That Michel developed a taste for "the most savage manifestations" in other people, would seem incompatible with love of progress; except that to get away from previous gains, congealed in convention, might make a backward step prerequisite. It is hard to go beyond good and evil without a bad start.

Marceline was recovering in the air of Switzerland; but he could not stand the decent sober people there and dragged her off to Italy, from one place to another, wearing her out. Sometimes they were fleeing bad weather, but always he was trying to escape from boredom, driven by "a demon." Michel would not settle down. Yet the worst for her to bear—and what all her suffering may be taken to symbolize—was the fear of his thought. She told him she understood his doctrine: "It is beautiful, perhaps . . . but it wipes out the weak." "Just what must be done," he answered, in spite of himself. He saw how she recoiled, and when reaching this point in going over his story for his friends he was afraid they would think he had not loved her. "I swear that I loved her passionately. Never had she been or seemed to me more beautiful. . . . Hardly leaving her any more, I surrounded her with continual attentions, sheltered her, watched over her each instant of her days and nights" (*L'Immoraliste,* 229). Yet when he did go out for a walk he tried to overcome his anxiety, as if it were unworthy of him, and prolonged his absence. Coming back with a profusion of flowers he was angered that their odor was too much for her. If she couldn't stand the spring! As she got worse and worse he took her farther and farther south, while she kept worrying about his ideas.

He was irritated not merely because his way of pursuing pleasure was making her miserable, but also because she clung to the religion he was rejecting. Though loving her he felt compelled to harden his heart against her, since she in her pain still appealed to the God who would condemn his pleasure-philosophy (cf. Fernandez, *André Gide,* 241). Such estrangement has implications beyond the circumstances of Gide's story and the parallel in his own situation (cf. *L'Immoraliste,* 179–180). For Michel's thinking to disturb his wife was unfortunate, yet except for occasional blunt expressions one may feel that what he thought was his affair. A man should be free to think, provided that he keep his views to himself when they distress a loved one. But this is impossible if he and the other are intimate and want to be sincere. It makes little difference whether he blurts them out or not if the ideas themselves, and the knowledge that he has them, are sinister to his wife. And Michel's ideas were motor. They drove him on his course. His behavior toward Marceline, leading to her death, must be blamed on what he was thinking. It kept him from the sacrifice that would have proved his love to her. Her death, however, only brings home what she suffered. The pain of alienation from her husband would have had the same quality even if she had been able to bear it.

The real question, though given the shape of a particular tragic narrative, is whether thinking is morally permissible when it hurts feelings, regardless of whether it is fatal. It is incidental that Michel is a cad and his bride dies. The problem lives. Men, good men, will think, and thinking will cruelly wound those they love; unless men

53

and women become critical and scientific enough to see that no value can be saved except as lost and recovered in more viable form. It may nevertheless be true that some value is lost in any transformation, so that intense attachment to sameness may not be loosened by the promise of novelty or of such identity as can survive change. Uncompromising conservatism must ignore change, refuse to take time seriously, and seize upon the image of eternity. People who believe in science and progress (though it is not clear that Michel does) must be ready to take chances, must to an unknown extent play fast and loose with their inheritance in the hope of enriching it, and even to secure it. They feel justified by such evidence as impresses them. Rejecting tradition and external authority, men have to rely on their own judgment; though it may be highly subjective, as when Michel says, "I feel nothing but what is noble in myself" (*ibid.*, 240). His subjectivity might have been corrected if he had consulted his friends while Marceline was alive. But his zest for doing needless things is essential to progress, and so is the impulse like his to share freedom with stevedores and drunken sailors. "I dreamed for everyone this leisure without which no novelty, vice or art can flourish" (*ibid.*, 238). That flowers of good and evil stem from the same relaxation of life, the same flirting with novelty, is sobering or exciting, especially as it may be hard to tell the flowers apart. The worse may seem better at least when more sincere, in a world where the good is largely conventional So Michel was attracted by men's vice rather than virtue. He could say, with regard to a young Arab friend who had lost his charm, settled in a butcher shop and looking

54

down on his former gay companions: "How stupefying are honorable careers!" (*ibid.*, 243). And: "I have searched, I have found that which constitutes my worth: a kind of stubbornness in the worst" (*Ibid.*, 245).

This repudiation of what is generally approved, this identification of worth with pursuance of evil, is unavoidable if values are to be transvalued. A puritan at any rate, for whom deviation from his strict principles will be considered backsliding, must, to become anything else, be at least provisionally a pagan; inasmuch as paganism connotes reversion to beliefs and practices left behind by puritanism. But Michel, like Gide, is groping for something novel. The spell of the remote past might serve as an antidote to yesterday, but not as a substitute for tomorrow. "I went to Paestum one day, alone. . . . Oh! I could have sobbed over those stones! The beauty of antiquity was there, simple, perfect, smiling—abandoned. I feel that art is slipping from me. It is in order to make room for what else? It is to be no longer, as before, a smiling harmony. . . . I no longer know the dark god I serve. O new God! let me know yet unknown species, unforeseen types of beauty" (*ibid.*, 246–247).

In *La Porte Étroite* Gide apparently comes back to the recent God of his mother and wife, instead of seeking an ancient or future God. The puritan Alissa, giving up happiness for holiness, counterbalances the ex-puritan Michel who is through with morality. But *La Porte Étroite* is not simply a repudiation of *L'Immoraliste;* for while Michel's immorality is found to have some justification as a groping for progress, Alissa's religiosity goes to an extreme that is hard to justify morally. And if she can be forgiven, it must be for the same reason that Michel can to some extent be exonerated: namely, that she, like him, upsets the ordinary table of values in the passionate quest for something ultimately better though immediately worse, because beyond established standards. In her way she is wanton as he, in throwing away her own and another's happiness. Her excess, her extravagance, in refusing to think that normal human happiness is good enough for her or her lover, while the rejected prospect of it becomes almost irresistibly blissful to her starving self, makes her as suicidal as Michel becomes homicidal. That she in effect kills herself, whereas he practically kills his wife, makes little difference; nor the fact that Alissa thinks in terms of sacrifice while he thinks of living ever more fully and will not forego anything that appeals. He is attracted by vice. She clings to virtue. Both have misgivings, compunctions; and thrust them away, fortified by the idea of going toward God. In the end both are humbled. The puritan and the pagan attitude are equally reduced by Gide, though he cannot give up either, in qualified form. He finds that Alissa, in pushing aside the human, becomes no less gratuitously cruel than Michel. Firmly as Gide believes promise to be found in the gratuitous act, he recognizes that it can be vitiated through needless sacrifice as well as through heedless egotism. This double hazard does not discourage him but must be reckoned with, on either side of the line of progress, before he can project it boldly toward the future.

Jérôme, who loves Alissa, was at fourteen "still undecided, disposable," with regard to a life-commitment. This was the state favoring creative advance in the Gidian scheme, though puritan training had already bent him toward virtue and confused happiness with unremitting effort. Alissa confirmed him in that direction. From her he was to learn that individual action was not ruled out by puritanism, as might appear, but emphatically called for. The discipline of its narrow path, steadfastly pursued, would open on to a trackless desert where only one's own courage was decisive. "Aren't you strong enough to march alone?" she asked him. "It is all alone that each of us must go to God" (*La Porte Étroite*, 1917 ed., 41).

This idea chills Jérôme just when he is expressing the need of being always with her. It does not comfort him to be told that they could not be closer than through forgetting each other in God. Heaven would mean little to him if he could not find her there. Thus is registered the dependence upon affection which complicates and limits Gide's enthusiasm for the gratuitous act. It can be heartless. The tensions between it and love may be resolved only by a love which is itself wholly gratuitous—a free gift, making no claim and no pretense. This is impossible without utter sincerity. But sincerity, baring any fluctuation of mutuality, may aggravate a difference that otherwise might be tolerable; whereas lack of sincerity lessens the chance of discussing and overcoming discord. Alissa reaches the point where she must belie her love for Jérôme, lest it undo the exaggeration of virtue which makes her false to him. Puritanism, after uniting them in a common zeal, separates them as she comes to feel that being happy together would keep them from something better. Her very love for him, in that context, convinces her that she must deny him for his good, though she

57

would not give him up for her own salvation. What she is aiming at is so vague as to get meaning only in the negation of every value shared with him; as if each good thrown away would augment the good in store. Inability to visualize that residual good, and fear of considering it a reward, make the future as blank for her as she tries to make her relation with Jérôme. Her virtue is gratuitous, but, instead of being rich with promise, it uproots every possibility except that of gratifying God—if he can be imagined to take pleasure in what is pleasing to no one. Rather, it seems that she is so proud of her prowess in virtue that she is more bent upon outdoing herself than upon honoring God or coming to rest in his peace. Henri Drain has said: "*La Porte Étroite* is the story of Protestant asceticism reaching Nietzscheism" (*Nietzsche et Gide*, 190).

If Alissa and Michel are comparable in sacrificing love to Nietzschean fervor, it may be welcome to think how Marceline and Jérôme would have been together: she with a piety that did not ration kindness; he with potentialities that would have been grateful to sustaining love. Since Alissa knew how much he required her support, it may be wondered whether he was treated less wretchedly by her than her father by her mother when that lady ran off with a lieutenant. Alissa was warned not only by the prolonged dejection of her father but by his plainly saying, when she asked what he thought Jérôme needed in order to be what he had it in him to become: "The affection and esteem which I have missed." Esteem Jérôme got, but the buoy of love, as he touched it, was jerked away.

FROM PURITAN TO PAGAN

This presentation of gratuitous conduct as blighting life, instead of giving it fresh impetus, brings home the need of guidance. To act disinterestedly is not enough, whether on impulse or on principle. Michel's impulses are not bad in themselves. They feel good. They are innocent in a man convalescing, and emerging from a system of excessive inhibition. His privilege is to float on the moment. But when, well and emancipated, he finds his wife ailing, it would seem time for him to exercise self-control again. Then it does not excuse him that he intends no harm. His exuberance is no longer ingratiating. Alissa, on the other hand, controls impulse quite as unjustifiably as he refuses to. Weakness holds him back for a while, and the only thing keeping her from what she wants to do is strength of will. It is often admirable to check inclination and rise above it; but not just to be admired. She is not seeking admiration any more than she is avoiding a penalty or hoping for recompense—unless it is heavenly preferment for Jérôme. Yet, misguided as he thinks her, so far as he can understand her, he has a quality of love for her that is evoked perhaps by her capacity to sacrifice their love for love of God. Up to a point Gide believes that to give up something precious is the way to get it back enhanced. *La Porte Étroite* apparently was written to show how this principle can be overworked, but it was written with irony. One cannot be cocksure of the meaning.

Commenting on this book in *Nouveaux Prétextes*, the author speaks of Alissa's "absolutely useless heroism" as a trait essentially French, warned against by Bossuet as false honor, and from which Rostand fashioned Cyrano's

59

panache. But to see the parade and swagger in this trait is not necessarily to depreciate it. Honor is falsified here, if at all, through too much fascination with it. This is extravagance of virtue, and if it is wrong it is difficult to say just where it goes wrong. To call it gratuitous will not condemn it if the finest things are gratuitous. That such are the finest is perhaps a feudal idea, growing out of the custom of serving an overlord not so much on account of what mutual obligations there were as because it was eternally "right." In return there was *noblesse oblige* which could proudly dispense largesse beyond obvious obligation. In a democratic society generosity is not resented among friends, the freely given, the radiant virtue that Nietzsche named *die schenkende Tugend:* the uncalled-for outpouring, exceeding what is called for, and disdaining calculation or advantage. So it is not easy to announce that Gide disapproves of Alissa when, after referring to her sacrifice as useless, he adds: "The thought of her lover immediately called out in her a sort of reflex of heroism, not voluntary, almost unconscious, and spontaneous" (*Nouveaux Prétextes,* 172–173). To let go an obvious good for a finer one is to take a risk. Yet disposition to venture is itself good, unless one has much to lose and nothing to gain. But what the odds are, and how to estimate them, is hard to arrive at when the value of spurning a rational appraisal is at stake; when happiness is balanced against the importance of refusing to think happiness fundamental.

Not only is there doubt in *La Porte Étroite* about the existence of a good above natural satisfaction. There is implied the question whether the right rises over the good, although Gide does not mention it. If the good is what satisfies desire, and the right is what ought to be done, regardless of desire, the right cannot be gauged by the good. The right is adherence to principle, whether it is convenient, whether it is agreeable, or not. What is right may coincide with what is good, but it is better to be right and pass up a good than to keep something good and be wrong. It may be argued, however, that there is a fallacy in a way of being right which regularly defeats the good; that in general the right course, the right principle, is one tending to satisfy desire and promote happiness. The right is a mere form if it does nobody good; and an actual wrong if it definitely benefits a few at the expense of many. Mistakes will be made about the good as about the right, and doubtful cases will occur. But it is clear that Michel forfeits the good which he and Marceline have, by failing to appreciate it except intermittently, and by rashly hunting a greater good; whereas Alissa, fully aware of the joy she and Jérôme might have, and unable to name anything better except to call it God, gambles on the belief that what she hopes to be right will surpass any known good. Even for her the approach to the right is through the good, though in reverse. If she is right she may know how right she is by the good she destroys; while she realizes that the loss she is responsible for exactly measures how wrong she is if she is wrong.

Her responsibility is so great that she dares not think of it as optional. When Jérôme writes that through hope of rejoining her he will follow her steep ascent, she replies: "But, my friend, holiness is not a choice: it is an obligation . . ." (*La Porte Étroite*, 1917 ed., 170). The good is

61

chosen; the right is respected, obeyed. The gratuitous act, when forced to the puritan extreme, cannot be grounded in the circumstances, any more than the most carefree spontaneity; but, whereas a genuine initiative needs no justification beyond its own assertion, the courage to throttle impulse depends upon the sense of a command. "I will" cannot conquer "I want" without becoming "I must." *Must* is melancholy without trust that life cannot be saved without willingness to lose it and its good. But Alissa leads up to this trust, and undermines it, by saying of Pascal: "If he had not first emptied present life of its joy . . . it would have more weight in the balance than . . . the uncertain felicity he proposes." Jérôme, surprised, would like to know if she does not believe in a future happiness after all. She says that does not matter, for she wants it to "remain uncertain, to avoid any suspicion of a bargain" (*ibid.*, 180–181). She dares not let trust become confidence lest "I must" slip back to "I want," and the door be opened again to choice.

Jérôme is "filled with a vague hatred against this 'virtue,' as I still called it" (*ibid.*, 188). By making him unhappy she is far from making him more of a puritan, as she had hoped. And as her own sadness deepens she calls it a state of sin that she must get rid of, as if it reflected upon the rightness of her sacrifice, or upon her integrity in carrying it out. She keeps a diary as an effort to recover happiness, after seeing that of her married sister. Yet the sister's happiness, being practical, disturbs Alissa because it cannot be gratuitous; and, easily attained, it could surely be surpassed. But has Alissa achieved more than sadness with all her effort? Trying not to be sad, she consoles herself with the idea that she would not accept a joy that was not progressive. How happy she would be if love and virtue could be fused! Still she will guard against identifying virtue with the natural inclination of her heart. What is given must be improved, if only in giving it up. The heroic cannot be reduced to contentment. But what value could a virtue have which her whole heart denied? "I realize that my life is all vain if it does not arrive at happiness" (*ibid.*, 239). In her final thirst for it she wonders if she can persuade herself that she has it. Dying, she is appalled by the bare walls and prays to reach the end without blasphemy. "I would die now, quickly, before realizing again that I am alone" (*ibid.*, 240).

Going back to Alissa's diary, after reading Martinet's analysis of *La Porte Étroite* as conforming to the course of love between Gide and his cousin as much as the *Immoraliste* does, one wonders whether Jérôme was not more to blame for the sacrifice of love and happiness than Alissa (*André Gide: L'Amour et la Divinité*, 147–154). He was not ardent enough. Taking her "virtue" more seriously than she intended, he forced her to exaggerate it by his renunciation. Ramon Fernandez also is quite persuasive in holding that Jérôme is no more understanding of Alissa than Michel of Marceline, and that Jérôme's passivity tilts the story toward holiness (*André Gide*, 107–115). No matter what heights Alissa might achieve in isolation, it was terrible to be alone.

With the loneliness of Emmanuèle is blended the memory of Anna Shackleton, for it pained her pupil to think of Anna dying alone, in a bare room. "During weeks and months I was filled with the anguish of her solitude. I went on imagining, hearing the desperate call, then the relapse, of that loving soul which all but God deserted; and the echo of that call resounded in the last pages of my *Porte Étroite*." (*Si le Grain ne Meurt*, Part One, Ch. IX).

Gide is for progress but finds new achievement empty if unshared. The great discoveries for him are to be made in personal relationships. There must be solitary stretches on the road, but it should not end in solipsism. The wrong turn in puritanism is away from physical intimacy and the values emergent from it, so that fidelity is shriveled to what might have been. The great good thing in paganism is mutual development through friendship and affection, whereas failure to go hand in hand is the pitfall of that good. It is sad to have this happen, especially when it seems unnecessary, as with Michel and Marceline. The unhappiness of Alissa and Jérôme appears equally avoidable. Yet the reach for more than the grasp, no matter how disastrous when criminal or fanatical, remains the mainspring of evolution. The present can be explained to follow from the past, but the future is gratuitous. It must come discontinuous and unbelievable when introducing something very new, until the newness is worn down to the point where a standstill would be reached if novelty did not continue to surprise the world. The characteristic of youth is to love the unfamiliar and rush out to meet it, disregarding dangers that make elders shake their heads. Yet the young want passionately to share their adventure as it takes them away from those who cling to them.

Lusting after the future breaks up families. They are anchored in tradition, though once nomadic, and are on guard against wandering from the fold. "Families! I hate you! close firesides; locked doors; possessions jealous of happiness." Gide exclaims thus in *Les Nourritures Terrestres,* because the family is centered on the child, the perennial vagabond, cherishing but frustrating him. "Sometimes, invisible at night, I have stood leaning at a window, watching a long while the way of a house. The father was there, by the lamp; the mother was sewing; the place of a grandparent was vacant; a little boy, near the father, was studying—and my heart swelled with the wish to take him out with me on the roads" (*NT,* in *OC* II, 116). Yet, while drawn to the child, Gide could not help appreciating the parental anxiety to keep him safe at home. In *Le Retour de l'Enfant Prodigue* the repentant young prodigal, wondering how he had the heart to leave his mother, prepares to stay and console her. He is scolded by his older brother, keeper of order, who knows how long it took man to become man, and simply wants to hold the House. The Father does not confine salvation to the House. Others built it. He made the whole universe and the runaway, who could have found the Father without returning. But a prodigal too weak to go on did well to come back. The mother wants him to discourage a younger brother from running off, and the contrite son promises. But his hardships are glorious to the little fellow who will not let advice, which sounds out of character from one who had the courage to break loose, discredit his example. Confiding that he means to get out that very night, the little fellow begs his big hero to come with him—not wanting to go alone, though he must go. The ex-wanderer, home to stay, cannot help abetting the escape of the youngster; yearning to spare him the return, but not at the cost of thwarting his departure.

What a prodigal might do if able to resist coming back, is the question which intrigues Gide in *Les Caves du Vatican*. Lafcadio is without a puritan upbringing or a family to inhibit him. He has "the advantage of being a bastard." He is not married or engaged. His mother is dead, he does not remember his father. The "uncles" who took turns in forming him have equipped him with languages and skills with which to get along wherever he wants to go. Fearing nothing, loving no one, respecting no one but the unscrupulous Protos, never at a loss, Lafcadio is free. The avuncular advice most valuable in making his freedom effective is to keep no expense account and "not to worry in advance about having enough to satisfy my whim, my desire or my hunger." The last should be taken care of last because desire and whim have a "fugitive solicitation, whereas hunger always comes back and is only more imperious for waiting longer" (*Les Caves*, 1922 ed., 102–103). Here Gide has conceived a human being who approaches the unconcern of a god.

Les Caves du Vatican, like *Paludes* and *Le Prométhée Mal Enchaîné*, is called a farce (*sotie*) by the author, and is full of fun. Yet his animus against puritanism is so deep that he is fundamentally serious in imagining how it would be to get rid of inhibition. This passionate purpose enables him, as he put it himself, "to depict the nude beneath the clothing" of Lafcadio, who "felt good in his skin, good in his clothes, good in his shoes . . ." Nothing is allowed to bind or chafe. The world for him is a "soft prison" like "the supple moccasin" in which his foot could "stretch and flex and feel alive" (*ibid.*, 220). He is emancipated from logic as from ethics. Though he receives a legacy he will not let it affect his life. He will find as much pleasure in opposing appetite as in catering to it. Necessity shall not dictate. Since "nothing holds him in Paris or anywhere else," he boards a train. Travel is the Gidian symbol of freedom. He breathes well-being and enjoys the ripple of possibility in every muscle. His thoughts no less than his body are untrammeled as he considers that, whereas he had recently done a kind act for an old woman, he might as well have wrung her neck.

The incongruity between his eagerness, his equipment, and the absurdity of what he thinks of doing, is ludicrous if one expects great things of him. With his resources and daring, with his dream of "some beautiful prowess," he turns out to be just delinquent. The point of inventing him was to consider the possibility of a person who does things which have no point beyond that of exhibiting unmotivated behavior and the unexpectedness of its consequences. He was dissatisfied with his kind act because, while it was spontaneous, there was nothing surprising about it. Even his feat of saving a child from a burning house, though thrilling to the crowd, was not to his taste, because entirely called for by the situation—given his agility and nerve. He was after something more gratuitous, and wondered "what the old woman would have said if I had begun to squeeze. . . . One can imagine *what would happen if,* but there is always left a tiny space through which the unforeseen comes to light. Nothing ever happens exactly as one would have thought. . .

That is what prompts me to act. . . . One does so little!
. . . 'Let all that can be, be!' is how I explain the Creation
to myself. . . . In love with what might be. . . . If I
were the State, I'd have myself locked up" (*ibid.*, 221).

Here is the sense of a world in which creation has just
begun, and also awareness of a social structure prematurely stiffened against possibilities which would shake it
up. The urge to explore them must not be checked in a
free mind by established law or prejudice. This is perhaps taking *Les Caves* too seriously, since it is called a
farce. Still such preoccupations may appear somewhat
adolescent for the heir of European culture, unless its
lagging authority has actually retarded the inhabitants of
its aura so much that one could think it stupid to be law-
abiding, creative to be truant or even criminal.

The development of science and technology at the turn
of the century had generated great impatience with the
past. Following the automobile, the motion picture and
the airplane, came esthetic theories flouting tradition in
pursuit of dynamic expression. Gide's admiration of action
unhampered by customary considerations may be compared with the ideas of F. T. Marinetti, the father of
futurism. Gide thought him a conceited bore when he
met him in 1905, but was charmed by his verve in 1911
despite his ostentation, and was on the point of admitting
his genius (*Feuillets* attached to the *Journal* of 1911). In
reading his *Manifesto of Futurism* in the Parisian *Figaro*
for the 20th of February, 1909, Gide must have felt a
kinship with his own manual of emancipation, *Les Nourritures Terrestres,* and even more with the glorification of
the gratuitous act in his *Prométhée Mal Enchaîné.* He

must have seen that the adventures of Lafcadio in his forthcoming *Caves du Vatican* would delight the man who was announcing an anti-cultural, anti-logical, anti-sentimental program, a cult of creative intuition, of sheer originality. Gide could not make the recommended attack on syntax, but strove for an imagination without strings. At least he let Lafcadio do it, who seemed inspired by these words in Marinetti's *Manifesto:* "We want to celebrate the love of danger, the habit of energy and recklessness. Courage, audacity, rebellion, will be the essential elements in our poetry. Literature exalted, until today, pensive immobility, ecstasy and sleep; we want to exalt aggressive movement, feverish insomnia, the run, the somersault, the surprising stroke, the punch." (Quoted in the article on *Futurismo* in the *Enciclopedia Italiana* of 1934.)

To Lafcadio, bent on having full freedom and exercising it, his fellows are despicably tame and unimaginative. "God! how few people one meets whose valises one would care to search!" On the other hand, anybody could be made the subject of an interesting experiment. The dullest might yield "a bizarre reaction." This attitude is more than anti-social. Protos admires the Chicago gangsters, but Lafcadio says: "Not voluptuous enough for my taste, those wolves: my nature is feline" (*Les Caves*, 1922 ed., 222). Half a dozen years after the publication of *Les Caves* Chicago furnished something of this nature in the case of Loeb and Leopold: rich and educated boys, bored with ordinary wrongdoing as with being good, who read up refinements of evil and pursued them purely for excitement. Their intention also was the thrill of unmotivated

69

crime: "what an embarrassment for the police!" as Lafcadio says. But Lafcadio is different in disdaining to plan what he does, preferring to act on the spur of the moment; though he can enjoy a whetting amount of premeditation, and will plan in a pinch, as in getting ready to visit his late-discovered father. Lafcadio likes to consider his capacity and wants to show himself that he is a superman not hampered by scruples, vanities or sentiments. He jabs a point into his thigh whenever he has given way to such a weakness. But he does not have to ward off the morbid after-thoughts of Raskolnikov. Gide's character only regrets losing his new hat in the scuffle. But he balks at calling himself a criminal, liking to think he is just an adventurer trying to see if he is capable (like Raskolnikov) of closing the gap between imagination and deed. He realizes that he has "done it very quickly, while I felt like doing it" (*ibid.*, 287). To believe that anything has really happened is hard, and it is tedious to wait for his crime to become known. He does not want to be found out, but wants at least to be hunted, "like a child playing hide-and-seek" (*ibid.*, 237).

He is brought to his senses when his half-brother, learning the worst about him, reproaches him unbearably, saying in a discouraged sigh: "And just as I was beginning to love you!" (*ibid.*, 289). Braced for anything but that, and from a man he despises, Lafcadio finds himself melting and is filled with resentment. The suggestion is clear that love might have kept him from his mad course, and from readiness to resume it in the end. But it would have had to be a love he could have reciprocated. Not that of the girl who comes to comfort him in the night. He speaks of giving himself up to the police, to be less unworthy of her affection. But in the morning he looks out the open window instead of at her asleep beside him. "What! is he going to forego living?" and for the esteem of Geneviève, whom he esteems a bit less since she loves him a bit more? Does he still think of giving himself up?" (*ibid.*, 296).

So ends the story of Lafcadio, on a theme close to the heart of Gide: that living might be saved by love, but that only a love which is free can be efficacious, at dawn when the trees tremble outside. More explicitly: Gide thinks a woman's love is likely to hold back a young fellow from the best in him, and even fail to keep him from the worst, because less gratuitous and less instructive than a man's love. But the man must deserve emulation, and the result will be according to his caliber. What the uncles had to offer Lafcadio was absorbed through affection. This he did not exactly have for Protos—but nearly enough for Protos to teach him much. Julius de Baraglioul, the half-brother, exerts influence only by arousing a reaction; but his just-heard revelation of tenderness comes closer to chastening Lafcadio than for Geneviève to give him all she can.

In *Pages du Journal de Lafcadio*, which is the original project of the novel published a decade after *Les Caves—Les Faux-Monnayeurs*—there is recognition that Lafcadio's lack was love: "what I expect of you is cynicism, it is not insensibility. . . . Emotion is hampering; yet all is lost if one eludes it, or even if it merely diminishes." Cynicism appears to be urged in the sense of wholesome impudence and effrontery, without which the desiderated

71

emotion might become sentimental. "I am afraid you might confuse emotion with a softness verging on tears, having nothing to do with what I called sensibility—which is usually just a joyous agitation of life" (*OC* XI, 16–17). This may seem too much an understatement of the significance of love. The idea is: to arrive at a kind of attachment which is not a rival to the ongoing adventure of living, but a powerful impetus to it—steadying, steering, and never holding back. Hardness must be kept, the saucy offishness of Lafcadio toward anything weakening. Yet he needs sympathy: not to unnerve him, but to help him find a way of living in society with its laws, and not lose his élan. His capacity for the gratuitous act is the essence of being alive and the source of every enhancement of life—if not allowed to fritter away in escapades or head into the noose of crime. It is not a little thing to say of love, but the highest, that it can keep life fresh and free: keep it generous and keep it vibrant.

Such love, as it figures in *Les Faux-Monnayeurs,* delicately but definitely is homosexual. In the meantime Gide had published *Corydon,* after being deterred for years by the fears of friends. This book, in the form of dialogues between Corydon and a narrator, is a defense of uranism or "homosexuality among males," not only as natural but as conducive to civilization. Evidence for naturalness is gathered from near and far in the animal kingdom; evidence for civilizing effect is drawn mostly from Greece in the time of Pericles, though periods of artistic efflorescence in Roman, English, Italian, French, and Persian history are cited. In taking this stand Gide's paganism has seemed most contrary to puritanism. But a puritan may have a pure love, and Corydon contends that none is nobler than that preferred by the Greeks.

If it seems odd for him to talk of "normal homosexuals," he says it is because the serious books in the field have been written mostly by medical men, concerning "cases" which have come to them. They have not been consulted by happy well-adjusted homosexuals, but by shame-faced complaining ones. Sick people and perverts, men who assume the role of women or find pleasure in cruelty, are not the concern of Corydon. Gide himself has been very much concerned to establish the unfairness of judging homosexuality as a whole by them. But his purpose in finally publishing *Corydon* was less to offset the narrowness of clinical studies than to defend "the love which dares not tell its name" from the misrepresentations of poets and novelists who sacrificed their better knowledge to convention. He was aroused in particular by the transposition of sex whereby Proust siphoned the ideal features of love from the homosexual relationship and assigned them altogether to the approved kind, while transferring everything reprehensible to Sodom and Gomorrah and using his imagination to make them more lurid than ever.

Gide would like to show that Corydon's kind of love "is just as capable as the other of abnegation, sacrifice and even sometimes of chastity" (*Corydon*, 1926 ed., 166). Desire may be of either sort but virtue is the same in dominating it—not through suppressing it but through cultivating its finest possibilities. Mere desire, focused on immediate pleasure, Gide never equates with love in the eulogistic sense. He learned in Africa not to condemn pleasure, and he never lost his loyalty to something more.

73

Yet he saw that the Platonic scale of ascending devotion could rise from the sheer enjoyment of another's company, when the other was a worthy person. A boy's love for a man, as for a girl or woman, "if it is profound, tends to chastity—but only, it goes without saying, if it absorbs desire into itself, as mere friendship cannot do—and may be for the youngster the best invitation to courage, to work, to virtue" (*ibid.*, 180).

But to appreciate that a young person may derive inspiration and guidance from the sympathetic interest of an older person is far from justifying homosexuality. Whatever the benefits which Gide wants to attribute to it, he should consider more seriously the social disadvantages and personal maladjustments it is likely to mean especially for the young. He does not seem to advocate seduction, but he fails to recognize the usual legal and moral distinction between homosexual (or other) relations freely entered into by adults and the relations of an adult with a minor. The reasonableness of this distinction, resting upon the evil of taking advantage of the young, cannot be dismissed. The young are not in a position to realize the probable damage to their whole life-structure. Nor can the views of medical men be lightly ignored. They are not agreed as to whether homosexuality is just an abnormality with no psychopathic dimensions or a form of psychopathology, but the latter may become the settled view.

It is evident that there are better answers to Corydon than the final silence of his interlocutor. Thus Ramon Fernandez effectively exposes the error in assuming that from establishing the frequency of certain behavior in the animal kingdom the human desirability of the same thing would follow. He observes that apparently only a small proportion of homosexuals in modern society are the kind Gide considers wholesome; that an affair with a man is likely to prejudice a boy against women and form habits unfitting him for marriage instead of preparing him for it; and that Gide is naive in thinking social attitudes could be changed in favor of a practice now shorn of the heroic associations it once had (cf. Fernandez, *André Gide,* Ch. III).

The ardent comradery which led to great things in Greece, and is still a key to creative advance in art and science, could not well take place between the sexes when intellectual and cultural life went on outside the domestic sphere to which women were restricted. This has been the situation also in the Arab world that crucially influenced Gide. In France the tradition of the *jeune fille* is similar. There a girl has been supposed, if well brought up, to be sequestered from adult life until marriage. Then she would not only be handicapped by relative ignorance but would normally devote herself chiefly to household matters, missing the free interest and activity making for a stimulating personality. The role of wife and mother, in this pattern, is kept apart from amorous adventures, so that young men have affairs with women they would not marry—who may be more exciting than wives, but are instruments for satisfying desire rather than persons who can take desire into aspiration. Corydon dwells upon the modern exaggeration of sex appeal in woman whereby she is made a perpetual lover averse to maternity. Uranism would protect her, he thinks, from becoming a toy for men. But Corydon does not consider that in America,

England and Russia, where women also have been exploited and patronized, a more democratic atmosphere has been developing wherein girls, having more of the freedom that has been thought masculine, are more often able to be full comrades, before and after marriage; and thus profit by as well as provide qualities which quicken the relationships of men. Plato appreciated the value of these relations in the great days of Athens, but believed the ideal state would equalize the education of boys and girls to put them on the same footing. And he was convinced that education could not be effective unless a lively sympathy joined teacher and pupil in the adventurous pursuit of truth, goodness and beauty.

A reader may be influenced by Gide to become more tolerant toward victims of homosexuality, is assured that a taste for it is not easily acquired, and is made aware that heterosexuality is not in itself a guarantee of morals. Gide may be admired for his fearless defense of people who have unduly suffered in our society. But the benefit of "Greek love," when it can still manage to be beneficial, he shows to be the same as in any love that is free and genuine. This plea need not be weakened, though it may be explained, by the hypothesis that the great love in Gide's life could not develop freely and naturally, once he had turned to his own sex after feeling obliged to renounce the object of his desire, as a result of puritan education followed by the refusal of his cousin (cf. Martinet, *André Gide: L'Amour et la Divinité*, 118).

The real lesson of Gide is to trust love. For him the secret of love is faith in human promise. Love is the free gift of nature that unlocks possibility, firing men and women to rise above circumstance and recompense. One may say that not love but its distortion made him and his wife try beyond desire for more than private happiness. She in her good deeds and he in his work reached out in the direction of philanthropy. But it is hard to imagine either of them not outgoing, regardless of their domestic situation. Their long striving for the ideal of self-surpassing generosity would have carried them beyond their own bliss as it lifted them over their difficulties. He was convinced, with the backing of the Gospel, that love is just as unselfish as it is adventurous: that it will not want the adventure of living to be at the expense of fellows, and will overcome indifference or inertia. Love is kind. Love can be trusted. It must be cultivated beyond the household, whether frustrated there or not. Love is too expansive to be fulfilled at home, in the best home, for the role of love is to move the world as nothing else will.

Love, in Gide's dynamic liberating sense, is fused with the pioneering love of knowledge and progress, as the Gospel love is one with the truth that makes men free. This learning and daring love, of human life and of what it might become, leads out of the swamps of puritanism, past the gardens of paganism, to a creative future; for the supremely gratuitous love of going on, as long as love does not fail.

3. GOD, SON OF MAN

"CATHOLICISM IS INADMISSIBLE. PROTESTANTISM IS INTOLER-
able. And I feel myself profoundly Christian" (*OC* VII,
532). This had long been Gide's position when the war
of 1914 forced him to reconsider, not only through direct
impact on him but also through the deepening religious
experience of friends. Several of them, becoming con-
verts to Catholicism, wanted him to join them. It was
a temptation to take a step represented as settling everything and relieving one of responsibility beyond what it
was well for a man to bear. Had he been indifferent or
hostile to the faith around him his friends would have
been less insistent. He seemed trembling on the verge of
going over, as they had been, and at times he was. But
the more his emotion rose, under the pressure of indecision, the more he felt the need of knowing what he
was doing.

True to his forward orientation, he wrote in his *Journal:* "If I had to formulate a credo, I should say: God

is not behind us. He is to come. It is not at the début, it is at the close of the evolution of beings that he must be sought. He is terminal and not initial. . . . And since time does not exist for him, it is the same to him whether that evolution which he crowns follows or precedes, or whether he determines it by attraction or propulsion" (*OC* VIII, 207–208). It may seem not very consistent that, while rejecting orthodox dogma, Gide thus sought an interpretation of God still in terms of it. In particular it appears careless that for a while he spoke of evolution as determined so completely that it might as well be controlled entirely from behind. Where then was the gratuitous act, which had been the great thing for him, because ungrounded, unlimited, unpredictable? Perhaps, however, nothing was more gratuitous than God: the goal beyond all going, the beginning for which there was no reason. But while Gide enjoyed a long look into the incomprehensible, his vision of God was less a metaphysical speculation than the felt exaltation whereby man refreshes himself and adds to his stature. In such a practical attitude, if God was the focus of beneficial contemplation, God was real enough. Or did this reduce God to a subjective idea, a merely human projection? Distraught by war work, devoting himself to the relief of Belgian refugees, Gide set aside time for meditation, morning and evening. It calmed him but the devil whispered that he was playing a comedy (*OC* VIII, 216–217). There was no use in calling on God for what hygiene would do (*OC* VIII, 267). But would it do?

The secret Gide needed he thought he found in the Gospel, though what it was he would have to work out.

79

The idea grew on him of doing this in a book of meditations or "elevations," as a pendant to his *Nourritures Terrestres*. "Except a man be born again" struck him in the English Bible (*OC* VIII, 210–211), and that was to be the burden of his subsequent thought about morality and religion, as it had actually been since the first trip to Africa. *Numquid et Tu* (from John 7:52, "Art thou also of Galilee?") was put at the head of the 24th or "Green" notebook of 1916–1919, the section of his *Journal* most given to religious searching. Somewhat earlier he had been reading about the authenticity of the Gospels in the appendix of his *Vulgate,* and comparing them with the help of concordances. He seems not to have gone seriously into recent Biblical criticism, much as it should have interested him. He was not in the mood to use a scholarly approach, for he said of the Gospel as a whole: "It is not a question of explaining but of admitting it. Commentaries are superfluous" (*OC* VIII, 311). He wanted to find out for himself, in religion as in life and art. Interpreting the Kingdom of God as being born again, he spoke of this as the Gospel's *esthetic:* "To forget what other men have written, painted, thought, and what one has oneself thought" (*ibid.,* 314).

It may seem paradoxical that while thus asserting himself he should seize upon the idea of dying to oneself as "the secret of the superior happiness of Christ" (*ibid.,* 317). He repeated that the mysterious center of Christian morality lay in the idea of giving one's life to get it back, and spoke of it as "the triumph of the individual through the renunciation of individuality" (*ibid.,* 321). The sum of it all was in the word Joy, which had been the keynote

of *Les Nourritures Terrestres,* when he was in revolt
against puritanism. But then he had sought joy through
forgetting good and evil; now he prayed to be delivered
from the stain of sin. This was so confusing that he was
afraid the devil was duping him. Gide's thinking was so
personal as to have no objective means of knowing whether
the too-precious self was being lost in a way to be saved
or just lost. He wanted to find his own salvation, go directly to God with no intermediary but the figure and
teaching of Christ. Balking at orthodoxy without yet being
ready to follow through a critique of it, he relied almost
entirely on his own study of various translations of the
New Testament: chiefly John, then Luke, then Paul.
He said he never had a conflict with Christ—only with
Paul. Yet the Pauline doctrine of the sacrificial death
was more in Gide's mind than his criticism of that position would suggest; and he used the theological title
Christ, almost never the man's name Jesus. To want to
bear the cross of Christ and to share his suffering, Gide
felt was to misconstrue the gift made through the cross;
but it was not until later that he questioned the idea of a
divine ransom for sinful men. The miracles did not strike
him as strengthening the teaching—which he would believe anyway. Logically then, he should have been more
interested in the difficulty of ascertaining what Jesus said,
and what it meant originally. How his teaching would
have been intended for Jewish hearers, how much it
was to be found already in the Psalms and Isaiah; and
how much of it was interpolated by gospel-editors more
concerned to register the views of the early Christian
church than to preserve historical accuracy—all this

should have been important to Gide. Repudiating both Catholicism and Protestantism, yet clinging to the Gospel, he could not say that for him it made no difference what Jesus did or said. He could not hold that the effective life of Jesus began with his death; that his significance was to be found less in his lifetime than in the church and tradition he supposedly established, then guided from on high. Without church or tradition to lean on, though cherishing the divinity of Christ, he was torn between belief and disbelief, according to his feeling and fear of mere feeling. The text of the New Testament was still there, but he had extended the Protestant freedom of private interpretation. Some things might seem perfectly clear, but his imagination could never leave anything obvious or literal. And if he was to believe in a divine Christ it was no harder, was even necessary, to believe in the devil: as a way of accounting for dryness interrupting joy that should have been indefeasible; as an explanation of doubt where faith wanted to be unquestioning.

Incredulity about the devil had to be overcome if he was to be real enough to take the blame for religious wavering. No devil, then no excuse for misgivings about Christ and God. That is, no excuse would be left but sheer personal infidelity—or rational rejection of supernatural figures as such. In either case the more than human comfort Gide thought he needed would be forfeit. To accept the popular image of the devil, he was too sophisticated; yet he feared a trap in his effort to be reasonable, as well as in mere feeling. The more he thought about the devil the more he found him at home in reasonableness. "The great mistake is to imagine the devil romantically. That is why it has taken me so long to recognize him. He is no more romantic or classic than the person with whom he talks. . . . He became classic for me when it was necessary in order to catch me, and because he knew I would not willingly regard a certain happy balance as evil. . . . Through measure I thought to master evil; and it was through this very measure that the Evil One took me in" (*OC* VIII, 334).

"It is in lack of love that the Evil One attacks us," Gide says toward the end of his *Numquid et Tu,* and it closes protesting devotion to Christ and God: fused in one presence, as the future life is absorbed in the eternal now for him who listens to the Word. The love declared there was to keep him out of the Catholic Church, for he became convinced that Catholics did not understand the Gospel. Remarking that they were not expected to read it save in excerpts, he quoted what he thought significant words, though not sure they could be attributed to Maurras: "I'll never quit the wise cortege of Fathers, councils, popes and all the great men of the modern élite, *to trust myself to the gospels of four obscure Jews*" (*OC* IX, *Feuilles Inédits,* 366). Such submission to authority and prestige distressed Gide in the conversion of a friend like Henri Ghéon. And Jacques Rivière admitted that he knew Christ only through the catechism. The Gospel did not appeal to him when he was persuaded by Gide to go through it for the first time. Because he wanted to approach God directly, Rivière said he did not like to read, "No one comes to the Father but through me," (*OC* IX, *Feuilles Inédits,* 370). What bothered Gide was that joining the

83

Catholic Church did not seem to mean coming to Christ, since it followed Paul. "If the Church had adhered closely to Christ, Protestantism would not have been possible. Christ did not say: "the Church is the way, the truth, and the life.' He said: 'I am . . .'" (ibid., 371). And Gide wrote that he could never "open the Gospel without feeling directly and individually addressed." He felt that one who understood it could not defer its urgency. Yet he found himself listening repeatedly to the devil, who always got the last word (ibid., 384–385).

Study of Dostoyevsky confirmed Gide's Protestant inclination to pit the Gospels against Roman Catholicism (cf. Dostoievsky, 151–152); and Dostoyevsky, along with Blake, was to help Gide think seriously about the devil (cf. ibid., 153–154, 172), although he was to differ from them in becoming a humanist rather than a mystic. To many it would seem the devil's doing when he considered the moral law to be more like the laws of harmony which the musician may elude than like the law of gravity for the architect (OC IX, 541). It might easily seem that the devil got Gide to interpret "Take all that you have and give it to the poor" as an injunction to strip off all that he had inherited in the way of "ideas, opinions, habits, modesty" (ibid., 452). This left him with a loving will "free for the first comer," but also with a "disorder of desire." If pride separated him most from God, and he was most proud of his virtue, it must not be permitted to stand in the way (ibid., 453). Though following the fiery pillar of Christ's teaching, Gide well knew how such "excess of renunciation, this renunciation of virtue for the love of virtue itself," would strike literal readers; but affirmed this paradox to be henceforth the guide of his life. He recognized that he would have to determine whether it was the dictation of the devil or not. But that could wait. "It is enough to say that for the moment I am going forward boldly on such a new route for me. A route? What am I saying! . . . Each step I take ahead is an adventure into the unknown" (*ibid.*, 454).

One may say that this was still the same adventure as in *Les Nourritures Terrestres,* with a difference quite as unexpected as might have been anticipated. When Gide was turning from puritanism to paganism it could not have been foreseen that his defense of *Corydon* would coincide with his deepening love of Christ. When Jacques Maritain tried to dissuade him from publishing *Corydon,* Gide's answer was his horror of falsehood. "Perhaps that is where my Protestantism is most enduring. . . . Catholics don't like the truth." Maritain of course replied that Catholicism teaches the love of truth. Gide demurred: "I have seen too often, too many examples of what adjustments were possible." He would not agree that the book was dangerous, or that it could be as dangerous as the lie of hiding its truth. As a last resort he was urged to promise he would ask Christ whether it was right to go ahead with publication. This he refused: "Understand, Jacques Maritain . . . I have lived too long and too intimately with the thought of Christ to consent to call him today as one would telephone somebody . . . never has my prayer been other than an act of adoration. . . . It has always seemed to me unworthy to demand anything

85

of God. I have always accepted everything from him, with gratitude. No; do not ask me that" (*Journal*, 21 December, 1923).

Gide must have meant that his own thorough consideration of the objections to *Corydon*, over the years, constituted a more genuine appeal to Christ than a belated interview which would have no point unless assuming that Christ had not been present all along in his thinking. It would be superstitious and presumptuous to summon Christ for an opinion, if his intimate influence day in and day out had been illusory. To summon him now, as if nothing had been settled, would suggest that all the hours with him should be outweighed by a moment with Maritain. He was sincere in his proposal, and felt the authority of the Church to justify him; whereas Gide felt the devil ready to discredit intentions and upset whatever appeared sure. There would be no security for Gide unless he could overcome the devil or find him better than his reputation.

Both alternatives were to be accomplished by emancipation from orthodoxy. A finite God, a human Christ, would not need the devil for a whipping boy. Relieved of opposing absolutes and of taking the blame for their apparent shortcomings, the devil could campaign against the conventional good and truth which stood in the way of something better. This would still· bring him obloquy and he might still deserve it, for downright evil as well as for unwelcome openmindedness. But whatever he had to do with limbering up old ideas was so much to the good. Gide came to say (in 1926) that orthodox Christianity was too exclusive, because "belief in *its* truth excluded belief in any other truth. . . . Humanism, on the contrary . . . tends to take in and absorb all forms of life, to reach an understanding with all beliefs if not to assimilate them—even those which repel it, even those which deny it, even the Christian belief. Culture should realize that trying to absorb Christian orthodoxy means taking in a mortal opponent. This is an attempt to admit something which can admit nothing but itself" (*OC* XIV, 320). Thus in Gide's mature reflection, as in his youthful paganism, he denounced his old religion for blocking progress. But now he was careful to attack intransigent orthodoxy and to isolate it from a Christianity that could march on to a fusion with humanism, becoming wholly a religion of human values found in experience and resting frankly upon it.

This is far from the nihilism he deplored in his friend Roger Martin du Gard. Gide could not see why choice should be limited to orthodoxy or emptiness, as if life could have no other basis. He felt he was going well beyond such a negative outlook toward a firm footing for morality. "It seems monstrous to me that man should need the idea of God to keep his balance on the earth; that he should have to accept absurdities in order to build anything solid; that he should feel unable to demand of himself what religious convictions artificially obtained from him, so that he would let everything go to smash at the moment his heaven was vacated" (*ibid.*, 378). But just as Gide repudiated orthodox Christianity and not what he took to be the religion of Jesus, so he was giving up the idea of a God mystically above the world and was working toward a God naturally derived from human ex-

87

perience. This may be understood as the implication of his saying, a little later: "I am an unbeliever. I shall never be impious" (*ibid.*, 387). Though he could no longer hold to a transcendent supernatural deity, he never lost reverence for the human content in the idea of God: the hope, gratitude, and worship or appreciation which the idea represents. This human meaning he found obscured in mysticism, though the mystical attitude itself might be explained as an effort to recover from the externality of staid religious forms the fervor of intense personal experience. Whereas conventional religion lacked the immediacy he felt in the Gospel, his own resort to mysticism was rooted in orthodoxy and not without precedent that had become almost orthodox; for Christianity had a host of mystics who could not have remained within it if their irregularity had not been tolerated; any more than they could have tolerated it if not in their fashion. Mysticism is the safety-valve which has kept traditional religion from being exploded by its volatile spirits. But the price of their saving independence has been irrationality. Heeding only their own feeling, they have been left with nothing else. This was Gide's situation in *Numquid et Tu*. There, as earlier in *André Walter,* he would soar to God on wings of emotion; but they were not strong enough, or the body of his naturalism was too heavy. He must come down where it was awkward to linger.

In ten years after *Numquid et Tu* he got over mysticism and was free to assail it, because he no longer needed its levitation to escape orthodoxy. He believed that in *La Porte Étroite* he had already warned against the extreme individualism in the Protestant form of mysticism (*OC* XIV, 408). But now he was through. "No matter in what form, there is no worse enemy than mysticism. And I hope my profound acquaintance with the question, through repeated personal experience and through sympathy—for theoretical, philosophical, historical, or scientific knowledge about the mystic state is not very informative—may give my testimony some weight. People have too readily believed with Souday that to shy from this [mystical] approach implies a certain mental inadequacy. . . . I think I am much better qualified to denounce or arraign mysticism than one who has never had any truck with it" (*ibid.*, 388). Later he said: "Mystical ideas: I slip back into them as into old shoes; I feel at ease in them, but I prefer to go barefoot" (*OC* XV, 199).

Gide's writing upon the whole opposes orthodoxy and the obscurantism associated with it, not simply through a new orientation but also from inside. He has been as imbued with traditional religion and its vapor of mysticism as anyone, and has found them wanting in their own terms, in their own scale, when experienced with their appropriate sensibility and imagination. The mere scientist or materialist or practical man has often been snubbed for obtuseness to the subtleties of the spirit. But Gide has been at home in them, expressing their indigenous mood with authentic eloquence, and cannot be patronized by people who pride themselves on being above science, which is the modern form of reason supported by experimental method. Gide himself feels that science has not reached the point of dealing adequately with the mystic state, but he believes in trying to understand it. "And what do you mean by 'mysticism?'" he asks himself. "That which presupposes and demands the abdication of reason" (*OC* XIV, 388).

It struck him that men would naturally rely upon faith in one another except in extremities where their combined efforts were of no avail. Then to call upon supernatural aid was tantamount to admitting helplessness, in a way to lessen the sense of human limitation for the moment but ultimately to exaggerate it. Thus he was horrified by prayers for men who could not be saved from a disabled submarine. "I wish people might be brought up so they would not be driven to despair when suddenly realizing that God is missing. Better to be convinced of that beforehand; for the best means of keeping Him from failing us is clearly in learning to do without Him" (*ibid.*, 394–395).

But it was only an impossible idea of God that Gide would do without—the metaphysical idea of a divine power at once so great and so concerned about men that the problem of evil became inevitable and insoluble. The name of God could not in the same sense designate the order and power of the natural world, and also the love and aspiration focused in Christ. It was easier for Gide to think of two Gods. There was no use praying to a God of nature. To ask such a God "to intervene in the operation of his own laws is impious" (Pléiade ed. of *Journal 1889–1939*, 1190). "This involuntary God, who makes it rain indifferently on all—the only true god that we confess upon awaking, each day—has nothing to do with the fierce Jehovah . . . any more than with the god of love who is incarnated in Christ. . . . Nothing is more likely to warp the mind, warp it irremediably, than this accord which is attempted between irreconcilable elements." He added that it took a mental acrobat "to believe that it was only man's weakness which kept him from fitting his liberty into God's foreknowledge." If liberty was genuine there could be no foreknowing what it would bring; and he believed too much in liberty to worship a God for whom it could not be real. He preferred a God who would "prefer insubordination to genuflection" (*ibid.,* 1173). After having accepted the orthodox conception of an omnipotent omniscient God, creator and controller of everything, he had to rebel against the very idea. But while denying the existence of a God who could prevent evil or freedom, yet recognizing a God of things as they are, an "involuntary God," he sought a more congenial God, in keeping with the figure of Christ.

Confused as Gide admitted himself to be in his private theology, he trusted his feeling of being drawn by pious souls. He seemed to have their sense of rapprochement with God, which was "not so much a situation as a state of mind," so delicious that to lose it was to be inconsolable (*Pages de Journal 1939–1942,* 129). But he made the exciting and comforting discovery that his *communion* was with a coming God—not one already existent. Then the puzzle of his doubts and affirmations could be put together. There was no God to save men from disaster when their fellows failed. The only real God, actually and adequately in the world already, was just a name for the laws of nature. Being everywhere they could not be what one yearned to have draw near. Self-sufficient and independent of man, they would not heed his prayer or need

91

his help. There could be no covenant between man and the God of nature. But a God whose coming depends on each of us has a claim on us. There is no question of his failing us but of our failure to reach out and make him real. Nor will realization of him conflict with human liberty but achieve it more effectively.

Such a view, if Gide could have maintained it, might have enabled him to reconcile his religious longing with his scientific outlook; but he slipped back from the idea of a God in the making to that of a Maker who was in the beginning. This reversal was recorded in the *Journal* of 1942: "Science, it is true, progresses only in substituting *how* for *why;* but, however far back it is pushed, there remains always a point where the two questions join and merge. To obtain man, millions of centuries would not have sufficed if chance alone had been at work . . . the mind cannot help admitting a propensity, a bent, which befriends the confused groping and unconscious steps of matter toward life, toward consciousness; then, through man, toward God." At the very moment when Gide was rejoicing to envisage a God ahead, who might consistently be the God of scientific discovery, genuine novelty and the sheer adventure of the gratuitous act, the dead hand of orthodoxy was felt. The prodigal son of Protestantism had to come home. In a few lines can be seen his brave departure and his loss of nerve, his fear of impiety toward the past. "As soon as I had understood that God was not yet, but was on the way to being, and that his becoming depended on each of us, morality was restored in me. There was no impiety or presumption in this thought, for I persuaded myself simultaneously that God was not to be achieved unless by man and through him; but that if man led to God, creation, to come as far as man, took off from God, so that the divine could be recovered at both ends . . . and that there had been no setting out except to arrive at God." Thus Gide had it both ways: emergent evolution and a cosmic scheme to control it. He had: "God creating man in order to be created by him" (*Pages de Journal 1939–1942*, 144).

But while Gide had two ideas of God which could never be quite compatible, they might be taken as symbolic of the past and future, as they somehow fit together, though they pull apart. Each departure is conditioned, the future could not be what it will be if the past had not been what it was. Yet it would not seem necessary for him to conclude that the future was prevised. And he made plain in some passages that he did not. He saw that to take evolution seriously was to open up the past and the future, in such fashion that neither could be known except in the tentative and hypothetical way of science. "If man is susceptible of changing in the future, one may be equally sure that he has not always been what he is." This takes man out of the scheme of traditional religion, in spite of the effort to make it reach around evolution; an effort which could succeed only if time were halted and progress frozen (Pléiade ed. of *Journal 1889–1939*, 1286). In the evolutionary view, humanity was not specially created any more than anything else, and was not the ward of a brooding Providence.

If, out of infinite possibilities, one world had been chosen and worked out, a divine mind back of us would be the only explanation. But to think of an original choosing and working-out is to presuppose a God who then had to be there. If the world did not need a creator, to think him necessary would not be logical; and we know nothing of the origin of the world, or even that it had a beginning. One could as well suppose that the world always existed, so solidly that it would have taken a God to prevent it. Therefore, since the world is, no God was there to interfere. That man should have appeared, and that just the combination of circumstances occurred to permit his appearance and survival, is wonderful; but the chance of any other phenomenon becoming a fact, when pitted against all possible rivals, should be just as wonderful. Granted a world of any sort, and that it would shake down to some adjustment of structure and process, the complication and interdependence of elements could not have been intended without awesome control. But to imagine the role of a creator to account for a wholly supposititious intention, on the chance that there might have been one, and might have been a world-beginning to be intended, is to invoke chance much more recklessly than to think that "chance alone" could have led to man through millions of centuries. For this "lone chance," though in retrospect the frail torch-bringer of our existence, with a universe of odds against it, was the hardy child of all the chances, sheltered by the jostling that shouldered out the dinosaurs.

Had this child not survived we should not have grieved. It is because we rejoice in human life and cherish it, that we feel it slender and precarious. We forget that it is nourished by the earth as much as trees and glaciers. The wonder of it all for us is in our own wonder, which so recreates everything as to make us think the origin of consciousness could not have been unwitting. But as children are often begotten without being wanted, yet become knowing enough, the eventual intelligence of the race does not verify the myth of a deliberate creation. For Gide the important question is not how we came to be here and to acquire awareness, but where we are going, now that we have religion, art and science. Up to a point we may simply have grown, without a God to sow or save us. But, having grown to the point of creating God, we must rise to that possibility or fall back. Ever since the sense of right and wrong dawned in Egypt, the idea of a deity worthy of man's idealism has been fashioned and refined, while men have sought, not too steadily, to live up to their finest insight. Shall this effort abate because no God in the beginning guaranteed a God to come through the blind evolution of man as picked up eventually by the self-reliant use of his imaginative intelligence? A haphazard origin does not detract from the dignity of man; it does not depreciate divinity to be the outgrowth of humanity. God, is not man's endowment but his possible achievement, to be had only by winning, and won only by going ahead.

That Gide tried at times to state this idea more or less in religious terms it outreaches, should not be allowed to compromise it; especially since he repudiated those terms when he felt they were wrong. Though retaining the God-word he realized that what he wanted to mean by it must be differentiated from some of its associations, and he cared more about affirming an attitude than about affirming a word. He said: "There is a certain way of adoring God which strikes me as blasphemy. There is a certain way of denying God which comes back to adoration" (*ibid.*, 1288). He was using the idiom he had, so far as he could. But while he put new wine into old bottles, he believed he found the new wine in the Gospel. He was solemn in asserting that he followed it, never twisting it to follow him. The difficulty of distinguishing what Jesus said from what has been ascribed to him makes it hard to know how accurately Gide adheres to him. But, having arrived at his understanding of the Gospel through reason and love, he said he would not deny reason and turn to the "blind belief" demanded by the Church in its conception of Faith (*Pages de Journal 1939–1942*, 158).

It is in a couple of imaginary interviews, put under the heading of *Dieu, Fils de L'Homme* (in *Pages de Journal 1939–1942*), that he most clearly removes this "blind belief" from what he considers to be an enlightened faith. He says: "belief in a personal God, in Providence, implies an abdication of everything reasonable in us. I even prefer, and emphatically, the '*Quia absurdam*' to every stretch of ratiocination whereby some insert in the divine plan the chance results of natural forces and laws, or the criminal follies of men. . . . I find it much more comforting to consider God as an invention, a human invention, which man develops little by little, tends to shape up more and more, through intelligence and virtue. It is toward Him that creation is moving, reaching, and not from Him that it emanates. And since time does not exist for the Eternal, it comes to the same thing, for Him" (*ibid.*, 159).

What place anything eternal has in the evolutionary

96

scheme of Gide, the philosophy of Whitehead might elucidate. Gide himself is not concerned with this problem, but with showing verbal support for humanism in the text of the Gospel. He would not express it this way. "I have said and I repeat: it is not the business of the true Christian to interpret the Gospel words in one way or another, but to believe them and put them into practice. That is not to say I pretend always to have done so" (*OC* XIV, 403). He has been quite aware of finding in those words a meaning at variance with Catholic and orthodox Protestant theology. For him that is because their adherents interpret and construe the Gospel. "I take these words just as they are given in this little book which confounds the wisdom of men" (Pléiade ed. of *Journal 1889–1939*, 1286). Yet he recognizes that the living truth is not received once for all but is something growing, something to strive for. The crucial divergence for him is between truth that is sought through a lifetime of research and the Truth of the believers: a Truth one "would not seek unless one had already found it," which is made all-sufficient (*OC* XIV, 159–160).

Gide's Catholic critics treat him primarily as a heretic whose fundamental fault lies in failing to accept their position. To them he has emptied the idea of God of its veritable meaning, has thereby lost all hold on the world, and is condemned to loneliness, without a goal. His search for new values they dismiss as the nihilism of a French Nietzsche (cf. Wittrock, *Der Gottesbegriff im Werk André Gides*). From their point of view it is overweening to think of new values, and one who tries it must be miserable. Thus René Schwob is convinced that Gide is des-

97

perately sad because he is not an orthodox Christian, and undertakes to explain his work as the effort of a man to deliver himself from an excessive burden of scruples, timidity and abnormal sexuality (in *Le Vrai Drame d'André Gide*). It is suggested that all this could be forgiven or considered as a handicap despite which Gide made a contribution, if only he were contrite, or confessedly unhappy like Rimbaud and Baudelaire. But Gide has insisted upon his joy. Instead of repenting, Schwob says, he seeks public absolution through his books; but owing to the absence of Catholicism they are only schemes without flesh or vigor (*ibid.*, 170–171). His work is a substitute for God, an esthetic transformation of the puritan heresy (*ibid.*, 180–181).

Charles Du Bos, though friendly and sympathetic with Gide, takes the same line: that his work shows a steady loss of orientation in the spiritual world, a diminution of the "sense of the invisible," of God (*Le Dialogue avec André Gide,* 301). The sad upshot for Du Bos is that Gide is left without a destination (*ibid.,* 344). The notion of his fundamental timidity and need of esteem is stressed by Emile Gouiran: after a gloomy childhood he was dominated by anxiety and the need for escape (*André Gide: Essai de Psychologie Littéraire*). For Gouiran the key to Gide is a "nervous process which goes from uneasiness to relief, in passing through timidity and anguish," and this is said to explain his attitude toward God (*ibid.,* 163). Since he cannot maintain the summit of this process beyond the exhaustion of the organism, he loses God (*ibid.,* 164), until he can work himself up again, and so he tries to imagine a world that will prolong his anguish

GOD, SON OF MAN

(*ibid.*, 179). The trouble is identified as failure to see his problem in terms of original sin and transubstantiation through Christ. "But, in fact, has he ever really had the Faith?" (*ibid.*, 232).

After reading Gouiran, Gide wrote that he would like to inscribe a sentence from Bossuet as a motto for "the book of Du Bos, that of Schwob, and this study: 'It is impossible that he teaches well since he does not teach in the Church.'" (In a letter to the publisher of Gouiran's book, reproduced in the front of it.)

Maintaining that disquietude was not characteristic of himself, at least on the days when he did his best work, Gide wrote to André Rouveyre: "I hold that the truly uneasy ones are precisely those who cannot live without a system: the Massis, the Maritains. . . . But our good Catholics today cannot admit that one can find calm, balance and serenity anywhere outside the dogma. I wish you would not join them in that; it would please them too much." (In a letter from Gide to Rouveyre, quoted in *Le Reclus et le Retors: Gourmont et Gide* by André Rouveyre, pp. 200–201. Cf. also pp. 206–207, a page from Gide's *Journal* for 11 November, 1944.)

Albert Thibaudet said: "This at least would be enough for criticism to keep an instructive place for Gide: that since the Edict of Nantes he is our only notable Protestant writer, not exiled, not an expatriate, but of an education and nature entirely French." Martinet quotes these words at the head of his chapter on *André Gide Protestant*, where he comments on the scandal that Gide's Protestantism has been to critics for whom it was axiomatic that an artist could not be of that extraction. His work must be a failure.

Yet the limpid magic of his style cannot be denied except through prejudice. And his being an artist has been less upsetting than his being a thinker.

Most disturbing is his Protestant encouragement of free examination in the individual, as against "Catholic immobility." Such liberty would blur the limits of religion and lead to atheism, to intellectual chaos, to Nietzsche. (Paraphrased from Fouillée as quoted by Gide and reproduced by Martinet, 79–80.) This could not foster repose, and Gide did not seek repose, any more than his admired Nietzsche. Gide defied his critics with the remark that there was a Catholic orthodoxy but not a French one. Henri Massis could not forgive him. For Massis the culture of France was at stake, and western civilization, since Gide was insidiously trying to "de-occidentalize us, de-catholicize us." The attempt seemed to Massis nothing short of "demoniacal." (Martinet, 90–91). It did not help matters that Gide quoted Jesus in justification. What the Catholic critics would not see or could not admit was the affirmation in his Protestantism, the constructive human promise in his drive for freedom from all that had bound him. To them his effort to go beyond Protestantism had its logical outcome in anarchy.

He seemed deliberately to invite such condemnation when he held up as the ideal the unprejudiced mind "or one which knew how to loosen its prejudices" (*Un Esprit Non Prévenu,* 9). He could say, "The troublous elements of the mind will tomorrow be the best," (*ibid.,* 35), and cast doubt upon his own virtuous declarations, such as the profession in the 1927 preface to *Les Nourritures Terrestres,* that fidelity was the keynote of his life—saying

100

it sounded a little hollow afterwards (*ibid.*, 36). As if he had no character of his own he would identify himself with the very different characters of his imagination, and observe: "It is coming back to myself that embarrasses me; for in truth I no longer know *who* I am; or, if you like: I never am—I am becoming." (*ibid.*, 39–40). He has often spoken of being drawn to whatever was opposed to himself, and he said he learned to like attacks better than praise because the bitterness of his enemies enabled him to realize his importance: "They fight me, therefore I am" (*ibid.*, 46).

But for all his refusal to be bound, and his ingratitude, one may ask whether he did reject the faith of his Huguenot fathers; or only puritanism, as Martinet thinks (*André Gide: L'Amour et la Divinité*, 95). The question is really whether the Protestant faith should be limited to the letter of its sixteenth-century formulation, or associated rather with its spirit of progressive liberation. Gide remained a Protestant in this freer sense. His instability, his impatience with anything settled, his preferring departures to arrivals, helped him to re-think religion and morality in keeping with his appreciation of the pioneering, world-changing spirit of science. His constitutional unrest helped him to feel what his restless age needed.

Sybrandi Braak, a Dutch writer, has well stated the case for Gide as revealing the widespread "uncertainty and anguish of the modern conscience," and trying to work toward a position more tenable and hopeful than the orthodox one. "We refuse to believe that the heterodoxy of Gide is fundamentally irreligious. We believe on the contrary that religion is for him what it is for many of our contemporaries: the instinctive need through which man is led to recognize his better self." Braak continues: "He alone is religious, in the philosophic sense of the word, who seeks, who thinks, who loves the truth that reconciles love of the ideal with love of humanity. This religion is not trimmed to any dogma." He notes that Maurice Barrès dreamed of a Catholicism which would not exclude freedom of thought, but replies that the Encyclical *Pascendi dominici gregis* of Pope Pius X in 1907 against the modernists shows the folly of this dream (*André Gide et L'Ame Moderne*, 191–193). Although covering Gide's stories only up to 1920, Braak's book goes far to establish that their significance consists in "marking the effort of a generation toward spiritual deliverance" (*ibid.*, 107).

Fernandez also maintains that what Du Bos deplored as "de-spiritualization" in Gide, his rejection of orthodox Christian spirituality, is today the necessary preface to a genuine "re-spiritualization" (*André Gide*, footnote, 152–153). Fernandez gives eloquent testimony to the gratitude of people who were young in 1914, and of French youth later, for spiritual encouragement found in Gide when they were unmoved by the spokesmen of traditional morality (*ibid.*, 136–141). Mademoiselle Nadejda Forch vividly put the redemptive power of Gide's sympathy with "those who are subjected by life." She said: "They are the children, the adolescents, the old." (*Cahiers de la Quinzième*, Sixième Cahier de la Vingtième Série, 25 mars, 1930, pp. 46–47). Gide's wholesome influence upon countless persons is also emphasized by Roger Martin du Gard (in *Hommage à André Gide*, 179–183).

GOD, SON OF MAN

The difference between Gide and his Catholic critics is that between a dogma not to be questioned and a view which thrives on inquiry and experiment. He knows the Church would not condemn Galileo today, and believes it slowly makes progress by retreating. The imaginary reviewer says: "And in this very falling back, orthodoxy grows stronger." He is answered: "My mind refuses to submit to any orthodoxy whatsoever." The dialogue continues:

He—And yet you recognize the excellence of the evangelical precepts. Without the Faith all significance evaporates from their most handsome practice.

I—Say that it takes on a different meaning, and that I am free to express it.

He—Yes; through pride.

I—I was waiting for that word. Believers are obliged to give a pejorative interpretation to everything great, noble, beautiful, which is done with independence.

He—Independence! Ah! this is surely the moment to speak of it! You recognize however that today it is more important than ever to group, to organize . . .

I— . . . One can always find excellent motives for repudiating reason and keeping man from thinking. It is fine to put wills together: nothing great is done without submission or discipline. But to demand devotion in order to prevent the exercise of reason, to regulate thought by a watchword, can lead only to a general stupidity.

(*Pages de Journal 1939–1942*, 160–162, Pantheon Books, Inc.)

But much as Gide looks forward to an open future for creative intelligence and hates to have it cramped by any sort of oath, he still looks back with piety and would like to join the two vistas. It bothers him to think of two Gods, though he has tried. At least he continues to find two dimensions in the idea of God: one indicating the power and actuality of existence; the other representing the love and aspiration of man. These two things are so different as to be opposed, he says in the same imaginary interview.

On the one hand the whole of the Cosmos and the natural laws which govern it; matter and force, energy; that is the side of Zeus; and one may well call that God, but in depriving the word of all personal and moral significance. On the other hand the bundle of human efforts toward the good, toward the beautiful, the slow mastery of brutal forces and putting them in service for realizing the good and the beautiful on the earth; this is the side of Prometheus; and it is the side of Christ as well; it is the blossoming-out of man, and all virtues converge here. But this God does not inhabit nature in any wise; he does not exist except in man and through man; he is created by man, or, if you prefer, it is by way of man that he creates himself; and every effort to externalize him through prayer remains in vain. It is with him that Christ is joined; but it is to the Other that he calls in dying, when he cries out in despair: 'My God, why have you forsaken me?'

He—In order that 'everything be fulfilled,' says the believer.

I—But since I do not *believe*, I see there only a tragic misunderstanding. There is no forsaking there, because there never was an agreement; for the god of natural forces has no ears and remains indifferent to human suffering, whether in fastening Prometheus to the Caucasus or nailing Christ to the cross.

He—Allow me: it is not the forces of nature that crucified Christ; it is the malignity of men.

I—The God whom Christ represents and incarnates, the Virtue-God, must struggle both against the Zeus of natural forces and against the malignity of men. That last word of Christ (the only one of the seven things the Crucified said which is reported for us by two evangelists, the naive apostles Matthew and Mark, who report only this sentence) would keep me from confusing Christ

104

with God, if all the rest had not already warned me. How can one fail to see in this tragic utterance, not a desertion, a betrayal by God, but this: that Christ, in believing and making others believe that he was allied with God, was mistaken and misled us; that He whom he called 'my Father' had never recognized him as Son, that the God he represented, that he himself was, was only, as he sometimes said, 'Son of Man.' It is only that God that I can and will adore.

(*Ibid.*, 163–165.)

For Gide the crucifixion obscured the heart of the Gospel. This was not a metaphysical idea of divine power exaggerated to the point of creating the problem of evil, and not a wishful effort to invent a friendly universe, but the insight that joy comes with substitution of self-abandon for abandon to self. It was this teaching that the cross interrupted so shockingly that the followers of Christ consoled themselves by coming to believe that the cross was the goal of the teaching, its "explanation and fulfilment." Gide saw that to regard the death of Jesus as an unforeseen accident and restore the importance of his message, it was necessary to consider reference to the cross previous to the crucifixion as interpolated in the Gospel to fit the myth of a predestined Savior. If Jesus was a teacher prematurely dying, his divinity had to be denied (*OC* XV, 392). This was a question that Gide often considered in working toward the flat 1942 statement of his humanism. The disciples, after going proudly with their teacher to Jerusalem, tried to justify his unexpected end as being foretold in Scripture for the salvation of humanity. That he died *on account of sinners* then had to mean that he died *for* them (*ibid.*, 504). To Gide, though the ignominious end had become indispensable to dogma, it was still the interruption of Christ's teaching; not part of it, but the obstacle over which his secret of joy must rise. That would not be easy, for: "the cross triumphed over Christ; it was Christ crucified that continued to be seen, and taught. . . . And thus it was that this religion succeeded in darkening the world" (*ibid.*, 505).

Gide was vehement in denunciation of organized religion. He could not calmly dismiss it, because of the hold Protestantism had once had upon him, and the pressure on him to become a Catholic. "I would not swear that at a certain period of my life I was not close to being converted." He was thankful to have had some converted friends (Jammes, Claudel, Ghéon, Du Bos) who saved him from that fate without ever knowing how much they had instructed him (*ibid.*, 172). Later he spoke of their conversions as being, like his own *Numquid et Tu*, products of the war, of "bereavements, thoughts of death, lack of outlet for the heroism generated, need to sacrifice to higher interests. . . . What warns me, consternates me, is that the tree can also bear frightful fruits. . . . Lord, you have taught me to judge the tree by its fruits." The worst for him was: "That which, for us, is an indispensable virtue—intellectual honesty—is in their eyes only an impediment to belief" (Pléiade ed. of *Journal 1889–1939*, 1284–1285).

He went back to preferring Protestantism, though he gathered from Siegfried that in the United States where Protestantism was strong, it was as dangerous intellectually as Catholicism. He decided that "any religion, whatever it is, when it wins out and can impose itself,

106

satisfies man and dissuades him from all progress" (*OC* XV, 172). Perhaps, if he had been more in touch with the American scene than reliance on Siegfried's book, *Les États-Unis,* would suggest, Gide might have appreciated the liberal modernist tendency in American churches, and especially the humanist movement in and out of churches.

As for the Catholic Church around him, Gide thought in 1938 it was remembering its "sovereign role" and trying to make up for what he spoke of as a pact with Hitler. "Danger, or attacks at least, have made her get hold of herself and many grievances that angered me against her are over" (*Journal 1889–1939*, 1326). The rebound of Gide from communism may have had something to do with this mood. "The flinching of communism restores to Christianity its revolutionary importance. Catholicism betrays when it becomes conservative. Conservator of what, Lord Christ?—of titles, fortunes, privileges. The *tradition* has nothing to do with that." Not only the Church but tradition, which presumably he had spurned for good, beckoned him again. "What matters is to bequeath the spirit; not 'the letter that kills.' That some Catholics feel this, I have never doubted. But it seems, today, that even the Church understands it; that she begins to understand it. Certain persons (of whom Péguy is first, then Maritain, Marcel, Mauriac, Berdiaeff, Bergamin) have helped a great deal there" (*ibid.*, 1327).

How helpful in the cause of progress he continued to believe these persons were, one may wonder. Upon the whole his utterance would indicate that he found Catholicism too aggressive and unscrupulous for tolerance

107

to be in order (cf. *OC* XV, 180). His general feeling has been: "Many roads lead to Rome. Only one leads to Christ" (*ibid.*, 186). Religion would be all right if really centered on Christ. "But religion is not Christ; it is the priest" (*ibid.*, 310). This is ironically stressed in Gide's *École des Femmes,* wherein the unhappy wife Éveline is forbidden by the priest to doubt her husband's sincerity, when she is fed up with his pretense of invoking moral duty for doing as he pleases. She finds that since she can no longer believe him she can no longer believe in God. The priest had persuaded her that Church and God sided with a man she could not trust, putting externals first. Scolded for pride she would pretend to be humble, but wished she could believe in God long enough to find out that gestures were all he wanted. The trouble with her, the husband Robert said in the sequel named for him, was insubordination. Submission, he quoted from a monsignor, was essential to being a Christian. Éveline's fault had lain in presuming to guide herself without a director. She had even admitted that she did not believe in revealed truth, but only in what she could find true for herself. What could that lead to but individualism and anarchy? One is reminded of Maritain's reluctance to approve self-searching in poetry ("Poetry's Dark Night," *The Kenyon Review,* Spring, 1942) when Robert says it is bad for people to examine their own conscience and discover its inner workings. Conscience and consciousness should remain a mystery for the Church to interpret. It was dangerous to introduce sincerity into morality— unless offset by a "higher" notion of duty—for sincerity could become the excuse of the natural man. The safe-

108

guard was to use the mind only for knowing God, but Éveline had reached the point of refusing to mention God. Robert could not believe that his piety had destroyed hers, for he had always been able to put her in the wrong.

So clever was he in this that she could scarcely formulate what she had against him. Her effort to face him is used by him to turn the tables on her. Even the reader, though seeing through him, is almost disarmed when Robert proceeds to build up his case. We try to discount the plausibility of what he says by comparing it with Éveline's perspective; and find ourselves in the embarrassment that overcame her when she went in to have it out with him. For he begins to put us in the wrong as well as his wife, even though we see his hypocrisy coming out more and more brazenly. The effrontery is so consummate that it becomes confusingly like her virtue of sincerity. His authoritarian attitude toward her, his disdain of women, reason and human feeling, are antagonizing enough. But a critic is jockeyed into a position where he cannot condemn Robert without challenging what have seemed to be the fundamentals of morality and religion. By using the dualism of the cultural tradition, Robert deftly identifies disapproval of him with wilful flouting of everything that is higher, wiser, finer than the natural man—damning the individual who dares to use his own judgment. Thus Robert does not allow himself to be discredited but strengthens himself by the fact that Éveline is naturally a better person. He admits and wants others to appreciate her inherent fineness. His point is that, since he is inferior, it is laudable that he should try to improve himself. She should have honored this effort in-

109

stead of denouncing it as hypocrisy. If it is said that his way of bettering himself is wrong, the reply is that he goes about it in the fashion socially and even divinely approved—according to local authority on the divine; authority claiming to be universal.

In short, if we reject Robert we must, like Éveline, reject God. We cannot avoid that conclusion without getting away from the terms in which the problem is presented. Our sympathy is aroused for Éveline, but we are shown that to side with her we must break with conventional Catholic assumptions. We believe in sincerity. That may be all right in painting. But in morals? Are we ready to be relativists, functionalists, humanists, like Éveline's doctor? We are disgusted with Robert but we have fair warning of the consequences if we follow Éveline—and so has the Church.

While *L'École des Femmes* and *Robert* satirize the Catholic assertion of institutional authority over personal judgment, *La Symphonie Pastorale* warns against the too loose interpretation of Scripture to which Protestants are exposed through their reliance upon private and literal reading of the text. The pastor's guilty love for the blind orphan he befriends, and his arrogation of her affection, he tries to justify by Gospel passages on love and joy. His son, shunted away from the girl by the father, is driven to preoccupation with sin in the Epistles of Paul, and gets her to become a Catholic with him; though they give up marriage, having both been poisoned against natural love.

One might draw a parallel between the blind girl in this story and the blind prophet Tiresias in Gide's *Oedipe*, in
110

the idea that the blind are inspired by God. Both warn against ill-founded and overweening happiness. But this would be far-fetched. The girl is enabled to overcome her handicap and to see quite clearly how a natural and appropriate happiness would have been accessible if she had not been imposed upon. She is symbolic of Gide's or anyone's awakening to the wonders of the earth and human relationships, and the danger of having them warped by religious narrowness which may be selfishly interpreted for the advantage of one person at the expense of others. But she is the victim of this abuse, and would have had no prejudice against happiness if it had been offered to her fairly, without damaging that of her benefactor's family. Tiresias, on the contrary, is constitutionally blind to the value of happiness itself, especially as resting upon human initiative and insubordinate to established religion. The conflict between him and Oedipus carries on that between the priest-supported Robert and Éveline, and culminates in the echo of Éveline uttered by Antigone when Tiresias has told her not to leave with Oedipus because she is promised to God and not free to dispose of herself. Antigone replies: "No, I am not going to break my promise. In getting away from you, Tiresias, I shall remain faithful to God. It even seems to me that I shall serve him better, following my father, than I did with you. I listened to your teaching about God until today; but still more piously I shall heed now only the instruction of my reason and my heart" (*Oedipe*, 119–120). Antigone does more than echo Éveline who feels obliged to give up the priest's idea of God. Antigone does not merely dare to reject a mean representation of

111

ANDRÉ GIDE

God but dares to see God afresh in human good humanly understood.

This climax is the more effective in Gide's play of *Oedipe* because earlier she had resisted the apparently similar suggestion of her brother Polynices that one could not think freely without first effacing the effect on the mind of religious practices, and approaching God by way of desire. Antigone had agreed that God was what she placed at the goal of her thought's thrust, but said thinking was vitiated by abandonment to passion. When Polynices interpreted her to mean that her God was just a reflection of her virtues she objected that the reflecting was hers, and that virtue came only from Him. As against her brother's proposal that he might be guided to her God if she would let him do what he wanted—marry her— she asked how one could hope to reach the good by doing wrong.

Thus when she comes to side with her father against Tiresias, it has been made clear that humanism does not mean selfish indulgence but adherence to right against wrong, more than ever; while what is right does not become wilful and subjective as a result of being based on the good; for the good is not just a matter of obeying impulse or of putting a single person's advantage first. The good is what seems best for everyone concerned, when a situation is considered as a whole and with sympathy—by trusting reason and the heart. The individual might suffer but it could still be sweet to him to bring men happiness, even at the cost of his own suffering, as Oedipus put it. Tiresias persisted: "It is not their happiness that should be wished, but their salvation." Oedipus

112

GOD, SON OF MAN

replied for the last time: "I leave you to explain that to
the people."

Tiresias had hated the happiness of Oedipus and determined that it should be cracked, because he seemed
too independent; while Antigone had worried about her
father's apparent omission of God. In contrast to Creon
who was attached to tradition, Oedipus was glad to think
of himself as a bastard, like Lafcadio, without a known
past to serve as model or to lean upon: with "everything
to create, country, ancestors—to invent, to discover. No
one to resemble but myself. . . . It is a call to valor, not
to know one's parents." He would avoid the incestuous in-
clinations of his sons by seeking a goal not too near, and
not behind but ahead. If he had heeded the backward-
pulling mysticism and morality of Tiresias, Oedipus would
never have guessed that the answer to the riddle of the
Sphinx was: Man. "All science which takes off from man,
and not from God, is worthless," said Tiresias. Oedipus did
not deny that he had committed a crime, a murder, and
that it had deflected him from the pursuit of a God. When
he discovered with horror that he had killed his father
to marry his own past in his mother, as guided by a God,
he understood why he had been prompted to turn from
Him toward the Sphinx.

Having blinded himself, Oedipus sought Tiresias and
asked if this was what he wanted. "Jealous of my light,
did you want to drag me into your night? Like you I contemplate now the obscurity of the divine. I have punished
these eyes which were unable to warn me. You can no
longer crush me with your superiority of the blind."

"Then it was still pride that made you put out your

113

eyes," Tiresias said. "God did not expect this new crime of you, in payment for your previous crimes, but simply for you to repent."

Oedipus replied: "I wonder that this idea of repentance should come from you, since you are the one who believes the gods lead us and that it was not in my power to escape my destiny. No doubt this expiation of mine was also foreseen, so that I could not have held back from it. No matter! It is voluntarily that I sacrifice myself. I had reached the point where I could not go ahead without dashing against myself." Having given up everything in the past, including himself, he would go away, hoping to do elsewhere some human good: and Antigone went with him.

That she did was vindication, for she personified genuine morality and religion: reflective, progressive, human, as over against authority, formality, mystical obscurantism. And whereas Sophocles had staged a predicament which was tragic for the audience as well as for Oedipus, with no way out, Gide shows the way for the modern reader. If God is to contrive all that men do, they cannot be guilty of crime. As Antigone said, Oedipus did not knowingly marry his mother any more than he intended to murder his father. If a man was to be punished for the crime a God made him do, and obliged moreover to offer him expiation, as if the deed were a stench to the divinity that ordained it, the man should be disgusted less with himself than with such a God. And any God would be such if actually the author of all that happened. If blame for what men do is to rest upon them, they must be responsible for themselves, and free to live according to

114

their own lights of reason and feeling. Then they must reject Tiresias and his God, to get along without God or find him in Man—with limited but growing power; with limited but human kindness.

This would seem to be the moral of Gide's *Oedipe*. He says in his *Journal* that he expects the reader to have the play of Sophocles in mind, but not to think Gide is posing as a rival. He has tried simply to present "what Sophocles was unable to see and understand, though offered by his subject; which I understand, not because I am more intelligent, but because I belong to another age . . . and it is to your intelligence that I address myself. I propose, not to make you shudder or weep, but to make you reflect" (Pléiade ed., 1151). Gide would not pretend that the tragic sense of life is disappearing through the mere lapse of time, or that because we live later than Sophocles we are happier than he could imagine. But Gide is optimistic enough to believe that science has entitled man to have more self-confidence; and that philosophy, though it has not solved all the hoary problems, has at least found the way around some of them. Evil is real, but the problem of evil, engendered by the idea of an all-doing and all-knowing God, is not real for one who gives up that inhuman conception and is ready to go with Oedipus and Antigone—ahead.

Then the gratuitous act of Lafcadio, though still capable of criminal manifestation, becomes focused on human value, through her eyes. The break with the past is more decisive for ceasing to be capricious and irresponsible; is genuinely creative, in reaching toward a progressive morality and religion, instead of just flouting common

115

decency. The blind old Oedipus is Lafcadio grown up and outgrowing the gods; thinking not of thrills for himself but set on the adventure of freeing men in general from the dead hand of the past, to increase their happiness. That Oedipus is not only breaking forward but going in the right direction is guaranteed, so far as a guarantee is possible for moral pioneering—in practical, understandable, and the most reassuring fashion—by the approval and guidance of Antigone. It is when weighed against her virtue that the very idea of the old all-powerful God is found wanting, and a new more human idea becomes promising.

In *Thésée*, Theseus receives the exiled Oedipus upon the soil of Attica, when he has failed in everything. Although his weakness and discouragement make it understandable, it is disconcerting to find him penitently agreeing with Tiresias that one must lose sight of the external world in order to see God. The blind king feels not only that everything he undertook was tainted by his crime, but that all humanity is vitiated by an original fault, from which man could not escape without divine aid. Oedipus is reduced to believing that suffering is redemptive, that misfortune was what enabled him to reach his healing union with God. The role which had been his, now is taken over by Theseus: who flouts superhuman wisdom, as Oedipus had done, proudly asserting himself a child of earth, a believer in man, and a better man than Oedipus. At the same time his moral inferiority to Oedipus, and similarity to Michel and Lafcadio in their egoistic individualism, might seem to make Theseus discredit the humanistic ideal. Certainly he cannot compare with Prometheus as its champion. But as Athens' legendary founder Theseus is associated with its progress from barbarism to the Periclean age, when religion was really devotion to the city-state.

It is no more surprising that he should arrive at appreciation of the high human values which Athens came to symbolize, than that Gide himself, beginning with much the same spirit of adventure, should turn out to have a social conscience. Theseus is made to say that he had always wanted to do good (*Thésée*, p. 20), as Gide would say that he had always been troubled by injustice. Theseus is presented as having lived simply and humbly, as being repelled as well as fascinated by the luxury of Minoan civilization, to which he comes a prisoner who will win freedom through personal charm and prowess. The situation is analogous to that of Thomas Mann's Joseph in Egypt. Both heroes feel overawed at first, and both recover a sense of inherited superiority to foreign grandeur; though Mann's elaborate reconstruction of it is just suggested in Gide's delicate work. The imaginative engineering of Dedalus rivals the technological ingenuity of the Egyptians, and the God-monologue of Icarus is reminiscent of Ikhnaton's mystical monotheism. As Joseph turns away from theological speculation to the practical solution of human problems, so Theseus leaves behind his own physical triumphs, and avoids the metaphysical flights of Icarus, to found Athens for man's happiness and freedom.

Thésée, although it revives all the Gidian themes in their full diversity, closes on the humanistic note of *Oedipe*.

117

4. CHRIST AND MARX

THE WAR OF 1914, WHICH INSTIGATED GIDE TO DEEPEN HIS ideas about religion, also spurred him to overhaul his morality. As further reflection upon God brought him to humanism, so a new consideration of man led to communism, though in neither development was there any sense of leaving Christ. And just as he relied upon his own reading of the Gospel, understood through his own thought and feeling, without benefit of Biblical criticism, so he was not won by the arguments of Marx and his followers, but was convinced by fellow-feeling and awareness of injustice that the old social arrangements would have to be changed. Again the advantage of studying Gide inheres in the fact that he is not so much an intellectual as a contemporary with the power to put in fully human terms what it is to experience the great issues of our time, to sense their drift and respond to their challenge. He does not isolate religious, moral or economic man within a set of restricted technical problems wherein a professional judgment has to be accepted by the ordinary mind. He simply confides in the reader how it is to be a man now, a man with no special knowledge except that of himself and of men who have known how to express themselves in words. Their gift of communication, their human touch, has enabled Gide to come from the utmost individualism to a social conscience; from the private and abstract notion of man, with a metaphysical soul to be saved, to men with a world to win.

For about a year in 1914–15 he worked in the *Foyer Franco-belge*, helping refugee families from northern France and Belgium (*OC* VIII, xvi, 96). He had the satisfaction of knowing he was usefully employed when he could not have lived with himself otherwise. The inconvenience and discomfort involved in the dislocation of habits, with the postponement of projects he could not have pursued anyway in such anxious days, reinforced the sense of doing his bit. The work was taxing, and when it did not take all his time he felt "devoured by sympathy." Leaving this post for a while, he found it demoralizing to be on his own and could not use his freedom: afraid he had no right to go back to his writing, and afraid this fear was not merely a sincere recognition of obligation but also a mask for laziness (*OC* VIII, xvii, xix). Again on duty at the *Foyer*, he wrestled with the conflicting claims of self and society. As his editor, M. Louis Martin-Chauffier, puts it, Gide felt himself a stranger in a world which the war had led him to discover: the miserable people who came to the office for aid made him "ashamed of every superiority"; and though he would recover somewhat from the painful sense of difference, he was to keep his "horror of a society which maintains that difference artificially" (*ibid.*, xx–xxi). When he was finally through with the *Foyer*, after his services were no longer needed, the crisis of being simultaneously drawn and repelled by the Catholic Church obliged him to clarify his philosophy of religion. That would occupy him indefinitely, though in a few years he got over his violent indecision about the Church. Meanwhile he could not put off thinking about morality. Rather, he could not stop, for it had long engrossed him and was continuous with his problem of God.

At home again at Cuverville in Normandy, he worried that children of relatives and friends in the house were gaily dressed, flaunting their leisure in the countryside (*ibid.*, 265). First-hand glimpses of inequality had more effect on him than theory, and were cumulative. Years later he mentioned being depressed by the miserable village of Criquetot near Cuverville—no hygiene, comfort, gaiety, though in a relatively prosperous region. His heart was clutched by a little neighbor boy who wanted to become a teacher instead of staying on the farm as his mother wished. Thought of the difficulties he would encounter in trying to rise above his station deterred Gide from helping him (*OC* XV, 316). Apparently in connection with this situation the *Journal* notes: "Only convinced Christians are in a position to bring to the afflicted, the disinherited, the bruised, the dying, valid consolations. The great grievance one may have against the Christian religion is that it sacrifices the strong to the weak. But how can one disapprove when strength is used to help weakness?" (*ibid.*, 325). On the same page it comes out that Gide launched the would-be teacher on his studies after all, and saw the troubles he was having. The brothers and sisters thought his scholarship money should be used to help out at home, and the mother was afraid he was aiming too high. Gide felt moved to say that if he could begin his career again it was about such families that he would want to write.

And he had not waited for 1914 to be touched by the unhappiness of others, not only as unlucky individuals but as denizens of social levels where misfortune was the common lot, fortitude the shining virtue. In 1914 he had published *Souvenirs de la Cour d'Assises,* giving his experience in the spring of 1912 as a juror in the criminal court of Rouen. He looked at his colleagues and then imagined them on the opposite bench: "shabbily dressed, unshaved, unwashed, tousled. What figure would they cut? What figure would I cut myself?" (*OC* VI, 386). Since this was at the period when he was writing about Lafcadio, the contrast between that young man's bravado and the sordidness of being caught must have been in mind. He simply wanted to act inexcusably, to vault over motive and intention. Contemplation of the vagueness and pettiness of human motivation, so far as it could be recovered, and the difficulty of ascertaining it in the courtroom, may have added to the fascination of the gratuitous act for Gide—as the emergence here and there of a new élan that might launch humanity beyond the morass of present problems, just as life may have sprung from unaccountable spores in stagnant water. At any rate Gide could not feel that there was a great difference between the people who got into trouble and the people who kept out or did not get in so deep. Lafcadio might be a caricature of a person, but his deliberate lack of direction was only an exaggeration of the footless and aimless state of humanity as a whole, that any human being might seem to be in if reasons should be demanded for his conduct. The artificial thing in Lafcadio's case was that he tried not to know why he would act as he did, whereas people who think they know why they behave as they do, might find it hard to explain afterwards—to a judge and jury.

Gide felt that often the judge should give way to the psychologist, but that many cases, such as he was to gather from newspapers in *L'Affaire Redureau*, in *Faits Divers*, and *La Séquestrée de Poitiers*, were beyond traditional psychology. He admitted that, strictly speaking, no human action was gratuitous in the sense of being entirely unmotivated. "Gratuitous act" was simply a provisional label for conduct that could not be explained by what passed for personal interest. (*L'Affaire Redureau suivie de Faits Divers, Documents réunis par* André Gide, in first volume of collection called "*Ne Jugez Pas*," Gallimard, 1930, pp. 108–109). In studying cases of such abnormal conduct, and getting people to send clippings for his collection, he felt not only that he was carrying on a scientific investigation that required venturing beyond the usual confines of specialization; but that he was on the track of the fascination, the curiosity, the daring that was the mainspring of science and progress. "Without curiosity, humanity would still be in the stone age" (*ibid.*, 170).

The absurd things he found real people really doing, in his quest for bizarre behavior, and the quirks of justice in dealing with them, make his Lafcadio seem naive in thinking that to act on impulse is more gratuitous than what habit and custom frequently produce, and in thinking his own impulsiveness extraordinary. He is obnoxious in assuming that his deficiency of social feeling makes him superior. His education and development are a parody of the emancipating but sane and balanced intelligence Gide was finding necessary for the advance of civilization—except in the important respect of not being bound by the past. Gide admired Lafcadio for wanting to act freely, and young readers were excited; but the author saw that creative freedom lay in yoking initiative to cooperative planning—not in irresponsible self-assertion or mere originality, any more than in sheepish conformity. In *Les Caves du Vatican* this deeper insight is only implied. That makes for fun and subtlety and is effective when appreciated, but the point might be missed if this farce were not read in conjunction with *Souvenirs de la Cour d'Assises*, published in the same year of 1914, where Gide's social conscience is plain. With this conscience in mind, despite its limitations, the reader can easily see the irony intended in the treatment of Lafcadio. He may be on the way beyond conventional good and evil toward a better world, but is a long way from it.

Meanwhile, as Gide realized while serving with the criminal court of Rouen, society must have protection from dangerous acts, no matter what promise might be latent in them, and difficult as it is to ascertain the degree of their evil. Though "judge not" was the attitude he wanted to take toward the accused, he saw that since tribunals were necessary their procedure should be improved. It seemed to him that miscarriage of justice was less the fault of judges, lawyers and juries, than of the machinery they had to work with, which was worse in its grinding, the more efficiently they used it.

The deepest effect of his court experience came during a trial in connection with the robbing of a sailor—reminding Gide of a story heard years before in Le Havre about an overcrowded lifeboat—hands and heads of the drowning struck with oars when they tried to climb in; wrists cut off with a little hatchet. He could not sleep, thinking of it (*OC* VII, 73). That hatchet made him a communist eventually, and enabled him to feel that becoming one was not a conversion, since he had long been ashamed to be one of the few in the lifeboat of privilege. Nor did he feel that becoming a communist was more than reaffirming the Gospel that for him was dictated by the love of man.

Back in *Le Renoncement au Voyage* (1903), in the midst of recovering the beauty of North Africa, he had exclaimed: "How good it would be, if there were not so many poor on the earth, to talk quietly with a few friends this morning" (*Morceaux Choisis,* 1927 ed., 233). It would be fine to be an Epicurean if one could stay with friends in a garden and forget the world outside. But Gide could not be a stay-at-home and he could not step out without seeing the "immensity of human misery" (*OC* XIV, 395). The love of life affirmed in *Les Nourritures Terrestres* made him feel that life should be lovable for everyone, while making him realize how far from lovely it was for many. *Les Nouvelles Nourritures* reaffirmed the natural joy of living, during the period when he had overcome the appeal of the Catholic Church and was becoming a com-

124

munist. Written between 1919 and 1935 this book was still sensuous enough, but the emphasis had moved on to the happiness found in working for the happiness of others—had moved from an irresponsible individualism to a loyal comradery. In writing the *Nourritures* of 1897 he had been no less sure of its inadequacy than of its significance. He had wanted it to be read but also wanted it to be thrown away. The reader of the later *Nourritures,* addressed fraternally as "comrade," is also expected to go beyond the author, but with a love he is confident will not have to be dropped like the "convalescent" or provisional self-indulgence that he had urged upon Nathanaël. Love would not stop without making life as worthy of love as the earth already was, and more so. In the early *Nourritures* God was identified with happiness but happiness was all placed in the moment, as might be possible for a person very fortunate or selfish. The idea then was: "I have called God all that I love" and "I have wanted to love everything" (*OC* II, 87). The illusion of loving everything was nourished by a litany of apparently random but actually controlled impressions—selected for their delightfulness. Thus the God of fortune's child would have to be outgrown by anyone aware of the harsh realities, or with any sympathy for the millions of people who could not escape them. The God of the new *Nourritures* is not reserved for the gratitude of rich travelers and vagabonds in out of the way places, but found also and rather in the joy of helping humanity toward a more generous and sharable well-being. This God is not just found but fashioned. He is invented every day, by everyone who joins in the great adventure of social progress.

125

The vision of values yet to be won must rest in part upon appreciation of goods already enjoyed, however selfishly and smugly. Without actual satisfactions it might be impossible to imagine a state of things more generally satisfactory. But Nietzsche was an example of the creative urgency in maladjustment, in contrast to the lethargy that infects euphoria. The reformer feels the need of seeking a new equilibrium, Gide said (*OC* IX, 128). It is not necessary to assume a physiological derangement in a man who sees values in a new configuration. But the joy of working toward it is fed by the pain of having meanwhile to tolerate the status quo, which may have to become intolerable before enough effort is generated to overcome it. Since effort must become cooperative before the world can be significantly altered, the role of the prophet is to develop a conscience that is social in extent as well as intent. And the writer, with his gift of communication, is in a position to be prophetic, according to his intelligence and sympathy. These very qualities may wobble him right and left in politics, as Gide realized in his own case. But while he had thought social and moral questions more important than political ones, in the sense that it was more decisive to reform men than a system (*OC* IX, 352–353), he came to feel that a system might be so bad and so powerful that men would be helpless until it was changed.

His 1925 trip to the Congo convinced him of this. He was distressed by the poor health of the people and the lack of proper medical attention (*Voyage au Congo, OC*, XIII, 132). Having observed that the less intelligent the white man was, the more stupid the black man seemed to him (*ibid.*, 102), Gide enlarged this idea in a footnote: "Colored people are represented as indolent, lazy, without needs, without desires. But I readily believe that the state of subjection and the profound misery in which these people remain plunged, will too often explain their apathy. And what desire could anyone have who never saw anything desirable? Whenever blankets, cloth, household utensils, tools, and so on, are offered to the native by a well-stocked company store, one is naively surprised to see his desires awaken—if on the other hand an equitable remuneration for his work enables him to satisfy them" (*ibid.*, 150). Gide was pained by the sight of women working on a sandy road while burdened with nursing babies, and learned that they often got caught in cave-ins of the ditches from which they filled in ruts (*ibid.*, 180). He was shocked by the sadistic treatment of natives who failed to deliver a fixed amount of rubber, by deserted villages (*ibid.*, 184), by the report of children taken from home to work and going unfed (*ibid.*, 291), by man-hunts for porters (*ibid.*, 371).

The attitude of some of Gide's Catholic critics toward this book is revealing. He was pleasantly surprised by Mauriac's warm response to it (*Journal*, 4 June, 1931). But René Schwob, after insisting upon Gide's self-worship and lack of genuine sympathy, had to make light of the *Voyage au Congo* as not very interesting or important. He says it bored him. He does not deny Gide's kindness, but thinks it is not really generous. He simply wants to be surrounded by good will, happens to like savages, and has: "a fear of hurting which is a kind of delicacy and modesty—if these diverse elements did not enter in, I

127

think Gide might not even have noticed so many slaves suffering around him and for him: the many-hued insects and flowers would have taken up his whole attention." Schwob says he does not mean to depreciate Gide's kindness, but thinks delicacy is more fundamental in him, and timidity still more so. In other words, he cares about the misfortunes of others because he is anxious to be well thought of, and does not want to be uncomfortable. The animus of Schwob's analysis comes out in his remark that Gide was trying in this book "to persuade us that, without the help of any religious sentiment, a profound disinterestedness draws him to those who suffer . . ." To Schwob "it is the contrary that he exhibits, for there is nothing fervent or human in his affection." The trouble is that Gide is just thinking about justice (*Le Vrai Drame d'André Gide*, 149–157).

Gouiran takes a similar tack in finding theological fault with Gide's social conscience because it is concerned with distributive justice, with things that can be possessed and monopolized. He recognizes that Gide has a religion of humanity, a cultural humanism, but complains that in writing of the Congo evils he lacks "that intimate penetration, that concern for the redemption of each soul, and that compassion for the crowd, of which the Gospels give us moving testimony on the part of Christ." (*André Gide: Essai de Psychologie Littéraire*, 238–239).

Gide was simply shocked by dearth of daily bread and ordinary decency, as Diderot had been in considering the problem of colonial exploitation (cf. Charles Lipton, "The Social Thought of Diderot," *Science & Society*, Spring, 1944, p. 130). Shuddering at what he saw, Gide wondered what demon had sent him to Africa at the cost of peace of mind. What could he do about it all? But he knew: he could talk (*Voyage au Congo, OC* IX, 184). The question was how to get a hearing. In the habit of writing without caring who was listening, and waiting for posterity, he envied the journalist whose voice would carry at once (*ibid.*, 189). Somehow he must convey the idea to his own people that here were human beings like themselves. He and his party got along so well with their "boys" that he wondered why whites in general thought they had to be rough with black domestics. Perhaps he was just lucky (*ibid.*, 220). "But I am quite sure that each master has the servants he deserves. Nor does all that I am saying apply only to the Congo. What servant . . . would heartily want to remain honest after hearing his master deny him every virtue?" (*ibid.*, 222). Gide could not admit that a greater experience with the natives entitled a person to be more abusive of them. "It is quite rare that experience enlightens us. Each uses everything to encourage him in his tendency, and pours it all into his proof. People talk about experience: there is no prejudice so absurd that it won't find confirmation there" (*ibid.*, 223).

But while it is true that people tend to find what they are looking for they can be trained through science to look for facts that may not fit preconception. Experience is thereby opened to discoveries that prejudice would not see. A sweeping dismissal of appeal to experience in value-judgment was a lapse in one who was through with mysticism, and in sympathy with science. Gide was moved by his Congo experience, and wanted it to reach others

129

at home, so that it would affect their thinking as it did his; though he insisted that his experience of social evil went back to his first African trips. Then he had not considered it his affair, but his belated feeling that as a writer he should do something about it was continuous with his early impressions of injustice.

His receptiveness to those impressions might be attributed to the orthodox religious training which he had largely repudiated. It was certainly part of his experience, but a part claiming authority above experience and passing upon it. Now, as a humanist, he would have to locate in man himself the authority to pronounce upon right and wrong. He might still refer to the teaching of Christ as the touchstone of moral distinctions; but could he expect other men to rally with him to this standard except as their own history inclined them to? If their background assured them that men were not all brothers, that it was all right for white to exploit black, what could Gide say? If there was no intellectual principle he could invoke, which all people were obliged to accept, how could he logically maintain that some men ought to change their ways? He could still assert it. And he might call upon persons who would share his feeling about exploitation to put pressure on the oppressors. If he could do this he might, with conviction of righteousness, cease to worry about using force against people who would not admit they were wrong. His task then would be that of emotionally arousing men who could be got to agree with him, and not the job of finding a philosophical foundation for his position.

Actually he went ahead and appealed to pity, fairness, and the fellow-feeling which were ignored by colonial companies and their agents. He mentioned as beyond his power of description "the beautiful eyes of these natives, the touching intonation of their voices, the reserve and dignity of their deportment, the noble elegance of their gestures" (*ibid.*, 346). He did not fear to be called sentimental; as he would be for not enjoying a hunting party because its purpose was killing. He would rather "sit down and watch the monkeys" (*ibid.*, 354), examine the immense mounds of extinct termites (*ibid.*, 150), study beetles, spiders, butterflies, bees (*ibid.*, 231, 235–236), make a pet of a little monkey-creature called Dindiki (*ibid.*, 244), or go back to reading La Fontaine (*ibid.*, 281). Should such a man interfere with the profits of men who had not come to Africa for fun or health? Was it just a matter of sensibility, and was that enough to justify raising a hue and cry?

Suppose that instead of admiring the natives and feeling sorry for them he had found them repulsive? Then would his sense of an obligation to champion them have remained? And, if so, on what basis? It could not be very reassuring for the merits of a case to rest upon something so fluctuating as personal like and dislike. The chasm of this consideration had startled Gide during his war work of 1914–15. "How many times at the *Foyer*, while nursing, consoling, sustaining these poor rags of humanity, just able to groan, too weak for a smile, for an ideal, for any beauty, I have felt rise up in me the frightful question: Do they deserve to be saved? The idea of replacing them

131

by others more promising is certainly part of the German *philanthropy*. It is logical and, by this token, monstrous" (*OC* VIII, 174).

If in such a fundamental moral issue logic is shockingly out of place, while feeling is too subjective, and experience cannot be trusted either, one can see why Gide was tempted to accept the guidance of the Church; and why, having refused it, he was attracted by another authority as the Russian Revolution loomed on the horizon. But much as he needed moral support, he could accept it only as it was consonant with the teaching of Jesus. The Gospel served him where logic, feeling and experience failed; and all three could be reinstated as long as he had a basis under them. Others who acted as if they had the same footing he could cooperate with, whether they acknowledged it or not. But there remained the problem of the proper attitude toward people who took a different stand. Were they simply to be coerced? And was that consistent with the Gospel?

The hurdle to be got over, whether people professed to be Christian or not, was the habit of thinking there were inherent differences in men, such that they ought to have differential security, comfort and opportunity; and the tendency to accept the familiar distribution as right, if one found it favorable. Thus the refugees at the *Foyer* often said they were not used to what had happened to them. "I'd like to say to each of these once happy ones: 'It is your turn.' But no; there is neither compensation nor profit in that. Those who were benumbed with egoistic comfort are incapable of getting a lesson from reverses; and, as for the others, how can they be

reproached for giving in to a chance for happiness?"
(*ibid.*, 177–178). On the other hand it bothered Gide increasingly that the happiness of some should rest squarely
on the unhappiness of many. But how could one go, and
help society go, from the biographical fact of being
bothered about injustice to the value-judgment that one
should be? He thought sensitiveness and awareness were
requisite for that transition, though he had to recognize
that the threshold of receptivity automatically rose enough
to spare the ego much discomfort. "X. perhaps is not insensitive, but he ignores it; he ignores immensely. And
he also lacks the imagination to represent to himself, when
he is in the room where people are having supper, what is
happening in the basement and the kitchen. . . . He is
tender-hearted, I know; he cannot bear injustice, where
he can see it; but he cannot see far. That thousands of
beings have labored to assure his welfare—this is what he
needs to ignore in order to go on being happy" (*OC* XIII,
428).

But the bliss of ignorance is doomed by communication,
which in turn makes possible and imperative a more
sharable happiness. The more effectively the ego is put
in touch with other selves, the less it can regard them as
mere outsiders or nonentities. In a broader view they
have the same urges and needs, essentially, as any precious
and private self in which intelligence is stationed. To
deny the reality and validity of that wider perspective is
to deny the fact and value of communication, of the social,
inter-individual structure which communication generates
and reveals. To question the existence of a society of
selves with values in common can be only rhetorical if

communication is a fact. Thus Gide's urge to speak out about social evil, and his equipment for doing it, implied the duty to do it. The fact that he had readers, however few, interested in what he had to say, obliged him to let them know what deeply concerned him—especially when violation of such human sympathy as bound them to him became his theme. As they valued the sense of being drawn together they must be disturbed to be informed or reminded of the fissures in society, of the paradox that exploitation is social no less than cooperation, and that enemies may be in communication as well as friends.

Gide was aware that reading a made-up story of man's inhumanity to man permitted a self-complaisance which could disappear in attending to a report of actual conditions. The self might easily enjoy sympathizing with imaginary troubles, and have a gratifying sense of generosity without being called upon to lift a finger; whereas in learning of real injustice the fear of inconvenience, expense, and loss of tranquillity would tend to dry up generous impulses. Yet the very reluctance to face cruelty and suffering indicated that apparently selfish people could maintain their indifference only by taking shelter in ignorance or callousness. That some people are downright selfish and even sadistic must appear as a problem for science to work at, and as probably a product of such divisions and antagonisms in society as could be got at through an improvement of communication. This would heighten awareness of evils in living conditions, education and economic relationships, which might then be ameliorated through the practical operation of something like the Gospel attitude of mutual love and responsibility.

134

Progress toward a more democratic society, and the rightness and goodness of such progress, cannot for Gide be proved by logic or feeling or any mere facts of experience. Instead of proof he has a faith which enables him to find encouragement in logic, feeling and experience, as they come to confirm his faith. That they have not always confirmed it enough to give him peace of mind is evident from his leaning toward the authority of the Church and then toward that of the Party. But he has dreaded absolutes more than doubt. He would rather be uneasy than unthinking; and good thinking is for him the scientific kind: tentative, experimental, adventurous. In the Gidian scheme, scientific procedure takes the place of the eighteenth-century faculty of reason as it had displaced the medieval idea of the soul and the fatherhood of God, as the foundation for mutual respect and fair dealing. His turning from Catholicism toward communism is a recognition that men's actual communion inheres in their human lot, more consciously and purposely as they leave their isolation and suspicion through the adhesive power of science. He sees that men are brought into closer, more understanding intercourse by new means of communication and transportation, and also through growing familiarity everywhere with similar tools and methods.

He calls it puerile to fear that acceptance of science and technology will "Americanize" the world, in the sense of degrading culture through mass production and standardization. He asks why America should stop there. "Thanks to her, humanity begins to glimpse new problems, to evolve under a new sky. A sky without stars? No; but in which we have not yet learned to discover the

135

stars" (*Journal*, 23 June, 1930). Even during the first world war he was thinking that arms alone could not be ultimately decisive; and the Russian Revolution made him say, "the enormous war itself will be swallowed up by social questions." He was thinking not only that peace could never be made lasting by force but also that France would no more be proved right by victory than Germany would be proved wrong by defeat (*OC* IX, 392). Only if national and other animosities could be outweighed by the sense of a common stake greater than any one-sided advantage, would peace have a permanent or peaceful basis. Gide's insight is that science is building such a basis, in spite of being used against it.

Many passages indicate his hope that "the stars" will shine out of new social relationships made possible and obligatory by the advance of science—relationships resting firmly upon common interest instead of rocking on the powder barrel of pride. He said conditions which might have been bearable if they could not have been helped became abominable when man was equipped to change them. "This state of things has become intolerable to me; all the more intolerable that I profit by it, that my brother suffers from it and not I. Intolerable this thought: what is today will be and nothing will change anything" (*Journal*, Pléiade ed., 1177–1178). This was in 1933. "There is nothing for it but to forge ahead, as the sciences have done for a long time. Though condemned to immobility by the Church, the earth has not ceased to turn, nor the mind of man to become more creative" (*ibid.*, 1175).

Science is used in war, but new weapons make everyone so vulnerable that war itself renders cooperation more

urgent than hostility. That men are now obliged and em-
powered to come out of their corners and form a common
conscience, thanks to science, gives more effect to the
teaching of good will than supernatural sanctions can. As
a freer and more sharable life is brought almost within
reach of all, the old words of love cease to be just an
ideal, if they ever were. As they take on new meaning and
plausibility a writer inspired by them and by science,
like Gide, really has something to communicate.

It may still be objected that the Gospel of love did not
originate in science and is not logically derivable from it.
But the origin does not matter, if the teaching is found
necessary and workable in a world being transformed by
science. Nor need it be intellectually embarrassing that
one cannot argue from science to love through a series
of abstractions ending in Q.E.D.—if science can actually
make love more effective by translating it into cooperation. That is valid enough for the creative intelligence.
That is knowing a tree by its fruit. Science validates the
Gospel by making all men neighbors and each man his
brother's keeper. It may have been poetry or prophecy
once, but now the way of life taught by Jesus has become
a working hypothesis which men must live by or perish.
That they want to live, and will like the new world they
are making, remains an assumption which Gide hinges
upon the capacity of men to treat one another fairly. For
they have reached the age when, more than ever, love is
viable, hatred fatal.

He does not assume that they want life merely because
they cling to it under conditions that are disheartening.
"When I think of all that I am spared . . . I wonder that

137

more people don't jump overboard, and I think humanity, everything considered, has formidable courage. It is perhaps also that they lack that little bit of courage which it would take to hurl oneself out of life" (*OC* XV, 165). As the two *Nourritures* affirm, he had found the possibilities of living so good that he could not imagine their being turned down by anyone who had half a chance at them; yet his own enjoyment of them was spoiled by realization that they were not available to mankind in general. "For too long now I have unlearned the art of being happy. My head is stuffed with a pile of atrocious considerations. Too few people are granted the simplest happiness. The groaning and protest of the others drowns all the harmonies of earth and heaven. To tell me that I can't do anything about it does not keep me from hearing them." In October, 1933, he was on the eve of joining the Communist Party. "Would he dare say he can't do anything, he whom unjust fortune favors? For a long time, without suspecting it, haven't I profited by misery? Was it not what others lacked that allowed me to lack nothing? These advantages which blinded me, which have permitted me my jauntiness, I vomit them" (*Journal*, Pléiade ed., 1187).

The spectacle of suffering had made him wonder how anyone could be smug. "With regard to it the indifference of certain rich people . . . becomes more and more incomprehensible to me. Preoccupation with oneself, with one's comfort, ease, safety, marks an absence of charity which grows ever more disgusting to me" (*OC* XIV, 395).

It was about a decade after the first world war that he was saying this. "We fortunate ones, we have no right to complain. If, with all we have, we are not able to be happy, it is because we have fashioned a false idea of happiness. When we shall have understood that the secret of happiness is not in possessing but in giving; in making people happy around us, we shall be happier ourselves. Why, how is it, that those who call themselves Christians have not grasped better this initial truth of the Gospel?" (*ibid.*, 396). Perhaps he should call himself something else? "In the presence of some rich people, how can one help feeling a communist at heart?" (*OC* XV, 125). Homely little experiences were adding to long thoughts. He was distressed by his landlady's overwork, on a stay in Zurich, but apparently felt unable to intervene, though he did not see how she could be gentle and resigned (*ibid.*, 353). In another case he spoke up in court in the effort to get the pension of a retiring concierge up to where it should be, and failed. He said he was no good in such a situation. His heart beat too fast, and he could not speak well "without assurance that he was being heard" (*ibid.*, 125–126).

It was borne in upon him that a lone individual, even with means at the service of good intentions, could only begin to do what anyone should see needing to be done. There was too much inertia, unless it could be met by men working together. But for them to get together they must get over the notion that things would somehow come out all right by themselves. "The rather naive wish for a comfortable victory of 'good' over 'evil' has lamentably retarded the progress of humanity" (*ibid.*, 200). In his mail came appeals for help; duties accumulated until he had to take refuge in sleep. How could one think it would

139

be easy to right the world? Trying to save a toad from children who had mistreated it, showed him in miniature the gigantic task of civilizing people. Talking to the children, he thought the only one who seemed affected was the one who had watched his effort to nurse the toad. He blamed thoughtless parents and a deplorable education (*ibid.*, 301–302). On another occasion neither Em. nor he could sleep, angered and depressed by "the imbecile cruelty" of some children to a dog.

While hope depended upon a quickening of sympathy he saw that revolutionary implications would harden many a heart. A new awareness of social needs would expose the limitations of old ideas and ways. He knew he was most bitterly reproached because of "having worked for emancipation of the mind. This seems unpardonable to the party which on the contrary aspires only to the most complete submission to authority, rule, tradition, etc. . . . The best reason it finds for proving that man *ought not* to change is that he *cannot* change. For from the moment one glimpses the possibility of progress, how can one not want to obtain it?" (*ibid.*, 357). Naturally some would be much attached to the established order, regarding any alteration of it as subversive. "No," said Gide, "I don't like disorder, but I am exasperated by those who shout: 'Let's not budge any more,' when no one is settled yet" (*ibid.*, 310). Alienated from such members of his own class, he did not feel disloyal or discouraged. His devotion was to humanity, not to those who held themselves above it. And he said: "To feel oneself on the side of the oppressed, *that constitutes part of my optimism,* and I know that bearing their suffering with them would not

140

crush my optimism. It is not at the mercy of hardship. A profound optimism is always on the side of the martyred" (*ibid.*, 359).

From wondering how the people had the courage to live without his exemption and privilege, he had come to feel that only by identifying himself with them could he keep his own cheerfulness. By giving up the pride of his station and the self that depended on it he was not trying to love misery in order to have more company. He was realizing that it was more blessed to give than to receive, that happiness was less in having and holding than in sharing and helping. For most people to achieve the life they should have would take a long time, but meanwhile there was no better way to live than in working with them. If there was postponement in this, the good of going in the right direction was not put off. And for Gide going had always been good, even though the going was hard. He counted on the most immediate and refreshing joys to spring up along the way. Travel, growth, progress, were the breath of life to him. To live meant to go forward, and that made it necessary to shake off inertia. This would seem risky to the timorous. Reasonable persons could prove the folly of it with logic. "But what imprudence to let everything be ruled by reason! The Christian ideal is opposed to that; and even the Greek. . . . We belong to an age when everything must again be put in question. . . . No progress for humanity is possible unless it shrugs off the yoke of authority and tradition" (*ibid.*, 373).

But while reason and reaction had to be defied, science was sealing their defeat. The engineering mind, sneered at by the literary, was moving up the timetable of con-

141

science. A man of letters with a mind, like that of Gide, could understand. Though in his youth consorting with a school which thought art should be kept pure of social questions, and suppressing in his *Amyntas* those noted on his first trips to Africa, he reconsidered. "It is not in the least that I feel myself more 'human' today than at the time when no trace of these preoccupations could be found in my work. I simply was careful to keep them out, thinking they had nothing to do with art. I am no longer so convinced of this, nor that anything can or should remain alien to art; for art is in danger of becoming and must become artificial if what the artist most cares about is banished" (*ibid.*, 359).

An artist who was also a man of intelligence and imagination could not look away when convents were burning in Spain, whether or not he agreed with Gide that Spain's inquisition of other days, and of less long ago, prepared the reprisals of 1931. He took it for granted that feudal arrangements could not be saved by rigidity in the age of science and commensurate social aspiration. "Let those who are angered by this violence tell how a chick is to leave the egg without breaking the shell" (*ibid.*, 384). He was not just resigned to change. He was eager. "But above all I'd like to live long enough to see Russia's plan succeed, and the states of Europe obliged to bow before what they refused to recognize. . . . Never have I leaned over the future with a more passionate curiosity. My whole heart applauds this gigantic yet human enterprise" (*ibid.*, 385).

He admitted being distracted from literature by the Spanish revolution and the Russian Five Year Plan; but
142

implied that it was a limitation of literature, or his conception of it, if it could not make room for his absorbing interest. To be passively interested in the great new developments of his time was not enough for a man whose life-long endeavor was to express what he felt and thought. "I wish I could shout very loudly my sympathy for Russia. And it is important that my cry should be heard." He not only wanted to see Russia's success but to work for it (*ibid.*, 419).

His way of working was to write, although he had not considered all his writing part of his work. The *Journal* he had thought of as being done on the side, in addition to his real effort or when he was not up to it. One reason, however, why projects which supposedly had priority often bogged down was that he could not pour into them the concern of the moment. He was in the dilemma of holding that art should be pure and also that it should come out of a life-struggle with real problems. The *Journal* was the solution. It was not just a way of occupying himself when he could not work at what he had on hand, or a discipline to keep his skill from rusting when he was not using it; or a method of heating up ideas for final casting. Here was a form which in its very lack of form lent itself to thoughts too fugitive, too homely and intimate, too pressing to be expressed appropriately or at all unless in jotting. Yet in the degree to which Gide has been of his time and able to sound it, his personal observations, in their cursiveness, have caught the feel of universal problems and the curve of their coming solution. Moving on while looking on, his *Journal* is harder to throw away than any of his books but *Les Faux-Monnayeurs*.

The scenes and soliloquies of Gide's temptation to join the Catholic Church were generated by experiences everyone shared who was awake in the first world war, and registered an access of emotion that had to find outlet in a religious conception whereby a modern man could live with eyes and mind open. The conviction of humanism led to fresh expression which could not be adequate on paper, even in the *Journal*. Home from the horrors of the Congo in 1926 he stirred up administrative inquiries and proceedings which led to substantial reforms (*OC* XIII, vii). Excited to find Russia putting humanism into practice, he wanted to help her effort with the energy he had refused the Church. Only in the *Journal* could he manage to write what he felt, and what he wrote not only shows him going toward Russia but challenges the reader to show what other direction a person or the world could decently take after seeing what was involved. What he was writing in the *Journal* was in the air for everyone to read. He wrote that at last people were "seeing what a state can do without religion, a society without divisions." In a footnote he added: "Without religion? Perhaps not. Rather a religion without mythology" (27 July, 1931). It would not matter if mythology came back for some who still liked it, after it was shown to be mythology and if used only to support human values. Meanwhile it was a tremendous stride for Gide, the lone individualist who had thought he must await posterity for company, to find millions of potential comrades. A mere writer's say-so could not possibly have the force of their triumphant progress, but a private diary might become a collaboration with history.

CHRIST AND MARX

How steadfastly Gide was prepared to go ahead with history, one may wonder when noting in the *Journal* that just ten days before his burst of enthusiasm for what a state could do without religion, or without mythology, he had exclaimed: "There are some days when, if I just let myself go, I'd roll right under the holy table" (17 July, 1931). He explained that it was intellectual honesty rather than pride which held him back. But the point is not so much what restrained him as the fact that he needed restraint to keep from throwing himself into the pre-humanistic attitude that would seem impossible for the author of *Oedipe*. Then his ensuing sympathy for the Soviet Union may have been not simply the rational consequence of his humanism but an emotional rebound from the headlong surrender he had nearly made to Catholicism. On the 24th of July, 1931, he was ecstatic about Thornton Wilder's *Bridge of San Luis Rey,* declaring it to be: "deliciously written, facing the past."

Vacillation is characteristic of Gide. Scientific interest and social conscience orient him toward progress, away from his restraining ties with the once revolutionary bourgeoisie, grown fearful of losing their dominant position through further developments. At times he has come back like a black sheep to a fold no longer white. His "gratuitous act" is akin to futurism in the proto-fascist lack of a clearly progressive principle. Yet he could never have accepted that part of Marinetti's *Manifesto* which glorifies war and destructive patriotism as "the only hygiene of the world." This was the aspect of futurism which could march with fascism. The rest was tolerated only as it seemed unimportant or irrelevant (cf. H. M. Kallen, *Art and Freedom,*

145

p. 796). But, although Gide never became a fascist, one must wonder how seriously he was taking his own revolt against the forces of the past when in 1916 he espoused the *Action Française.*

This was a movement which had sprung up at the turn of the century, when the Dreyfus affair brought defeat for the enemies of the republic in the army and clergy, resulting in the separation of church and state. The *Action Française* fed on fear of the principles of the French Revolution, hatred of the republic, and hope of restoring "order" through authority, through an élite devoted to tradition and monarchy (cf. *French Royalist Doctrines Since the Revolution,* by Charlotte Touzalin Muret, Columbia University Press, 1933, pp. 217 ff.; and *Les Idées Traditionalistes en France de Rivarol à Ch. Maurras,* by Alphonse V. Roche, in *Illinois Studies in Language and Literature,* Vol. XXI, University of Illinois, 1937). Democracy was condemned because it did not provide enough "safety," or seem to assure enough national prestige and power.

A letter Gide wrote in 1898 painfully reflects this hysteria: "If to save an innocent Dreyfus would be the undoing of a guilty France, it is necessary for Dreyfus to become guilty and for France to be made innocent. But this would require acting with authority and not letting the ranting begin. Now that it has begun you cannot stop it. . . . Too late now, dear friend, to hush up the affair." And the letter continues: "For I don't like the Jews . . . and never thought them more dangerous. But when authority is lacking, a formidable cleverness is necessary— and the clever thing now would be at least to simulate frankness if one does not dare to have it—if it is too dangerous to have it. Or else let us sweep up—sweep up. For, it is already too late to simulate." He did not feel very good about this in a following letter where he reflected: "what you say about France I think terribly just, but it is a sorry thing, you must admit, if what is to save France takes on the aspect of infamy" (*OC* II, 486–492). In January, 1914, he was not yet ashamed of anti-Semitism. He was distinguishing between French and Jewish races and wanting to have a history written of Jewish literature in France and elsewhere, to bring out its peculiar nature. "That would introduce some clarity into our ideas, and doubtless hold back certain hatreds resulting from false classifications. . . . They speak more facilely than we, because they have less scruple. They speak louder than we, because they do not have our reasons for sometimes lowering the voice, for respecting certain things. . . . Certainly I don't deny the great merit of some Jewish works. . . . But I could admire them with a lighter heart if they reached us only in translation." One might remark that, fortunately for his favorite reading, the French Bible was known to be translated. "For it does not count with me that the literature of my country is enriched, if in a way detrimental to its significance. Better for it to disappear the day the Frenchman's vitality gets low, rather than leave an ill-bred fellow to play his role in his place, in his name" (*Journal, OC* VII, 575–577).

On the 29th of July, 1914, jittery over what was coming, he was feeling sorry for himself because he had talked only with Jews the day before, who struck him as outdoing themselves in a show of patriotism, although he admitted

147

enjoying the conversation of one of them—the philosopher Xavier Léon. One would like to think that Gide outgrew this limitation or that he learned to control it, except perhaps in the kind of antipathy he kept for Léon Blum. It may not be indicative that in *Geneviève* (published in 1936) friendship with a Jewish classmate, the daughter of an artist, is disapproved by the heroine's parents. Their attitude is presented as part of "the conventional banality" of their bourgeois status, and the issue of anti-Semitism is confused with that of prejudice against the artist. Since the trouble comes mostly from Geneviève's father, the already discredited Robert of *L'École des Femmes* and its sequel, one might argue that his prejudice is discounted here by the fact of being his. Yet as late as April, 1938, Gide was not free of it himself, in an article he published on *Les Juifs, Céline et Maritain* (in *La Nouvelle Revue Française*). He chides Céline for playing on anti-Semitism to exercise his lyrical powers—saying it is cynical even if no harm is meant. In reference to Maritain's lecture on *Les Juifs parmi les Nations,* however, he ridicules the idea that Jews are not inherently a race apart, though admiring Maritain's generosity in holding this idea. For Gide the Jews will be Jews and nothing can change the fact. He objects to Maritain's view of the Jews in each nation as an "inconvenient element that must be charitably tolerated," on the ground that this view does not bring out sufficiently the positive contribution of "the Jewish race." He means to honor Jews, apparently, in describing their contribution as an "urgent sense of justice," without which morality would deteriorate; yet he

148

finds Israel's message of justice "somewhat limited" except as "Christian charity comes very happily to temper its intransigence." Does he think justice can be carried too far? Is he afraid it might lessen the need for charity? His conclusion is that in general it is salutary to offset the tendency toward uniformity by having the inconvenience of minorities. He said less charitable things about charity when he was becoming a communist, as well as kinder things about justice and the common needs of humanity, than in this parody of the cultural pluralism a true democracy would seek.

There is for the admirer of Gide a disconcerting intermittence in his moral development. His youthful sentiments in connection with the Dreyfus case indicate that his African struggle to free himself from a narrow code had not broadened him as much as he liked to think. Adherence to the *Action Française* during the war of 1914 would suggest that in middle age he was still not very advanced in some fundamental respects. He, who was going beyond Catholicism and Protestantism, was lured by propaganda that liberal Catholics could not stomach. As part of the effort to unite Catholic and non-Catholic conservatives, the *Action Française* denounced his dear privilege of reading the Gospel for oneself, as leading to moral anarchy (Muret, 267). Maurras, an editor of the movement's daily paper, said: "One must come out of liberty as out of prison" (Muret, 252). Priests were forbidden to give absolution to readers of that paper (Muret, 272). The whole thing was too much for the Vatican. There was no diplomacy in the way Maurras was urging a return

149

to religion, and there was a feeling that he was using religion for royalism. Finally in 1926 Pius XI forbade belonging to such a group as his (Muret, 270, 272).

What Gide, loving the creative intelligence and trusting experimental method, with his crusading against the dogmas and "certainties" of tradition, was doing with people who made tradition their watchword, he tried to explain when called upon in 1935. He said that in the desperate days of 1916 the *Action Française*, although not the best organization, and although he was not a royalist, seemed the only one to rely on for the necessary unity (*André Gide et Notre Temps,* 28). This was practically what he had written in the *Journal* the 3rd of March, 1918. In a letter not dated but appended to the 1919 *Journal* (*OC* IX, 466), justifying an article attacking the *Action Française,* he said it had aroused his moral indignation even during the war, and that he had refrained from speaking against it only to spare some dear friends. On the 4th of February, 1930, he wrote in the *Journal:* "This revival of Thomism, and the writings of Maritain, and the quarrel of the *Action Française,* etc., about which we flay each other, will soon appear mere historical curiosities."

But if alarm for national safety had drawn him into an illiberal camp, and friendship had kept him from denouncing it, during the first world war, he found it harder to explain his desertion of the cause of freedom in 1931. It was then that his *Journal* was taking on the character of a collaboration between him and history. It could be expected that the coherence of such a joint product would suffer from inevitable divergence of the collaborators, when one misunderstood the other or they simply

CHRIST AND MARX

disagreed. Just as Gide was regarding the rise of Soviet
Russia as history's contribution of a magnificent chapter
toward better living, he hesitated to touch the part where
his co-author wanted help in crossing out the mistake of
the fascist passage. When the poet Lauro de Bosis had
scattered anti-fascist leaflets over Rome and his fate was
unknown, although his old airplane probably had been
overtaken by Mussolini's swift fliers, Salvemini asked Gide
to intercede, in October, 1931. He could not read the
words of the new Icarus without emotion, "but what to
do? . . . I'll have to explain myself to Salvemini: despite
my admiration for the exploit of the young hero, something
fails me here: the belief in liberty. I can barely succeed
in making my own thought clear. The notion of liberty as
taught in our time strikes me as most false and pernicious.
And if I approve soviet coercion, I must equally approve
fascist discipline." Gide went on to say he wished he
could be sure he would still think lightly of liberty if he
were not free himself: "I who hold above all to my own
freedom of thought." He meant simply "that man does
nothing worth while without constraint and that very few
are capable of finding constraint in themselves" (*OC* XV,
449).

In this passage he continued: "constraint for constraint,
that of fascism seems to me a return to the past, that of the
Soviets an immense effort toward the future. This costly
experiment is important for all humanity and may deliver
it from a frightful burden. The bare idea that it might
be interrupted and made abortive is unbearable to me—
that such a gigantic struggle toward the never-before-
attempted should remain in vain. The idols they are smash-

151

ing over there have long struck me as the most oppressive among the false gods" (*OC* XV, 450, end of October, 1931). Yet he was not clear enough about Mussolini to come out against him with Salvemini.

Perhaps the limitation of the man's radicalism is suggested by the fact that he expressed it best in philosophizing about God; since it is a temptation, even for a humanist, to separate God from the realm of Caesar. Ominously Gide had appealed to the wisdom of this separation when trying to rationalize his refusal to intervene for Lauro de Bosis. "On the side of God, liberty—that of mind; on the side of Caesar, submission—that of actions. Only concern for the happiness of the greatest number, on one hand; on the other, only concern for truth" (*OC* XV, 450). Would this mean that truth belongs to God and to the freedom of the mind, while the happiness of men is turned over to the mercies of a Caesar who scorns to consider truth? No wonder Gide noted that he was hardly satisfied with what he wrote here!

His trouble lay in the confusion of two ideas of liberty: the negative notion of it as absence of restriction, which is untenable except in "pure thought," and might as well be assigned to the aura of obscurely "spiritual" things clinging to the word God, even when its meaning is humanized; and the positive notion that individuals and groups should participate democratically in all matters affecting them. Instead of differentiating these two ideas of liberty, Gide ignored the second when he paired liberty of thought with submission of action. If he had been thinking of effective freedom he could not have divorced it from practical life; and if he had been considering happiness at all concretely he could not have calmly identified it with submission to Caesar while removing the question of truth from Caesar's realm. This was a strange taming of the rebellious gratuitous act. But Gentile made the "pure act" basic in the official philosophy of fascism, for which authority and liberty were one, by exaggerating the Hegelian principle that the true freedom of the individual was in the strength of the state (cf. H. M. Kallen, *Art and Freedom*, p. 867). From that point of view it was only a rash poet's gesture to oppose Mussolini. Yet one would like to regard Gide as a champion of free intelligence against arbitrary force, and a recrudescence of the authoritarian past. Perhaps one reason for his inconsistency is that, as in his play *Oedipe*, he thought too much in terms of kingly individuals who would lead the people forward, without appreciating the capacity of ordinary men to think for themselves and provide their own leadership.

But, while his individualism avoided the onus of attacking fascism when he was urged to, he was uneasy about slurring liberty and retiring it to a bosom above the battle. The paragraph after the squirming provoked by Salvemini in the *Journal* was more affirmative, more in keeping with Gide's progressive morality. Here he remembered that the constraint of fascism was clinging to the past, that of the Soviets planning for the future. Nothing should make more difference to the author of *Les Faux-Monnayeurs*, *Voyage au Congo*, *L'Ecole des Femmes*, *Robert* and *Oedipe*.

Gide said he was deterred from communism by the "frightful means" which seemed necessary to attain it,

153

although it was awkward for him to applaud what he thought were the fruits of revolution and refuse to help. He hated to think of people getting hurt. It moved him deeply to read the letters of German students killed in the war he had been glad for France to win in 1918. With his horror of bloodshed he was thankful that the transition to the future had been made in Russia, and hoped it would be accomplished less painfully elsewhere. Meanwhile he was uncomfortable in the midst of class conflict, not liking to have on his side "hatred, injustice and arbitrariness" (*OC* XV, 459–460).

He was seeing in 1932 that the cooperating society of the future was dependent upon science-begotten industry. "This new society can no more be imagined without the machine than the isolated farmer without tools" (Pléiade ed. of *Journal*, 1108). Yet he also saw that progress hinged upon the recognition of need and aspiration as well as upon machinery. People who attacked the U.S.S.R. and denounced the Five-Year Plan as a mirage were combating hopes that could not be discouraged, because these were rooted in the process of their realization (*ibid.*, 1111). That such hopes were collectivist he did not like to think without qualification. After quoting his uncle Charles Gide as saying, "It demeans the role of cooperation to make it serve individualist ends. Its true role is to serve collective ends," André Gide said there should be no conflict between communism and a properly understood individualism which would also serve the community (*ibid.*, 1113). If there was no conflict here for him, either he had a very individualistic conception of communism, or he had come a long way from saying thirty years before in *Prétextes* that individualism was for only a few great men, at the price of discouraging the rest. Henri Drain finds in this passage (*Prétextes*, p. 163) an echo of Nietzsche's "invectives against egalitarian, democratic or socialist doctrines" (*Nietzsche et Gide*, p. 118). Perhaps that echo will help to explain how Gide in 1932 would "understand" individualism as compatible with the Soviet experiment. He thought he would not need to change his spots in the process: "At heart, in temperament and thought, I have always been a communist. But I have been afraid of my own thought and have, in my writings, forced myself rather to hide than to utter it" (*ibid.*, 1118). This might strike one as surprising from a man who had striven for truth and sincerity; or as a confession of confusion; or perhaps just an effect of the complexity of the subject. He was quick to admit incompetence in political and economic matters. But, finding them so entangled that specialists were often deceived, he seized upon the psychological and imponderable aspect as belonging to the field in which he might be considered a technician (*ibid.*, 1120). If it was true that the future society would depend not only upon machinery but upon attitudes, the writer's technique of dealing with them would be as crucial as any skill, once he appreciated the social possibilities of his calling.

With Gide's growing interest in communism, however, came a loss of creative power, as he termed it. But perhaps this may be considered not so much a loss as a transfer of energy to things which seemed more vital: upon which he had to express himself, though only in jottings in the *Journal*. He had moments of regretting this, and even thought social questions were occupying his mind because the "creative demon" was retiring. But much as he loved poetry and elevated prose, he saw them becoming dead letters through divergence from life; and he loved life more. He saw also that their refinement had been fed by inability to solve social problems. When his wife chided him that his poetic force had diminished with his Christian sentiments, he wrote: ". . . rather with my perplexity. Each of my books so far has been the development of an incertitude" (*ibid.*, 1139, July, 1932). He might have noted that doubt and indecision are bound to fragment the self in a fractured society; and that while some art could flourish and relieve some people in that broken situation, he would rather see the works of the whole self in the whole world to come. He did say plainly that he hoped a Soviet state could achieve the finest flowers of thought without "enslaving a class and denying it the benefits" (*ibid.*, 1139). And he could not get away from social questions, no matter how he tried. Even the previous war had not obsessed him so much. As on the Congo, he must again speak out or be the accomplice of abuses. Trying to sleep one night in July, 1932, he opened Whitman, *By Blue Ontario's Shore:* "O days of the future I believe in you—I isolate myself for your sake . . . Lead the present with friendly hand toward the future" (*ibid.*, 1141). It was more than ever for the unborn that Gide wanted to write, though he realized they would not need to hear what he needed to tell them. He would not let this sadden him; but in his sense of isolation the ideal companionship of Christ was comfort, to offset what Em. said about loss of Christian sentiment. "Do you think Christ would recognize himself today in his Church?" (*ibid.*, 1125).

That Christ would be for the U.S.S.R. seemed more likely, though in his time the social question had not arisen in anything like the modern form. Communists were opposed to his teaching of resignation and submission, because "in disarming the oppressed it handed him over to the oppressor. But the oppressor, in taking advantage of the betrayal of the oppressed, betrays and deceives Christ. In putting hope off beyond life, religion drugs and discourages resistance. To understand this is to be angry with religion, without quitting Christ on that account. Judas himself was less a traitor to him, and less perfidious than those who pretend with his words to authorize a society which first of all makes dupes of those whom his words disarm" (*ibid.*, 1126). Far from leaving Christ, Gide insisted that he was being led to communism by the Gospel (*ibid.*, 1176).

Yet he remarked that the atheism of the Soviets was what most antagonized some pious souls who failed to see "that only false gods could ever be suppressed." Though coming to communism Gide never could be identified with those of the humanist and naturalist persuasion who are through with the idea of God. He said: "The need of adoration dwells at the bottom of the human heart" (*ibid.*, 1131); and added that the pious believers in a revealed religion of which they are the repository "prefer humanity miserable to seeing it happy without God—without their God." For himself he would repeat that he had always been a communist in mind and heart; "even while remaining Christian; and that is of course

157

why I have found it hard to separate them and harder to oppose one to the other" (*ibid.*, 1131–32).

He did not pretend to have arrived at this position by himself. His confession of growing faith was generous. "It took people and events to instruct me. Do not speak here of 'conversion'; I have not changed direction; I have always marched straight ahead; I continue; the great difference is that for a long time I saw nothing before me but space and the projection of my own fervor. Now I advance while orienting myself toward something; I know that somewhere my vague wishes are being organized and that my dream is in a fair way to become reality" (*ibid.*, 1133).

He still felt unqualified for politics. "Don't ask me to join a Party." His habitual individualism and independence were against that, while his thought and feeling were threatening more and more to overflow all inhibition. The discrepancy between his declared sympathies and reluctance to take the final step could not last. As friends who were converted to Catholicism unconsciously taught him the folly it would be for him, so the ineptitude of those who tried to keep him from communism had the contrary effect. In 1933 he wrote in the *Nouvelle Revue Française* that if they thought it funny for a rich man to go left, he found it more surprising that a rich man could call himself a Christian. The Gospel teaching against possession and privilege was perverted by the Church, which could have headed off communism by absorbing all that is best in it, he thought. Now the Church was so allied with essentially anti-Christian forces that it was too late. It was not the fault of Christ that his words had been twisted. Even "It is more blessed to give than to receive" was made abominable in reserving the joy of charity for the rich and letting it also entitle them to paradise. "Thus one can say that from the betrayal of Christianity, Communism is born. . . . Christianity played the game (indirectly and involuntarily, no doubt, but effectively) of capitalism (just as it had played the game of feudalism); so that it was to the greatest interest of capitalism to favor the Christian religion . . ." (included in *Pages de Journal 1929–1932*, Gallimard ed., 167–168). Christianity might still be a perfect thing in the vision of some adherents who should not be blamed for its abuses. But communism could not remain private and subjective; could not be realized individually. Suppose communism was half illusion, as patriotism was, or any love—here was an illusion that would bring reality (*ibid.*, 172).

But a movement relying upon workers and peasants, and for them, was disdained by nice people who did not find them "interesting." Gide himself had misgiving, as when he was appalled by the ugliness of a crowd in Marseilles and said: "Who speaks of loving humanity is above all mystically taken with what it might be, with what it doubtless would be but for this shocking atrophy" (Pléiade ed. of *Journal*, 1135). And while the individual continued to attract him more than the masses, he saw that there must be favorable conditions for them if the individual was to be healthy in any complete sense. The smugness of the comfortable aroused in him the ire of a prophet. "That class of workers, suffering, oppressed, upon whom you have seated yourselves and have installed your well-being—not to understand that it is you who have brought it about and have forced it to be what it now is: this strikes me as monstrous. You have stupefied it, debased it, stained it, and you have the audacity to say: look how dirty they are! Just give them the means to wash, to rise, to learn, to blossom out in the sun, and we'll talk again about that. What matters to me is what they might become. And that is what frightens you. For you know quite well that their 'inferiority' is imposed. . . . What I admire in the U.S.S.R. is the equality of departure, of equal chances—and the abolition of that abominable formula: 'You shall earn MY bread in the sweat of YOUR brow'" (*Pages de Journal 1929–1932*, 172–173).

In 1933, he was spurning tradition, with all its works of "intelligence and taste." Instruments developed for conquering nature would always be honored, but the future would not bother with the rest. "Homer will be as if he had never sung. Child's play, all that! We are entering a serious era." (Pléiade ed. of *Journal,* 1164). Still he thought he could help the cause more if not enrolled in the Party, fearing it would inhibit his contribution, which was writing. He could not write to order (Pléiade ed. of *Journal,* 1147). He could not speak in public. It was only alone that he could count for anything, he said (in a letter to Barbusse, 31 August, 1933, included in *Pages de Journal 1929–1932,* pp. 193–194). But in 1934 he was able to say that one could be an individualist and a communist (Pléiade ed. of *Journal,* 1216). His *Nouvelles Nourritures* of 1935 celebrated this discovery. That he joined the Communist Party, even after this, does not seem to be established, either by Gide or his critics. Pierre Naville, in his preface to Claude Naville's *André Gide et le Com-*

munisme, merely speaks of his "conversion" as having occurred in the period covered by the *Pages de Journal* of
1929–1932. As Claude Naville says, these pages "testify
with precision to an ardent sympathy for the U.S.S.R. and
a progressive adhesion to communism" (*André Gide et le
Communisme*, p. 37). Compared with such testimony it is
of secondary importance whether Gide ever had a party
card. He, the retiring individualist, reached the point of
addressing workers in a Communist mass-meeting. Klaus
Mann heard him do it, praising the republics of Spain and
China, denouncing Hitler, Franco and Mussolini (*André
Gide, the Crisis of Modern Thought*, p. 249).

In March, 1935, Gide admitted in his *Journal* a sense
of shame that he had never had to earn his living; and
thought the time was coming when a bourgeois would feel
inferior beside a laborer (Pléiade ed. of *Journal*, 1221).
This would be a return to what he found Lenin calling
"the democratic revolutionary spirit . . . of primitive
Christianity" (*ibid.*, 1228). A really strong personality
Gide thought would be glad to blend with the mass, unafraid of losing itself. It seemed that people cling to
property through inner poverty, and clutch the past
through inability to imagine what might be; through lack
of confidence in man, kept lacking by religion (*ibid.*,
1231). Perhaps the idle rich were worse off than the
poor. The latter at least were not bored. They would seem
to have the ground of happiness in work, except that too
often their work was reduced to drudgery (*ibid.*, 1234).
The remedy lay in radical change of the social order. He
no longer thought the moral question was more important
than the social, in the sense that individual men should

161

be reformed first. They could not really be reformed in great numbers unless social conditions were made over (*ibid.*, 1241). Regretting that under Mallarmé's influence he had long been unpolitical (*ibid.*, 1237), he looked more to the Soviet Union. He expected so much there that he knew he might be disappointed. But he was sure of the ideal represented there, even should his devotion to it oblige him to turn away from the U.S.S.R. (*ibid.*, 1241).

What he hoped Russia and the world would achieve, through systematic and scientific attack upon social problems, never was expressed in a novel he might have written at the height of his creative power. Yet, while no work comprehensive, complex and sustained enough for such a subject was forthcoming after *Les Faux-Monnayeurs*, in that novel he showed why the world had to be remade. And poetic force did blaze up again, with the intensity of a dedication fanned by all the winds of perplexity and doubt. Above the *Journal* rose the flame of *Les Nouvelles Nourritures*—prose poems of joy in Communism, and Christ.

Verily, the happiness which gets impetus from misery beneath, I want no more. Wealth which deprives another, I want no more. If my clothing denudes others, I shall go naked. Oh! you keep an open table, Lord Christ! and the beauty of the feast in your kingdom is that all are invited.

(*Les Nouvelles Nourritures*, 1938 ed., 58–59.)

Comrade, don't believe anything, don't accept anything without proof. Nothing has ever been proved by the blood of the martyrs. There is no religion so mad that it has lacked followers or failed to arouse ardent convictions. It is in the name of faith that people die; it is in the name of faith that they kill. Thirst for knowledge is born of doubt. Stop believing and begin to learn. No one ever tries to impose except in the absence of proof. Don't be gullible. Don't be imposed on.

(*Ibid.,* 149.)

Every unquenched thirst, every unsatisfied hunger, the shivering, the vain waiting, the exhaustion, the insomnia—that all this be spared you, oh! how I wish it, comrade! Bend to your hands, to your lips, the branches of all the fruit trees. Throw the walls down, knock down before you all barriers upon which jealous monopoly has written: "Keep out. Private property." Manage to get at last the whole reward of your labor. Lift your head and let your heart at last fill up, not with hate and envy but with love. Yes, at last let all the caresses of the air reach you, all the rays of the sun and all the invitations to happiness.

(*Ibid.,* 159.)

Comrade, do not accept life as men offer it to you. Do not stop believing that life might be more beautiful; yours and that of other men; not another, future life, which would console us for this one and help us to accept its misery. Do not accept any longer. The day when you begin to understand that men are responsible, and not God, for almost all the evils of life, you will no longer be resigned to these evils.

Don't sacrifice to idols.

(*Ibid.,* 163.)

After about five years of enthusiasm for the Soviet Union he went there in the summer of 1936, and published his experience in *Retour de l'U.R.S.S.* The book expressed admiration and affection for the Russian people. He was charmed by the smiling faces, the happy children, the rest homes, the zest for learning, and the whole atmosphere of hope and affirmation. Nothing he saw with his

163

own eyes repelled him, beyond the poor quality of consumer-goods for which people waited in line, the ugliness of Moscow buildings, the lack of individuality in dress and living arrangements. It seemed naive for the people to think everything they had and did was better than any other country could show. He was disturbed by what he heard about disparities of salary and status, regimentation and shackled thoughts. Yet his own favorable first impressions stood out from the disillusion of his traveling companions. He cooled during his stay, but his book was apparently criticism of an experiment still cherished.

When he found his *Retour* regarded as an attack upon the U.S.S.R., and was attacked by its friends, hailed by its enemies, he was forced to take sides. His second book on Russia, *Retouches à Mon Retour de l'U.R.S.S.*, was the consequence of his first book more than of his trip. He dwelt upon his embarrassment from the privileges heaped upon him by his hosts, but instead of adding much in the way of personal impressions he offered a compilation of charges made against the Soviet Union by its expert long-time opponents. (He said: "It is only after having written my book on the U.S.S.R. that I have finished informing myself. Citrine, Trotsky, Mercier, Yvon, Victor Serge, Legay, Rudolf and many others have given me their documentation. All that they have taught me, which I had only suspected, has confirmed, reinforced my apprehensions"— *Retouches à Mon Retour de l'U.R.S.S.*, 53.)

In 1936–37, when Gide's anti-Soviet books were papering the book-shops of Paris, his words were appropriated by Rightist and pro-Nazi forces. It would doubtless be exaggeration to think his opinions had very much to do with the dissolution of the Popular Front, preventing aid to Loyalist Spain, or preparing for Vichy betrayal. His books were more a symptom of the times than a cause. Yet he was aware of his potential service to the Right, for he had written in his first book on Russia: "I do not hide from myself the apparent advantage which the enemy parties—those for whom 'love of order is confused with a taste for tyrants'—will pretend to find in my book" (*Retour de l'U.R.S.S.*, 16). There he reproached the Soviet Union for slowness in deciding to help the Spanish Republic, and felt encouraged about the Russian future when that aid was finally forthcoming (*ibid.*, 70, 98). If heading off Hitler and Mussolini in Spain or elsewhere was what he wanted, it is strange that he did not explicitly disavow the comfort which the fascist cause might find in what he wrote at a moment when the Franco-Soviet accord against Hitler was hanging in the balance. But hatred of fascism was no longer to him a reason for loving all its enemies.

In 1937, Gide could find no distinction between what he saw in huge letters on the walls of Italy and what he had observed the year before in Russia. He thought he was seeing everywhere in Italy the very slogan adopted by Russian Communism: "which still pretends to be anti-fascist, but no longer is except politically," since it also was requiring "those who joined the Party to *believe, obey,* and *fight* without weighing what was involved, without criticism, with blind submission. Three-fourths of the Italian inscriptions would go just as well on the walls of Moscow" (*Journal,* 5 August, 1937).

165

It would seem that Gide's views on the U.S.S.R. after his visit wrought a sea-change in all his political thinking, regardless of whether his criticisms of the U.S.S.R. were justified or not. Still convinced of the historical necessity of socialism, yet disillusioned about the one country where he had hoped to find it, he could not help being cynical. Having no other focus for his aspiration, he was headed for doubt and despair. Yet he was at home with these attitudes. It may even appear that he drew a sense of relief and renewed self-confidence out of his disengagement from the embarrassments of left-responsibilities.

In ceasing to be a Stalinist he did not become a Trotskyist. Both camps felt that he was alienated from them and from the contemporary scene, a self-communing individualist. Trotsky dismissed him with a remark: "Gide has removed himself too far from us, along with the epoch he reflected in his deliberate and leisurely disquisitions. Even his latest books, interesting though they are, read rather like human records of the irrevocable past" (in a review of *Les Javanais* by Jean Malaquais, written by Trotsky in August, 1939, and published in *Fourth International* for January, 1941).

Claude Naville (who died in December, 1935, before his pamphlet on Gide was published) tellingly pointed out how incongruous it was for Gide to become a communist, with his background of individualism, symbolism and Nietzsche. If the man's scientific interest and training had been taken into account by Naville he might have found there a connection with scientific socialism, though it was the individualistic rather than the social features of science that attracted Gide. Naville characterized Gide's

166

communism as vague, idealistic, utopian; and felt that it was just his former religion with the supernatural and eternal elements left out. He thought Gide was confused in identifying his individualistic humanism with socialism; as well as deluded in imagining that either individualism or socialism was tolerated in the U.S.S.R. Yet Naville thought Gide's confusion registered the pressure of the time; and said it was enough to see him "denouncing injustice . . . believing in human progress . . . sympathizing with the workers' movement and its revolutionary doctrine, not opposing the class struggle." The young anti-Stalin communist concluded that the old individualist represented the best of the bourgeoisie: "that in it which can still lean toward a better future, more intelligent and just" (*André Gide et le Communisme*, 67).

This was far from making Gide a Marxian. *Das Kapital* was hard going. He had read it "patiently, assiduously, studiously," and quite a bit of Engels and other Marxist writers. "I have read all that with more constancy and care than I have brought to any other study; and also with more effort; solely in the hope of letting myself be convinced, even of submitting myself, and becoming instructed. And I came out of it each time with cramps, my intelligence bruised as by instruments of torture" (Pléiade ed. of *Journal*, 1289, summer, 1937). He knew he should not expect literary charm, but he had come to think "that the theory itself was at fault, that it was irrational, at least artificial . . . fallacious and inhuman" (*ibid.*, 1289). He thought people must be impressed by the difficulty of it. He saw that it required initiation and interpretation. He had not made the common observation

167

that people are seldom convinced of Marxism by reading Marx; that usually it is through belonging to a workers' organization, meeting its problems, and observing Marxist thought in practical operation. The experience of the workingman for whom Marx wrote would give content to the diffuseness of which Gide complained; although perhaps most workers get Marx in simplified form through popular pamphlets by contemporary Marxists.

Disdaining the theoretical approach, Gide declared: "Oh! how right you were to see in my coming to communism a sentimental affair; but how wrong you were not to realize that I was right!" (summer, 1937, *Feuillets* included in *Journal*). For him there were two passages in which Marx attained density. One was "Workers of the world, unite!" (last line of the *Communist Manifesto*). In the other it is interesting that Gide's anti-intellectual bias led him to a seemingly characteristic misreading. He quotes Marx as saying: "It is not a question of understanding the world but of changing it" (summer, 1937, Pléiade ed. of *Journal*, 1289). Instead of saying anything against understanding, Marx wrote: "The philosophers have *interpreted* the world in various ways; the point, however, is to *change* it" (No. XI of Marx's *Theses on Feuerbach*, in the appendix to Engels' *Ludwig Feuerbach*).

Gide was relieved not to worry any more about whether his writing conformed to Marxism or not, but thought this very anxiety had taught him what was lacking in the theory. He still maintained upon occasion that the U.S.S.R. was a good stroke, but put it in a way to suggest that what was good in it had been taken over by its enemies; saying that the fear of it had brought reforms even under fascism,

168

and had forced the Church to remember social questions (*ibid.*, 1290). Christian charity and communism still had much in common for him, though charity did not attack the root of misery, and some Christians liked to perfect themselves through charity, so that "they would feel themselves altogether impoverished without the poor to aid." But whereas Christian charity might thrive on injustice, he wondered if it was not worse to make justice a substitute for love. Apparently he was troubled by the attempt of Marxism to be thoroughly scientific in its humanitarianism. Well as he understood and much as he admired science, he seemed to be afraid that to apply it wholesale to social problems would somehow miss the heart of them. For him the teaching of Marx should never be divorced from that of Christ. "I feel myself the brother only of those who have come to Communism through love, through great urgency of love" (*ibid.*, 1291).

Gide wanted to overcome antagonism and hatred, not to have them deliberately fomented (*ibid.*, 1292). He could not share the dream of crushing one part of the state with another part (*ibid.*, 1294). This was the ugly thing about class dictatorship. That it was intended to be temporary and expected to wither with its enemies, did not enter seriously into his thinking. In October, 1938, his satisfaction when the Munich episode had averted the use of force, showed how disillusioned and rudderless rather than Marxist his world-view was. His Dutch friend Jef Last pointed out to him that the shameful capitulation would encourage Hitler. Gide felt carried beyond his depth—wondering whether war could assure the triumph of justice, or only of force. He found himself clutching

169

once more at privacy; asserting that the domain of his worth was separate and inviolable. He would be at sea "in that other domain where events would drag me," yet he felt guilty in holding aloof at such a juncture. "If it strikes me as indecent to speak of anything else, silence would be better" (*ibid.*, 1323). And if he would not look at what was coming, there was again nothing before him but space and his own projection.

At the time of Munich he had just lost Em. as well as the comrades he had hoped to have. But something was coming. He, who loved to look ahead, did not want to see it. He was a refugee from the future, with his values on his back. All he had left was culture and that was disappearing. He could carry more of it than another, but how far? In 1939, he met war with memory, furbishing it until it was better than ever. "Long passages of poems come, as of their own accord, to lodge there; successive verses of La Fontaine, Racine, Hugo, Baudelaire, which I repeat tirelessly as I walk" (*Pages de Journal 1939–42*, Pantheon ed., 14).

The reader of Gide, wanting to estimate him, must face the question of his depression after the fall of France. Some admirers have seen a subtle but brave stand against the German occupation in the fact that for a while in 1941–42 he published weekly in *Le Figaro*, a paper allowed by the Germans in the free zone. Malcolm Cowley, in the introduction to his translation of the *Interviews Imaginaires* which appeared there, praises him for his nerve and ingenuity in outwitting the censor by inserting into literary criticism an attack on the regime (*Imaginary Interviews*, Knopf, 1944). Disapproval of Hitler is plain,

170

once a few cues are given which the educated Frenchman would find for himself. Whether this stratagem should be lauded as a kind of "resistance" or should be contrasted unfavorably with the decision of other writers to publish only in the underground press, is a question that must be settled by a riper time with a fuller knowledge of the specific acts and decisions involved.

Gide let his 1940 *Journal* stand, although it could be used against him. "I don't make myself out more valorous than I was" (Foreword to *Pages de Journal 1939–42*). The fine things he had said about siding with the oppressed and the martyred, the idea that his optimism was rooted in sympathy for their suffering, would seem forgotten on the 20th of August, 1940, when he found no protest in himself against the "ineluctable," although he was not quite ready to accept disaster. He would have liked to think—fortunately for his integrity he could not make it convincing to himself—that his scheme of life remained "untouched by the defeat" (*ibid.*, 66). He was able to distract himself somewhat by reading Goethe. It was admirable that he saw no incongruity in comforting himself with a German writer under the circumstances. But the fact of looking for solace in literature, the fact of looking for private solace exactly as he was in the habit of doing when there was no such public emergency, would not appeal to men who joined the resistance movement. How could he have the egoism to worry about the shortness of his days and his inability to fill them? to wonder whether his trouble was just a matter of growing old, and to be wishing he could "harness himself to a long project?" (25 August, 1940, *ibid.*, 69). To remark that the war had precipitated the ruin of a state already worm-eaten was not treasonable. To doubt whether it was prudent to attempt any reconstruction before the ground was more solid, and to prefer patience, might be called defeatist (24 September, 1940, *ibid.*, 78). It was more spirited to speak of the solution of human problems as up to man himself (27 September, 1940, *ibid.*, 80); to say that adversity had always stimulated him, and that he was suffering only through sympathy, since personally he was not molested. "At the most the right to express myself might be taken away; and I shouldn't feel myself much impoverished by that" (29 September, 1940, *ibid.*, 83). But of course not—if there was nothing he burned to say about a war that was not only killing millions but threatening to snuff out belief in freedom. It was a satisfaction to be progressing in German at his age, reading Thomas Mann (14 October, 1940, *ibid.*, 85). Could more be expected of Gide at his age? He was seventy. Still he was able to consider the values at stake, and sometimes he did. He could denounce the inhumanity of Hitler (12 January, 1941, *ibid.*, 96), and had been disappointed in Pétain (24 June, 1940, *ibid.*, 36). He missed his piano, might have got another, but was apprehensive about disturbing neighbors. This was delicacy; but what made him, almost a life-long challenger of authority and tradition, say that he was "little given to insubordination" (12 September, 1941, *ibid.*, 132)? The answer is found in his next sentence: "We have first of all a need of order, of discipline, just as a severely wounded man needs tranquillity to get well." He added that he feared there would not be a very good recovery "from the major opera-

172

tion which we have been forced to undergo." Then order and discipline would be needed permanently.

This sense of needing order might not be reprehensible in itself, but words have connotations that give special significance, and the connotations are largely given by events. If it was subtly significant that he developed fondness for the word "resistance" in the literary criticism he submitted to the German censor, it might be equally indicative that he used the currently Nazi-and-Fascist terms "order" and "discipline" in a private diary not to be published until after the Germans were driven out, to designate the prime desideratum. This follows painfully well the refusal to help Salvemini and de Bosis against Mussolini, and the denunciation of liberty in that connection; fits also with the previous adhesion to the order-mongering, liberty-loathing *Action Française.* But it is unfair to see a continuous thread of reaction between Gide old-and-disillusioned and Gide young-and-foolish. It is less a question of his remembering old folly than of forgetting subsequent wisdom. He had learned much in the interval between his *Action Française* days and the Vichy regime of Pétain. Indeed on the 24th of June, 1940, he recorded his shock after hearing Pétain say on the radio that France was "intact" after half of it had been abandoned to the enemy. But a good member of the *Action Française* could have written as Gide did on the 10th of July, 1940, though he did so with uneasy realization of what his sometime comrades in a very different party would say: "In the eyes of obstinate partisans those will appear shameful and despicable 'opportunists' who . . .

173

have above all a horror of disorder and demand scarcely
any other rights than that of thinking and loving freely.
But if that were granted me, I'd accommodate myself
quite willingly to constraints, it seems to me, and I'd accept a dictatorship which alone, I fear, would save us
from disintegration. I hasten to add that I speak here only
of a *French dictatorship*" (*ibid.*, 50).

He should have seen, from the time that friends of his
were fighting in Spain against the fascist dictators, that
such men had a way, for all their vaunted nationalism,
of getting together against their own nationals; and that
people who put "order" first were not squeamish about
who imposed it. He was not far from being one of these
when he had the cynicism to say that nine out of ten
Frenchmen would accept the German domination if it
brought abundance—"three out of four of them with a
smile" (*ibid.*, 49, 9 July, 1940). It would seem that each
time the pressure was strong he reverted to the pattern
of dependence against which he rebelled. Was it class-
conditioning, despite his long effort to overcome that?
He said on the 7th of February, 1940: "It is easy to remain
a conservative when well provided for oneself and little
touched by the troubles of others." Perhaps he never succeeded in offsetting this, as he was trying to do in the next
breath: "I cannot take pleasure in anything I buy at the
expense of others." And: "It is through augmenting that
of others that I fashion my greatest joy" (*Pages de Journal
1939–1942*, 18). This was clear and firm, but that was in
February. When France had collapsed in June, he brooded
over the situation, and over himself. It troubled him to
realize that he was relatively untouched by the disaster.

174

On the 17th of July, 1940, he wrote: "I'll not have known anything of it after all except by echo; will not have suffered except through sympathy. The 'intellectual' who seeks first of all and above all to shelter himself loses a rare chance to learn. The imagination remains powerless to supply the real contact and the uninventable experience" (*ibid.*, 57–58). This had been supplied him to a significant extent in the previous war, though what he had learned from it was the need of further thinking. *Numquid et Tu* had a tone of finality but was the beginning of a quest. Now he said: "It is not with impunity that for a lifetime my mind has been trained to understand the *other side.*" If he were free to speak he might say things seeming to favor the enemy, and he did say in his *Journal* on the 12th of January, 1941: "Haven't you, since the time you were occupied with gardening, understood that the only way to preserve, protect, safeguard the exquisite, the best, was to suppress the less good? You know well that this cannot be done without the appearance of cruelty, but that this cruelty is prudence" (*ibid.*, 95, 96).

Was this what he had meant on the 28th of September, 1940? Then he had written: "If tomorrow all freedom of thought, or at least the expression of thought, is denied us, I shall try to persuade myself that art, that thought itself, will lose less thereby than in excessive freedom. Oppression cannot debase the best; and as for the others, it matters little. Long live repressed thought!" He added: "It is in non-liberal epochs that the free spirit attains the highest virtue." The next day he reconsidered: "But we are entering, alas! an epoch in which liberalism is going

175

to be the most suspect and the most impracticable of virtues" (*ibid.*, 80–81).

And on the 12th of January, 1941, after speaking of the preservation of the best through the appearance of cruelty, he went on to correct himself. "Immediately the other voice is raised, which perhaps my head does not hear as well as my heart: 'What are you saying about the *best?*' The work undertaken by him who thinks he is the great gardener of Europe, this work is not so much super-human as inhuman." If it were accomplished there would be none to ask the value of what was destroyed. "Do not say, Hitler, that I am unable to understand you. I under-stand you only too well; but to approve you I should have to understand only you" (*ibid.*, 96).

This was the Gide who in 1933, at a meeting of Revolu-tionary Artists and Writers, arraigned fascist terrorism unequivocally (*Pages de Journal 1929–1932*, pp. 187, ff.); who in 1934 went to Berlin with André Malraux in the effort to free the latter's son and others from arbitrary detention (*ibid.*, 202); who on the 30th of March, 1941, would dissociate himself from the once great magazine *La Nouvelle Revue Française*, which had owed its exist-ence chiefly to him, when he realized that its new editor was a fascist (*Pages de Journal 1939–42*, 105); and who in April, 1941, would attack in *Le Figaro* the book in which Chardonne welcomed Hitler's order. Yet Gide re-mained essentially a spectator and questioner. This kept him from being a good partisan, and when the lines are drawn it does not seem enough to be good-hearted on the sidelines. He was not idle, however. His very vacillation guaranteed a wide consideration of alternatives in a quest for orientation, which was his contribution in this war as in the last. He made blunders. It was a morally dangerous undertaking, and he was injured. But, with others, he found a formula for a morality and religion to carry the world beyond its death-grapple with the past toward a future that opened again as the tide turned against Hitler. In 1942, Gide wrote *Dieu, Fils de l'Homme*. This peak of his thought during the war against fascism expressed his discovery that God was there, ahead: the focus of the love men had to have if they would still go forward.

5. ART FOR ART

IF FROM THE POLITICAL OR MORAL POINT OF VIEW THE DIF-
ficulty of pinning Gide to one position is held against him,
it should be remembered that he is an artist as much as
a moralist; that his work if not his life should be seen
from the esthetic angle; for he has called it the only one
which does not exclude other approaches (*OC* IX, 444).
But what his philosophy of art is, and how it has developed, is an intricate problem. Had his conception remained that of art for art's sake, his esthetic perspective
would have served to exclude other standpoints except as
they might be drained of seriousness and made abstract
figures in the carpet. This esoteric idea of art dates back
to his puritan youth when he held himself aloof from
experience. "Intuitive knowledge alone is necessary," he
wrote in *Les Cahiers d'André Walter* (*OC* I, 110). As the
André of the *Cahiers* wanted "to love with the soul alone
a soul who loves you the same" (*ibid.*, 124), so the young
author, in writing about his alter-André, wanted to drop
studies and human contacts, everything, to shut himself
178

up and believe that he worked in the absolute (*Journal, OC* I, 468–469). His book would swallow the writer; his vocation, if he was an artist, must be so irresistible that he could not help writing. As the puritanism of André-author and André-character was an attempt to overcome the tumult of the flesh with the radiance of an ideal, so their art was a refuge from the conflicting enticements of life. The dreamer looked forward to coming out of his dream into "a full and potent life" where he would "feel robust and normal," but he was not ready; he would put it off, savoring his aloofness and the anticipation of giving it up. "What I like about the work of art is that it is calm; more than we no one has wished repose, or loved uneasiness" (*ibid.*, 502–504).

In art he would keep his calm and enjoy losing it too. Art should come first. He must hurry before his privacy was invaded. "Oh! someone knocks at my door! Someone is coming to see me—horror" (*Feuillets, OC* I, 535). He wished he could shut out all solicitations, and be forced to do the one thing he wanted. He longed for blinkers. In dead earnest he drew up a set of writer's aids and incentives. First the intellectual ones. These included the idea of imminent death, and contemplation of the labor of the poor: "in my eyes only furious work can excuse my wealth." He must always aim at doing as much work as on the day he did the most. Among his "material devices (all dubious)" were eating lightly, keeping his feet warm, not oversleeping, and not reading too much before working. He found it helpful to read a few lines (piously) of Virgil, Molière, or Bach "without recourse to the piano." And he gave the secret of just how he went about the

179

magic business. "In my room, a low bed; a small space, a wood stand with a broad horizontal plank breast-high; a little square table; a hard chair. I imagine lying down; compose in pacing; write standing up; copy seated. For me these four positions have become almost indispensable." The only books in the room would be dictionaries. "There should be nothing to distract or charm. Nothing there should stave off ennui but work" (*ibid.*, 536, ff.). It was unnecessary to add that he would avoid politics and seldom read the papers.

One may be amused or irritated by this self-importance in wanting everything right for writing—for work that avowedly had nothing to do with the world's work. Gide himself, in a preface to the 1930 edition of the *Cahiers*, calls André Walter a "very bad example, and his *Cahiers* pretty mediocre advice." In retrospect the author considers the reader's annoyance to be the value of that book, saying: "it is to warn that I write, to exalt or instruct, and I call a book a failure which leaves the reader intact" (*OC* I, 203). Marinetti had said almost the same thing in his 1909 *Manifesto:* "No work which does not have an aggressive character can be a masterpiece." But that anyone should be wholesomely jolted by the defects of Gide's early expression could hardly have been its original aim. If so, he would not have become chagrined to think that he had been occupied with problems not worth the effort he had spent on them; and would not have wished to change "the languors and inversions of style" he no longer liked. He let them stand because: "Any amelioration would be factitious and would answer to a need of cleanness I did not know then" (*ibid.*, 202–203).

180

ART FOR ART

What the young Gide did know and seem to want in the sphere of art is indicated by his relation to Mallarmé. In the recent *Interviews Imaginaires* he is venerated as a kind of saint whose way of life was more significant than his work, though his intention was to make art all-important. His willingness to support himself quietly as a high-school teacher of English, rather than make his real interest in any degree the means of livelihood, struck his disciple as "disinterestedness," in contrast to the temptation for an artist to lend himself to propaganda and debased entertainment for the masses in the newly industrialized world. The market place appeared so inimical to anything fine that, like Flaubert, Mallarmé felt justified in withdrawing to privacy and a circle of friends. Among those attracted by him were several young and unknown but loyally confident that the bond of coming together with him was better than recognition from without. Though this was to follow, it would deflect very few of them from the view of art upheld in the "quasi-religious atmosphere" of his apartment. That view might be roughly designated as art for art's sake, but it is well to be more precise by comparing the spirit of Mallarmé with that of Hérédia, as Gide does (*Si le Grain ne Meurt,* Part One, Ch. X). He found Hérédia utterly unspeculative. Aside from art his interest was in external things, and his interest in art had the same quality. He seemed to have no knowledge of other people except through their most overt behavior. Unaware of any shortcoming, he had no sense of limitation. "He was rather an artist than a poet; and still more an artisan." That is to say that he was an artist in the sense of his Parnassian school which emphasized

181

metrical form and minimized human interest in general.
At his gatherings, which included diplomats and journal-
ists in addition to poets, Gide was terribly bored. And he
felt the same dissatisfaction with Gautier, who also represented the Parnassians though he preceded them. He
was the writer who could say: "The inexpressible does
not exist," because he ignored the existence of what he
could not express (Gide's *Morceaux Choisis*, 454). This
approach to art was so technical and professional that it
did not seem to make an artist the least uncomfortable
in the company of people who swam in the main stream
without thinking of criticizing it.

The Symbolist school of Mallarmé, who had been a
Parnassian, turned away not only from the harshness of
"real life" at the end of the nineteenth century, but also
from the Parnassian substitution of form for feeling.
Young men went out from Mallarmé with the emotion of
apostles and thought of their circle as the cénacle. Only
poets were chosen, except for Whistler and Gauguin. The
tone was mystical, metaphysical. Art for art meant that
art as form was for the sake of art as content—content so
ideal that form could only symbolize it vaguely. In reaction against realism the aim was the absolute: à la
Hegel for some, though Gide much preferred Schopenhauer. A poet might not yet be a finished artist because
of having too much to say. He would need to develop his
own mode of expression. He would experiment with ir-
regular verse forms. He might write very little, like Mallarmé himself and Gide's lifelong friend Valéry. In contrast to Parnassian confidence, a Symbolist would usually
be tentative, with a sense of much to learn. And, as Gide

said, "the mistake was not in trying to detach some beauty and some truth of a general order from the inextricable confusion that 'realism' then presented; but indeed in deliberately turning the back on reality" (*Si le Grain ne Meurt,* Part One, Ch. X).

He added that he was saved by *gourmandise.* He would seem to mean that greediness for the good things of life took him out of the tower of Symbolism. But that tower itself looked out, and was used in looking for an affinity between the self and things which in the casual relationships of life could all seem alien. This search has been carried on by Symbolist contemporaries of Gide as different as Valéry, Yeats, Proust and Joyce. They have shown considerable antipathy toward science as a possible aid in their search, though not averse to borrowing its results and some of its techniques. Gide is unusual in the extent to which he has adopted scientific method as his own. Despite the incongruity between its capacity for controlling reality and the Symbolist genius for shunning it, there has been a tie between them which he never severed. For science also is looking for secret connections, and its discoveries not only release its workers from the banalities of everyday life but turn the whole world away from what was reality toward what is to be. The difference is that, whereas the Symbolist sought an absolute behind the scenes, the scientist finds everywhere a relativity more transforming and transporting than any absolute dreamed of by the philosophers. Science, which has put art (or at least art-lovers) on the defensive, turns out to be its most powerful ally in the enterprise of making life over, closer to desire. Seeing this, Gide could remain

183

something of a Symbolist, could retain the banner of art for art, while developing a social conscience that would enlist art for life.

Art as artistry was for art as effect, and the effect he came to ask was an impact, a shock, in no superficial sense of pleasant thrill, but shaking complacency. For the mature Gide, a book was no good if it left the reader where he was, unshaken in his assumptions and prejudices. He must feel that the author wrote out of a fierce intimacy with life-problems. A full appreciation of art for Gide was transitive. It carried over from art to life, where art came from. And he did not need to leave Symbolism to think so. Symbolism was a reaction against the Parnassian cult of art as intransitive, as leading nowhere beyond the perfection of its own form. Whereas art for the Symbolist opened to a metaphysical vista beyond reality, Gide learned to conceive art as instrumental in recasting reality. Far from insensitive to what is called intransitive in art, he still values that phase of it, referring with reverence to the incantatory quality of Mallarmé's poetry. One may limit esthetic experience to appreciation of that quality, and call extra-esthetic every tie which art must be admitted to have with life at large. Sometimes Gide would seem a strict constructionist, as if he thought the esthete's ecstasy were the whole end of art. More often he speaks not as if the leverage of art upon the business of living were an alien use of art, an exploitation of it beyond the sacred confines of the purely esthetic experience, but as if art were intended for extensive use, and as if appreciation of such extension must enter into the fully esthetic moment, to qualify the heart of it.

The young man he was may be thought sentimental and self-centered, but the lushness of his *Cahiers d'André Walter* was remote from the Parnassian separation of art from human feeling. His preoccupation with religion and sex may have been far from a social conscience, but was not reducible to art for form's sake. He started out as an idealist, a puritan, and his artistic début was full of moralizing if not of moral purpose. How much Platonism there was in Symbolism may be gathered from his statement of its theory in *Le Traité du Narcisse* (published in 1891 and dedicated to Paul Valéry):

Verities remain behind the Forms—Symbols. Every phenomenon is the Symbol of a Verity, with the sole duty of manifesting it. . . . We live to manifest. The rules of morality and of esthetics are the same: a work which does not make a manifestation is useless, and by that token, bad. . . . All the morality of the artist, the savant, is that he must not prefer himself to the Truth he wants to utter; nor the word or phrase to the Idea he wants to show: I could almost say that here is the whole of esthetics (*OC* I, 215).

Thus the disciple of Mallarmé; and this the theme of Valéry in the celebrated *Cimetière Marin*. The poet seeks a symbol to reveal the archetype. The vision disappears, leaving Narcissus with his own lips: "an image should not be desired; a move to possess it tears it . . . Contemplate" (*ibid.*, 218).

This is romantic, but with a difference. Whitehead has observed (*Science and the Modern World,* Ch. V) that Romanticism enabled tender souls to escape the mechanistic world-view based upon seventeenth century physical science, by affirming that imagination gave access to a dimension of being more congenial to the heart. Edmund

185

Wilson (*Axel's Castle*) has followed up this observation by pointing out that, in the wake of Darwin, determinism spread so effectively to thought about sentient and social levels that a literary man had to accept it and work within it or seem ignorant. The result was Naturalism and Realism. When again the poet felt the need of a freer, more congenial and imaginative view, he returned part-way to Romanticism, but could not forget the lesson of Naturalism, to respect the observed facts, even though discounting them as mere symbols of a Platonic otherworld. If, as Gide suggests in *Le Traité du Narcisse*, paradise never existed except ideally, it could not theoretically be displaced by Zola's world of fact. But that scene of action could hardly fail to beckon eyes which had been open only to contemplate. And Gide was to insist that Zola belonged very high "as artist and quite apart from 'tendency'" (*Journal*, 1 October, 1934).

Like the celibate youth in *Paludes*, who was nerving himself to venture across the marshes around his tower, so the "I" in *Le Voyage d'Urien* (published in 1893) dreamed of pushing off from Symbolist contemplation. But his voyage was only another vision; his daring was still confined to make-believe. Knowing that he would have to become bolder, he confessed at the end:

One day, however, you know I wanted to see life, and we leaned toward things. But they struck me as so serious, so terrible, so responsible in all respects, that I have not dared to speak of them. If I have turned away from them . . . I have preferred to speak a lie. I was afraid of crying too loudly and ruining poetry by speaking the truth, the truth which must be heard, preferring to lie some more and to wait—to wait, to wait . . .

ART FOR ART

The mood of contemplation continued in *Les Nourritures Terrestres,* though focused on the earth. The dreaminess of this attitude and the ideal of expressing it in art were well put in *Le Renoncement au Voyage,* wherein Gide was renewing his youth in North Africa and recalling his convalescence there ten years before. The night was more beautiful than he remembered, and he hated to waste the splendor of the day in work. All the haunting ennui of the desert was felt in the song and silence of a flute. "I wish that, from page to page, evoking four moving tones, the sentences I write here might be for you what that flute was for me, what the desert was for me— of diverse monotony."

One might wonder why such yearning over things and places did not take the form of poetry. Gide scarcely attempted it after *Les Poésies d'André Walter,* though he liked these better in retrospect than the *Cahiers* they followed (cf. 1930 preface to the *Cahiers, OC* I, 201). Poets found in his father's library had been the companions of adolescent walks and thoughts. "A poet is what I want to be! A poet is what I am!" (*Si le Grain ne Meurt,* Part One, Ch. VII). It would seem that Gide could have been one as well as master of diary, essay and sketch, story, novel and play. There is no doubt of his being a poet in the sense of writing with imagination and using language creatively. Why did he not become one also in the use of meter and rhyme? The fact is that, after his early "passionate predilection for verse," he came slowly to recognize "the superiority of beautiful prose and its greater rarity" (*ibid.*). The reason was not just a change of personal taste. He never ceased to enjoy and admire Racine,

187

La Fontaine, Hugo, Baudelaire, Mallarmé, Goethe—for their versification as much as anything. A letter of 1902 explains: "Borne by another epoch, perhaps I could have found without difficulty the tongue of verse which I seek (you have sensed it correctly) and the regret of which makes my prose—but to be a poet in an age like ours, it would have been necessary not to see, not even to know, that it disdained you. All recent poets have been hallucinated. When a clear awareness of the surrounding world is added to inner fervor, a cruel and lovely culture may result, but also embarrassment, fear, the struggle of a divided self—prose. That is what made Flaubert—it is what undoes me" (*OC* III, 559).

Yet this undoing would be Gide's making too, and not only keep him from writing poetry but break him of prose that hankered after it. That versified writing can deal effectively with the changing world, he handsomely granted in the 1920 tribute to Émile Verhaeren, and in recent praise of Aragon (*Interviews Imaginaires*, 208). But Gide's conception of what it would mean to be a poet himself was colored by the Parnassian separation of art from feeling, and by the Symbolist separation of art from everyday reality. He saw that the Symbolist, reaching for a "higher" reality, was forfeiting most emotion by disdaining quotidian problems, quite as much as if he were to join the rival school in ruling out emotion per se. An "astonishing passage" in the *Journal* of the Goncourt brothers showed Gide in a flash the underlying error of both Parnassian and Symbolist—the error he must avoid: that of not being interested in the issues vital to their fellow men: "One cannot conceive except in the repose and sleep (so to speak) of the moral activity. Emotions are contrary to the gestation of books. Those who imagine should not live . . ." (Quoted by L. Martin-Chauffier in his notes, *OC* III, xiv). "That is exactly the contrary of what we think," said Charles-Louis Philippe to Gide. And the same poet said on another occasion: "I think we should seek something absolutely different. . . . Perhaps the sense of *justice* is destined to play for us the role which the picturesque played for the romantics" (Gide's *Journal*, 20 January, 1902).

Neither a Parnassian nor a Symbolist poet would like having his aim reduced to the picturesque. Each would think himself beyond such a romantic quality. Yet they both clung to something close to it, whether putting technique or personal and esoteric evocation in place of response to the massive values of human good and evil. Romanticism itself was a step in this direction, asserting the at-homeness of feeling in nature. Even to exaggerate the importance of a composition supposedly "objective" and free of feeling was wholesome in establishing self-confidence. But the self at work here was too private. The Symbolist imagination was too dreamily egoistic to satisfy the social self awakening in Gide and his friend when they felt the advance of justice over the picturesque, over the formal or the incantatory, as the focus of aspiration for the artist as for anyone else.

Awareness of reality and a fervor at variance with it bred the same conflict in Flaubert and Gide. But whereas the former found a solution in hating the existence around him and living for his art, the latter cultivated love of life: first his own, then that of others, and altered his art accordingly. Flaubert's constant blasphemy against life (in the third volume of his *Correspondance*) was to pain Gide later, when he would say: "I feel this *duty* to be happy, higher and more imperious than these factitious duties of the artist" (*OC* X, 477). He could also say: "I do not reproach Gautier for this doctrine of 'art for art,' outside of which I cannot find a reason for living . . ." Yet Gide brought the positions of "art for life" and "art for art" together by adding that he did reproach Gautier for "having reduced art to expressing only so little" (*OC* VI, 351).

If "life" was to mean just existing in external reality, drab as it was, and full of fear and want as well as petty frictions, for most people so far in the industrial age, Gide preferred art—if art meant the freedom and imagination lacking in all that. If art meant what humanity must have in order to move on, let there be art and let it be for the sake of more art. But if a private fervor and a perfection of form to enchant a clique of esthetes was what art amounted to, let them have it. He did not long accept as final the bourgeois society Flaubert hated. It should not be identified with life and the possibilities of life. Nor would Gide cut art to a cult mystifying and shocking the bourgeois, as if art could remain an escape from or attack upon a class in a passing stage of history. The opposition of art and life was owing to a static and meager conception of both. What there was of genuine human value in any school of art belonged to the movement of the whole human enterprise. He preferred the "still inchoate beauty of things" to the purified work of art. Life was more interesting, "more dramatic and quickening on account of

190

its very fugacity." No imaginable harmony was as good as the disruption of it for further growth. "The trail of *man* was what I looked for in every work" (*ibid.*, 370).

When Gide spoke of "art for art" as alone making sense of life to him, he meant art for art—for the sake of human life. His esthetics must be considered part of his ethics. He may have had lapses when he separated them. But even his reflections on technique usually come back to a moral basis. "Less painter than musician, it is certain that what I sought was movement rather than color for my sentence. I wanted it to follow faithfully the palpitations of my heart" (*OC* IX, 407). In the same vein he said the sentences of Flaubert's *Tentation* "seemed just as beautiful to me as at first, but today the most beautiful form of style touches me less than its limpidity and the movement of a soul which shows through the words" (19 September, 1917). It should be noted that by heart or soul Gide came to mean not egoistic emotion or a guarded privacy so much as a social sympathy. That makes it understandable that he became impatient with virtuosity, patient as he had been in striving for it. He thought it "never produced anything but the banal. The only technique (*métier*) which counts is that which feeling itself has created, and which it invents afresh as needed. I want to write nothing except from urgency (25 September, 1915). The word "urgency" amplifies the word "feeling" or "emotion" which alone might seem too subjective to motivate him adequately. The use of "urgency" shows his motivation to come from awareness of the larger human situation, as it appeared ever more urgent to him than any personal exigency, especially after he had done

191

a stint of war work. When he spoke of urgency in 1915, it was after greeting that year in his *Journal* with the announcement: "I tell you that it is a new civilization which begins." He wanted to uproot in himself everything unworthy. He wanted to be more natural and honest than before, but knew that letting himself go would not be the way. He would have to work harder to please himself with his work, more modestly and patiently than when he had prided himself on fine writing. "I have a horror of all rhetoric and all romanticism, and of that verbal effort by which thought tries to add an inch to its stature" (*OC* VIII, 228).

But, while he hated virtuosity, he said he could not help being impressed by it, as in Proust; and would like to be capable of it in order to disdain it without being like the fox in the fable (*OC* X, 516). Deeper than vanity, however, the reason for continuing to cherish formal excellence was the sense that without it there was risk of laziness and chaos. The pendulum swung between need of control and avoidance of constraint, in his esthetic as in his political reflections. "The problem of the artist is to realize maximum liberty in the most perfect form," he said in praising the Flemish French-writing poet Verhaeren for overcoming the Parnassian stiffness, like Rimbaud, but without his brutality. Verhaeren also "came at the moment when the Symbolist movement was in danger of immobilizing itself in an attitude, was becoming contemplative and losing interest in life" (*ibid.*, 6). But while Gide had learned to be alert to that danger, he was afraid after the first world war that literature suffered from lack of the patience the Parnassian and Symbolist writers had.

Though it was silly to parade the affectations of an artist, they would be effaced by the hard work of a serious one, so completely that his art might not be recognized at first (*ibid.*, 477). Annoyed to be accused of "coquetry in the arrangement of my sentences," Gide said, "nothing is more false. I like only the strict and naked. When I began to write my *Nourritures* I understood that the very subject of my book *was* to banish from it all metaphor" (*ibid.*, 480).

The progress of his art lay in avoiding each complaisance of lush and luxurious effect that came to nauseate him in his youthful over-writing. "I wanted above all to obtain from myself a kind of expression more vigorous, more incisive, more plain; not to yield henceforth to that weakness for rhythmic phrasing, the lulling of which I abhor" (*ibid.*, 505). This did not yet mean he wanted to be careless. He would be as meticulous as ever, and find his comfort therein, saying that the most atrocious attacks on his work would not trouble him as much as finding a sentence that did not satisfy him in his *Morceaux Choisis* (*ibid.*, 531). What he wanted, more explicitly, may be gathered from scattered passages in the *Journal*. He wanted to express his thought succinctly rather than eloquently (14 February, 1932), to overcome the notion that good writing consisted in amplification (*OC* XV, 458). "The *good writing* I admire is that which, without being noticeable, halts and holds the reader and keeps thought from advancing except slowly. I want thought to sink at each step in a soil rich and profoundly mellow. But what the reader usually looks for is a kind of good smooth carpet to lead him on" (*OC* XI, 380). As Montesquieu put it, "one cannot write well without skipping intermediate ideas"; or, as Gide added, "a work is not right without shortcuts" (*ibid.*, 399).

But it came over him, while seeking compression with the assiduity once devoted to elaboration, that it would be better yet if he could just let himself go. Obviously he could not grow effortless without trying, and he mentioned several times in the *Journal* that he was trying by forcing himself to write rapidly. "Too often I wait for a sentence to finish forming in myself before writing it down. It is better to take it by the end presented first, head or tail, without yet knowing the rest—then pull, and the rest will come" (*OC* XV, 325). Somewhat wistfully he said, "I have wanted to make my sentence an instrument so sensitive that just moving a comma would spoil its balance" (*ibid.*, 458). He would discipline himself by tearing up pages that were not spontaneous, learning to wander rather than be vain of saying things well (*ibid.*, 488). He wanted to follow the example of Stendhal. "The great secret of Stendhal, his great malice, is to write *right off*. His tremulous thought keeps as vivid and fresh in color as the butterfly which has just come out . . ." (3 September, 1937). But even if the result were colorless, Gide would rather not have it retouched. He admired the strength of Roger Martin du Gard, thinking it exempted him from the studied style that goes with "exquisite uneasiness. . . . I do not know a more neutral writing, which lets itself be more completely unnoticed." Beside his *Thibault*, any other book seemed "over-refined, recherché, precious" (*OC* XV, 536).

That Gide brought himself to prefer the plain could not

be asserted without reservation. He did not give up his passion for Racine but declared late in the *Journal* that he loved his verses "above all literary productions," and made an instructive comparison with Shakespeare. "I admire Shakespeare enormously," he said, and proved it by the loving labor of translation; "but in the presence of Racine I experience an emotion that Shakespeare never gives me: that of perfection. . . . Man and nature, all creative imagination (*toute la poésie*) laughs, cries and trembles in Shakespeare's plays, open to the winds; Racine is at the summit of art" (27 October, 1933).

The glory of French letters was this altitude and the approaches to it. There was more room for roaming in English and American literature, fondness for which grew on Gide throughout his maturity. He especially liked *Moby Dick*—not for the pessimistic philosophy he did not take seriously, but for the sea and air and adventure, as in Defoe. In 1940 (23 November), he was to write in the *Journal* that to restore his peace of mind he was turning from a stretch of German (wherein he had found much comfort) to English: "Each time I plunge again into English literature, it is with delight. What diversity! What abundance! This is the one that it would most impoverish humanity to lose." That he included American books in his love of reading English, he left no doubt in the "interview" he wrote on *The New American Novelists* after his liberation by the American capture of Tunis in 1943. "There is no contemporary literature that arouses my curiosity more than that of the United States; not even that of the new Russia" (*Imaginary Interviews*, 141, translated by Malcolm Cowley, Knopf, 1944). What he

195

says about Hemingway, Steinbeck, Faulkner and Cald-
well, shows that they were far from giving him repose.
But he was fascinated by their break from Europe's burden
of the past, as he had been in Thoreau and Whitman.

In 1934, shortly after comparing the perfection of Racine
with the humanity of Shakespeare, Gide began a new notebook of his *Journal* by complaining about the lack of value
in the last one, because he had let it fill up with "social
and political preoccupations which I want to banish from
my mind for a while" (6 February, 1934). The phrase
"for a while" suggests that before committing himself
further to Communism he wanted to refresh himself with
formal excellence. At 65 he was again like the youth in
Paludes, looking out toward life, yet hugging his tower.
In such a mood he had said a year or so earlier: "I prefer not to write anything more, rather than warp my art
to utilitarian ends. To persuade me that they should have
priority today would at the same stroke condemn me to
silence" (Pléiade ed. of *Journal,* 1149). Now weighed
down by life's problems, and girding himself to share in
a gigantic effort to cope with them, he rejoiced in a sphere
where perfection was achieved. He could hold it in his
hand by opening Racine's *Phèdre.* "What verses! what
chains of verses! Was there ever, in any human language,
anything so beautiful?" (footnote to entry of 18 February,
1934).

Gide was refreshing, not fooling himself. July 25th, 1934
he said in the *Journal:* "For a long time there can be
no more question of artworks. . . . There is scarcely anything left in me which is not touched by compassion.
Wherever I turn my eyes I see nothing but distress around

196

me. He who remains contemplative now shows an inhuman philosophy or a monstrous blindness." On the first of September he spoke of having lacked until the last two years a sense of the time he was living in. The influence of Mallarmé and German philosophy had strengthened his "anti-historical nature" and let him "pretend to work in the absolute." Now he saw how a sense of the absolute would serve to justify the existing state of things, and considered that *Paludes* might be transposed from the private-moral to a social key. "Woe to him who is satisfied with this imperfect world which could be so beautiful!" (28 March, 1935).

As the effort to improve the world became imperative to Gide, he could not exempt art from the general obligation. A "perfection" which ignored the great human need was more or less specious. Even the *Phèdre* of Racine had struck him, in the midst of ecstasy over it, as "a little artificial, a bit contrived, somewhat external to Racine as to myself, something of an 'artwork'" (18 February, 1934). The pejorative use of the term 'artwork' (*'oeuvre d'art'*) in quotation marks, in this context, must be taken to disparage not just a particular work of art but art itself; for on the same page he referred to *Phèdre* as Racine's masterpiece—still not long after putting his work at "the summit of art." Though Gide stuck to "art for art" up to a point, he was coming to hold that the highest art was not up to life.

Art would have to be regarded as respite from the real business, or as promoting it, to be vital. Then the final criterion of art could no longer be formal or stylistic. He would have to develop his conception of esthetic

197

worth beyond this level or admit that esthetic values were subsidiary. Two years before the passage exalting Racine to the pinnacle of formal art, he wrote: "Recently these questions of style have ceased to be of primordial importance to me . . . it is not that they seem less important to me; but that other questions, which were growing in me, which have now grown up, have taken the lead, drawing the rest in their train. So be it!" (14 February, 1932).

But if art in essence was more than form, art might keep a place in the van of progress instead of trailing behind. In one fashion or another he had always been for progress (except when knocked off his base), but he had formerly confused progress with the gratuitous act, conceived as the contrary of anything useful. When he had, like Flaubert, thought of the useful in a narrow bourgeois sense, then anything hateful to that sense, anything not crudely and selfishly gainful, appeared gratuitous, "disinterested." The bourgeois, as envisaged by Flaubert, could "admit only utilitarian art or literature"—utilitarian in terms of his limited vision—and would "hate everything he could not rise to understand" (22 August, 1937). But when Gide had won a more generous conception of the useful, there was no longer any point in opposing it to art and literature. Flaubert, in doing that, had in effect depreciated art as much as he accused the bourgeois of doing. So had the Parnassian and Symbolist schools. For it became clear to Gide that only as art was really useful, however perfect it might be otherwise, could it have a serious role in the evolution of human life.

It dawned upon him that art, to have a larger significance, had to sacrifice something of the beauty he had loved. The beauty of formal excellence, difficult as it might be to achieve, was after all too easy. At least it was too easy to contemplate, whatever it took to produce it. What it took was skill, a sense of rhythm and pitch rather than a heart, rather than a head, rather than full awareness of the human situation and a resolve to change it. Of course, not just anybody would find it easy to contemplate formally fine art. One had to have easy circumstances to do much of it, and a little might not be enough. Long exposure, habituation to "the best," and easy relationships with people who knew what that was, people of taste who almost had to be people of leisure—all made art-contemplation hard to come by.

Gide did not put it in just these words, but many words of his declare dissatisfaction with contemplation as an ideal, moral or esthetic. He did not deny its charm, but he saw how blinding it was, how it lowered the visibility of all that needed to be done. The insidious thing about upholding esthetic contemplation was the emphasis upon what was already done, with the separation of it from what men were doing and wanting to do. To the contemplative eye even what had been done appeared less important than the do-nothing sweetness of appreciating, with a slowly acquired taste, a thing of beauty as if it were out of time and out of human power. The work in a work of art was not like other work, and its art was not like the fitting of means to ends in other arts and crafts. The otiose attitude of pure contemplation, bestowed retroactively upon the artist, made him an honorary appreciator, as if he had done nothing himself; or as if the main thing he had done was to get an inspiration enabling him to con-

199

template his own work, from the first, before he had done a stroke, laid up in a Platonic heaven, waiting for him to appreciate the pure idea enough to reproduce it.

Gide refuted tomes of leisure-esthetics when he said the test of a good book was that it would not leave the reader intact. It would not leave him a reader, but would reach him as a human being and put him in touch with another human being, out of whose struggle with life had come a new awareness of its poignancy and possibility, a creative realization that would shatter complacency and transmit a will to think and act with sympathy. This view of art as transitive, as including its ulterior moral effect, instead of being short-circuited within form, or within a response to mere form, puts the artist again on a par with the appreciator. The latter, as the recipient of a vital impulse, cannot remain passive but must react to the activity of the artist, or fail to appreciate his art. Gide's artist becomes a worker who elicits cooperation by operating on another with an instrument that is good if it works. The spectator-view is relegated. Art is a process in which the appreciator participates with the artist; not an inert thing before which life should stop. Art is like any undertaking which unites men in common effort to cope with problems in a way to facilitate the organization of experience for greater freedom and control—for more satisfactory living.

If this conception threatens the distinction between art and work in general, that would seem better than maintaining a distinction which depreciates art in a working world. Art might still be the word for work that is unusually significant. This evidently is Gide's reply, as applied to writing. Literature for him, in the honorific sense of art, is not produced by people who simply want to relate what they happen to have seen or picked up. That is reporting. Perhaps, to be consistent, he should grant that journalism can be excellent. The point is rather that literature begins with authors who have something to say beyond what they have seen or received over the wires of news-gathering agencies (cf. Pléiade ed. of *Journal*, 1229). The way to learn what he means by this is to read or recall the writers he admires, and notice what they have to offer beyond the best reporting. But attention to what he says about some of them will suffice.

His comparison of Racine and Shakespeare brings out two desiderata which to some extent come together but which tend to diverge: formal excellence and vivid portrayal of man in nature. Back in 1905 he had suggested a third category of literary value—that of social idealism—in commemorating Hérédia, last and most perfect of the Parnassian seekers of perfection. His faultlessness was made possible by the fault of not being troubled by emotion. He had no problems outside the province of his technical skill. Everything of interest to him was familiar, final, external. His work was arranging and exhibiting to advantage the pieces in the museum of his mind. Over against him Gide posited the writer who lives in a changing world of outer and inner conflict, who cannot be perfect because he is not a custodian of hushed things but a voice of the people. These two kinds of writer are designated by Gide as "the imperfect innovators and the perfect conservators," and he attributes the force of the former to the solidity of the latter (*OC* IV, 444). This

201

would seem to mean that Shakespeare owed his success to the Racine-like achievement of his predecessors. Whether that could be maintained or not is somewhat irrelevant, however, because Shakespeare's human warmth and richness, as opposed to the exquisite formality of Racine, is not quite what Gide was opposing to Hérédia. What he said of Hérédia's formal perfection is close to what he said of Racine's classic qualities. But Shakespeare, with all his originality of vision and expression, and capacity for formal excellence when he tried for it, is not the only alternative to Racine-Hérédia. He is less formal and more human, but his humanity is that of individuals, not that of masses. Problems in his plays focus mostly on personal morality. There are social implications, but they have to be drawn out. He is no checker of umbrellas, no arranger of glass cases. He speaks for the hearts of men, but not as a tribune of the people. He does not intercede for them *en masse* before conscience. Their wrongs belong to his drama, they fill out soliloquy, but will not rise from his lines to shake the world. In a better one his work would have a lasting place, but it is not a lever of transition now. He is more sympathetic than Hérédia or Racine, but without a passion for social justice.

Dostoyevsky had compassion amounting to that, despite his prejudices. Here was Gide's "imperfect innovator" heralding the future in store for what may be enduring traits of human nature in Shakespeare's characters: a future in which multitudes will have the leisure and culture to enjoy Racine too, if they choose. Although nowhere compared by Gide with these twin peaks of his literary admiration, the also-admired grandeur of Dostoyevsky would appear to be not only comparable but of a third order in the Gidian esthetics; for Gide's devotion to him was different.

Perhaps in the long list of writers honored in the course of his *Journal* could be found some who should be put in still another category. But most of them to be taken very seriously would come under the formal appeal headed by Racine and Hérédia; or the lively human but not activating interest culminating in Shakespeare; or the revolutionary penetration of Dostoyevsky; or a combination of these qualities. The beloved Goethe would ride a hyphen between Racine and Shakespeare. Nietzsche would scale the same ascent as Dostoyevsky, though with a harder look in the eye. It would be fun to figure out the place in this scheme for those Gide took the trouble to translate along with Shakespeare—Tagore, Conrad, Whitman, Pushkin— as well as the place of Stendhal, who was the "dry bone" he kept to gnaw on; or of Montaigne, whose "nice soft pillow of ignorance and incuriosity" about social questions Gide had to reject—although without it he said he could write no more (*André Gide et Notre Temps,* a report of a meeting of the *Union pour la Vérité,* pp. 56–57). It is easy to see where to fit in the treatment of such questions by André Malraux in *La Condition Humaine,* which Gide found "profoundly plunged into life, engaged, and quivering with an anguish at times unbearable" (10 April, 1933). Where would the *Arabian Nights* go? And the Bible? He spoke of *The Song of Songs* and *Ecclesiastes* with the same held breath as in praising the verses of Racine. He called "beautiful above all human speech" Christ's teaching (in *Numquid et Tu, OC* VIII, 310); spoke of the

203

Esthetic of the Gospel: "to forget what other men have written, painted, thought, and what one had thought oneself—to be born anew;" and felt that Dostoyevsky was close to Christ (*OC* IX, 371).

Yet he said it was irreverent to think of Christ as an artist: "no matter how art strives for the divine it always retains something of the diabolic" (*OC* XIV, 409). This is understandable in terms of Gide's early orthodoxy, and of the highly formal, rather decadent esthetics he once accepted. But when he had reached a humanist ethics and philosophy of religion, thought better of the devil, and found "art for art" inadequate except as amended to mean art for what art can do for human life, it should no longer have seemed blasphemous to think of Jesus as an artist.

Otherwise Gide would have had to say that it was apart from being an artist that Dostoyevsky was close to Christ, and Nietzsche to both. But to separate thought of Dostoyevsky from thought of his art, or to split his art from his moral and religious quality, would be impossible. Certainly he was more than an artist, and it would be grotesque to call Jesus an artist, in the sense of concentrating upon "a work of art," regarded as perfect in itself and fitting Baudelaire's "perfect definition" of such a work in five words: order, beauty, luxury, calm, voluptuousness. Ample as the esthetic might be which Gide said he could write, using these words for chapter-headings (*OC* IX, 125), it would hardly accommodate the art of Dostoyevsky, Nietzsche or Jesus. An esthetic that would have room for them was suggested in *Nouveaux Prétextes* (1925 ed., 242): "the only works which matter to us are those with a beauty which *responds* to some anxious question; we are not interested in replies that come crowding after the question is no longer posed; those are works *which no longer answer to anything*." In fairness to the poetry of Baudelaire, perhaps some of this reflection should be inserted into the word "beauty" in the verses Gide seized upon as defining the artwork. But Gide's own understanding of "beauty" in Baudelaire's context was: "Line, élan, profile of the work" (*OC* IX, 125). This would seem to be still the formal idea of beauty that Gide was trying to replace with a more creative one, by suggesting the esthetic quality of a question, and an anxious one at that.

The Romantics had preceded him in dissatisfaction with pure form. Goethe had caught up the demand for human expressiveness through form, or at the expense of form if necessary. Tolstoy came in at this point; the Symbolist school also, in another fashion. Hegel might have helped Gide here, and Schopenhauer did. But he was to need an esthetic less idealistic metaphysically, and socially more idealistic, than theirs. He would need the one implied in Goethe's tremendous lines to Prometheus, and in his own *Oedipe*. In the midst of the slow effort of that play Gide exclaimed: "How easy it is to work according to an esthetic and a morality already given! Writers who are submissive to a recognized religion advance with the confidence of a sure thing. I have to invent all. Sometimes it is an immense groping toward an almost imperceptible light. And sometimes I wonder: what for?" (*Journal,* 29 July, 1930).

The esthetic he was inventing on his own initiative has

205

affinity with that suggested by Diderot, in his article on "Art" in the *Encyclopédie* (cf. Charles Lipton, "The Social Thought of Diderot," in *Science & Society,* Spring, 1944, p. 128); also by Guyau in the nineteenth century (cf. Van Meter Ames, "Social Esthetic, With Special Reference to Guyau," in *The Journal of Philosophy,* Vol. XLI, Feb. 17, 1944, pp. 91–97); and being worked out by American pragmatists. Perhaps they did not have the time or mood to do much with this field until lately. But they have added it to moral and social reform, and have done so quite in the spirit of Gide, though not noticing his work. Like him they could not rest with the spectator-esthetic of academic tradition. The esthetic experience for them is not one of spell-bound contemplation, but of active participation in a process.

William James was on the way to this, perhaps, though he put it humorously in saying that after hearing a concert one should use the stimulation of it in a kind act, if only in giving a seat to an old lady in the horse-car. He is the only pragmatist Gide seems to have come across, and they should have been brothers in arms against all absolutes. But Gide put down the *Psychology,* convinced of its "mediocrity" after reading the chapter on instinct (*OC* XIII, 451). He must have been disappointed to see there: "the sexual passion expires after a protracted reign; but it is well known that its peculiar manifestations in a given individual depend almost entirely on the habits he may form during the early period of its activity. Exposure to bad company then makes him a loose liver all his days; chastity kept at first makes the same easy later on." He would have to qualify each of these assertions so much from his own point of view that they must have seemed an expression of Bostonian primness.

But Mead would have intrigued Gide with the view that esthetic experience is "a creative process that puts things together in such a fashion that we can enjoy them" (*Movements of Thought in the Nineteenth Century*, 68). Esthetic experience has for Mead the role of introducing into the press of life more appreciation of what ends are being fashioned—and what are not but ought to be. By eliciting a cooperative attitude toward qualities and processes, and detachment from usual bias and commitment, a work of art can draw attention to points where a sensitive individual feels the need of social reconstruction, so that the appreciator will be moved to do part of the thinking that is called for. This is exactly the kind of response Gide wanted from a reader of *Les Faux-Monnayeurs*. Mead thought much about the novel as a means of leading from the individual's "meanderings of idea and purpose and imagery," which are "infected with privacy and therefore subject to disintegration," to the "universal meanings of common discourse and cooperative effort." His theory was that the creations of the artist, like the hypotheses of the scientist, enable the "inner life" of man, his reverie, to overcome its isolation and work out the implicated meanings that otherwise remain cut off "because of the incompleteness of social organization" ("The Nature of Aesthetic Experience," in the *International Journal of Ethics*, July, 1926).

For Dewey also, the enjoyment of art is continuous with the creative act; artistic-esthetic experience is the enhancement and deeper sharing of ordinary experience. Art is a communication whereby men project their needs; a working with materials and meanings to satisfy desire and to make it more satisfying (*Art As Experience*). Kallen holds that the liberty of the artist "has become the avatar of all the freedoms men fight and are ready to die for. It is the spontaneity and fertility of the very life of us, and so contagious that where the artist is free no other man can remain bond" (*Art and Freedom,* Preface). Thus Gide is not alone in developing an esthetic to go with a social ethic and a humanist philosophy of religion. He has contributed much to the view of art he needed: by realizing the need; by showing in his literary criticism that there is art which cannot be adequately assessed with the inherited conceptions of the artwork; and by producing such art.

Transference of his artistic allegiance from Flaubert to Dostoyevsky is the key to the new esthetic. Flaubert suppressed life to do his work. Dostoyevsky suppressed nothing: "he has wife and children, he loves them; he does not disdain life; he writes upon leaving prison: 'At least *I have lived* . . .'" (*OC* V, 47). All that he felt, thought, did and suffered went into his art. The complexity of his experience was one with integrity he could not omit (*ibid.*, 65). Gide speaks of how human and anxious this complexity was. The characters of Dostoyevsky are made vivid by their problems, and the problems are incompatible with a definition of art as cleaving to formal excellence and shutting out life-situations. The characters may be fictitious and their difficulties may be called imaginary, but are none the less representative of those which beset real men and women who feel the con-

208

flict between traditional ideals and new techniques. As Gide points out, he presents people not only as having the gamut of social relations but as having deep wells of intimate life and God-yearning (*OC* XV, 149–150). The novels of Dostoyevsky, "charged with thought" and "panting with life," are not works of art if art must be intransitive, insulated, sterile. Yet Gide feels that here is great art. Is it great because it is not "pure" art? Is it art in spite of provoking thought and communicating a sense of reality? Gide does not separate the intellectual and cultural burden of *The Idiot* or *The Brothers Karamazov* from their worth as art. Their esthetic value and their pervasive anxiety about the fundamental things of human experience are found to be indissoluble.

The same broadening and vitalizing of the esthetic shows up in Gide's estimate of Henry James: his work is highly artistic in being cunningly contrived, but it never overflows a formal pattern. He uses "just the steam he needs" for an artificial design. Though it may be good for the English (and Americans) to have this example of craftsmanship, since their writers have had less of it than the French, James lacks the vitality that Gide loves in English literature. The James-intelligence is too thin: "all the weight of the flesh is absent, all the hairy leafy element, all the savage shadow" (*OC* X, 547). This is an esthetic judgment, and it condemns not only a man's work but the purist esthetics for which formal excellence is enough. When Gide says that he is interested in James only for his technique, for "his prodigious virtuosity," he seems to set up again the dualism of esthetic form versus non-esthetic content. But he finds fault with the

James-form and shows that fault to be more than formal. Yet his criterion is definitely esthetic. It cannot be detached from what anyone would call an esthetic response to the sensuous qualities of a work and awareness of their configuration. He objects to the compulsion to put in everything, to leave nothing in shadow: "all this minuteness of indication fatigues and wears me out; behind none of his completely lighted figures the cone of shadow that cannot be explored where the suffering soul hides; but his characters do not need it; they have no soul. And I cannot succeed in persuading myself that this patience, this meticulousness . . . no, that is not great art; his brushes are too fine; he is afraid of robust touches; he proceeds by subtleties." The trouble is that James dominates his story from on high, that he "never commits or compromises himself in it; as if he had nothing to confess" (*OC* X, 548–549).

Whether or not one agrees with this criticism of James (and there is much to challenge it), the point is that if such criticism is esthetic it strikes at the prejudice that the work of art should be intransitive for esthetic appreciation proper. Holders of that prejudice tend to dismiss objection to it as coming from the esthetically uncultivated. But it comes from André Gide: "A character doesn't interest me unless created complete from the flesh of the author, like Eve." And this is the decisive trait in the art of Dostoyevsky: that his characters "are the projection of personal and private anguish." To clinch the point, Gide adds that lack of interest in the character of James himself is the crux of his artistic deficiency: "he is only intelligent; there is no mystery or secret in him; no *figure in the carpet*" (*OC* X, 549).

Again, whether Gide is wrong about James and right about Dostoyevsky or not, here is plainly a development of esthetic theory beyond the academic variety, away from the isolation of the artwork from its maker, from his time and place, for the pure contemplation of an appreciator who cannot be a proper one unless he in turn sheds the biological and social self. For Gide the literary artist succeeds by having a self worth imparting, by means of work which works through being transitive.

When he speaks of Dostoyevsky projecting his "personal and private anguish," it should be noted that he shows Dostoyevsky's individualism to inhere largely in his devotion to others, in keeping with the Gospel teaching that a man must lose his life to find it. That is, Gide recognizes that the personal and private self is social if at all developed. He sees that the self of Dostoyevsky, with its deep inwardness, was yet so social that he could commit and communicate it only through the delineation of contradictory characters: "they drag him pathetically into life, and us after him. Yes, that is truly it: the secret of the great novelist is not in the domination of situations, but in the multiplicity of his possibilities, of his intimate complicities. The qualities in James are those which can be got by arrangement" (*ibid.*, 550). In short, what can be completely controlled by the artist is only clockwork. Great art comes from being involved in life, with sympathy and awareness, and the expression of what is felt rather than the invention of what is feigned. Over against the esthetics of perfect form, exemplified by James, Dostoyevsky represents what for James would be an esthetics of less perfect form—but a form which is closer to life and therein superior, at least for one who loves life even in art.

Gide wanted a form for problems and questions rather than for answers. Especially in *Les Faux-Monnayeurs* he was dealing with moods and enigmas pressing upon him, as in his *Journal*. He wrote most of this novel in diary form, the form of experience as it comes and is felt in the flux, in the midst of adjustments that have to be made without foreknowledge of the outcome. Beginning with *Les Cahiers d'André Walter*, he had frequently resorted to this form, notably in *La Porte Étroite*, so that he was well prepared to use it. Thus the gap was narrowed between his formal literary projects and the notebooks where he jotted his daily doings and reflections. The growing desire to write more naturally, more cursively, and the fact that he used the *Journal* as a deliberate discipline to that end, make the *Journal* not something on the side of his main effort, but an essential part of it. Instead of using art to achieve art outside life, his endeavor was to hide with art the art that made life stand forth more vividly and promisingly, even in its problems.

For him the belletristic separation of art from life was resulting in dead letters. He would recover the power of words to establish community through communication. He would realize that as the self becomes the heir of society through speech, so the individual renews the group through speaking out. He would still love words, less for expressing his own moods in forms which might mean little to the uninitiated than for calling the conscience of mankind to look at problems that but for him would cry only to heaven. He would still celebrate the

212

lovely things, including the picturesque as it could be enjoyed by a person alone or with friends. But justice would be more beautiful to him than all the vistas of his travel notes. And justice must be shared to be genuine, though it has to be sought by individuals. They develop by taking over the symbols of the group to furnish their own consciousness, but they are not effective members of a common body until they appreciate the needs of one another. The self, in shedding selfishness, becomes more of a person. A fully human self, like that of Dostoyevsky, is one which cannot be itself without striving for justice. Such a self and its justice are social, however private also. Together they form a goal already operative, but only as individuals become aware of their solidarity as human beings. To foster that awareness is the use and the beauty of literature, above any other beauty of words or verses.

Such a humanistic esthetic was dawning on Gide early. In his lecture *De l'Importance du Public* (1903) he said the separation of art and life had been dangerous for both. "From the day when the artist no longer felt his public close to him, from the day when art no longer found its raison d'être, its significance, its use in society, in daily life (*les moeurs*), it did not waste away . . . it went mad . . . the artist who is no longer in touch with a public is obliged not to stop producing but to produce works without destination." Remarking that the great artists of the renaissance and antiquity would have found the doctrine of art for art unintelligible, he suggested that it arose at a time when art found no place or motivation in life, and "had to disdain what did not appreciate it"

(*OC* IV, 187–188). His Symbolist friends had been in this predicament, and his own work was long ignored outside their coterie. This was painful to him, though the coterie included Paul Valéry, Paul Claudel, Jules Laforgue, Henri de Régnier, the American, Francis Vielé-Griffin and the German, Stefan George. Gide was excited about life and wanted to share his excitement with more of his fellows. When the living would not listen he counted on the unborn for a hearing. His audience would come, his books would patiently await their readers and pick them out. Communication might be delayed but it was his aim.

To be sure, at the time of writing *De l'Importance du Public* he was thinking of the artist's public as necessarily small and select, because he shared Goethe's and Flaubert's superiority to a heterogeneous crowd. In the split-up modern world it appeared that only a few people could have a common taste or culture, without which the rich communication of art would be impossible. But it bothered him increasingly that the fundamentally sharable values of art should be pre-empted by the few who also monopolized less sharable goods. Fond as he was of traditional culture he came to realize that neither it nor art based upon it could appeal to people with new problems and anxieties brought about by the advance of science and changing methods of production—unless such adjustment were achieved that the mind might be free for interests beyond the immediate exigencies. But with his love of the gratuitous act, of youth and progress, and his aversion to anything like squeezing new directions into a final mold, he did not anticipate that any settlement of problems

214

would make passive contemplation more natural to man than participation in the ongoing process of life.

He talked about the need of constraint in art to compensate for the freedom of life. Art thrives on struggle with obstacles—but wants to conquer them, not to be confined. "It loves to burst each sheath, hence prefers a tight one" (*ibid.*, 206–207). Yet this is not to oppose art and life. This is rather to think of art as the concentration and enhancement of life. In art and life Gide has had the same scorn of comfort, the same prodigal love of adventure, the same conviction (upon the whole) that it is better to go on than turn back. In art he was early concerned with life-issues; in life he was ever fascinated by their artistic expression. He was not speaking in character, or at least not in the character that became most truly his, when he said the artist should not cater to the crowd because it demanded treatment of moral and social questions—"which were quietly settled for the cultivated public" (*ibid.*, 195). In his *Lettres à Angèle* (1898–1899) he explained that by the *crowd* he did not mean the *people*, and that "between a crowd of people and a crowd of bourgeois, my sympathy would go rather to the first" (in *Prétextes*, 1903 ed., 140). In his later stature, he would not quibble as to whether the people who asked art to face life-questions were just a crowd or not. The demand would be legitimate in any case, for he would no longer consider such questions to be settled except for a culture that was through. To wish them quietly out of the way was to ignore the people and to identify the "public" with a set—the set that wanted everyone to remain seated when scarcely anyone had a place to sit down.

215

This snobbishness was knocked out of his esthetic by Dostoyevsky, whose life and work were one in love of people, his own and all others. Gide noted that his letters at the end were "mostly to unknown persons, to console and guide them." At his death not only did the whole of Russia seem "united in one communion of enthusiasm for him," but Gide saw his work going on to unite Europe (*OC* V, 70).

The conflict between art and life was overcome in a man for whom they moved on together. In Gide the sense of their disparity derived from the fact that his initial taste in art had been classic, whereas he was keenly aware of living in a changing world. "Only the *finished* can take on style," he wrote in 1902 (*OC* III, 560), though he had a sense that everything but art was just beginning. No wonder he felt wistfully that in an earlier age the language of verse would have come more easily to him. Hallucination was necessary to being a poet now. To be one with eyes open to the contemporary scene was impossible. Only prose could result. Yet he would learn that prose could be finer than verse. Verse-writing could have a "sublime" verbal beauty, yet be "gigantically" absurd, as he observed after trying to read Victor Hugo's *Eviradnus*. "Imagine a foreigner drowned in that!" (26 October, 1918). For a foreigner could be substituted anyone whose interest would not be purely technical, who sought in art some relevance to living reality, and to intelligence about it. Instead of a formal esthetic of mere surface, Gide would have to have one of human depth and modern scope. Much as he loved the poetry of the past, and while he long continued to identify art, style and culture with a

216

perfection that was dead, or lingering outside time, he developed in his own performance and preference a sense of art as expressing the travail of the present, and helping the birth of the future. He said that he had spent four years not in writing the *Immoraliste* but living it; "and I wrote it to pass beyond" (*OC* III, 562).

This was to project an esthetic from the standpoint of the artist, for whom art was work to be done while a man was alive and confronted with the problems of his time and place—against the esthetic of the spectator for whom art is not so much a piece of work as an object of worship, not something to be done but to be revered, because the like could not be done in the press of any present but that of its own making. For the appreciator, coming after the fact, art is safe from effort and error. For the artist his work is a venture subject to failure, and he is likely to be quite conscious that he might fail. Gide was. He knew how his work was torn from his vitals. Each volume was part of his struggling self, though never the whole of it. Each volume was a private thicket he pulled through. In that sense he could accept Aristotle's theory of art as purgation of passion—the artist's (*OC* IV, 618).

The thicket was always partly one of technical problems in the writer's craft. Gide recognized that in painting and sculpture the emotion which drove the work might come out of the problems and possibilities offered by the medium. He said Maillol "does not proceed from an idea which he wants to express in marble; he takes off from the stuff itself, clay or stone" (*OC* IV, 425–427). And he was weaned away from the Parnassian and Symbolist schools by realization that the art of writing does not attain its full power when it uses words as if their use in life were not an essential or material part of the writer's medium. To work with a language and ignore its meaning in the activity and history of the men who speak it is not, like Maillol, to begin with the matter in hand but to throw away the best of it.

To a limited degree, questions of style seem to remain independent of content. At times Gide appears to be thinking of thickets they may constitute in their own right, and to consider whether it is better to plunge through them blindly, or take stock of them, as in the distinction he likes to make between poet and artist. He remarked, apropos of Francis Jammes' fear that a critical and revising reason would spoil the freshness of sensation: "to be a poet it is necessary to believe in one's genius; to become an artist one must *doubt it*. The man truly able is he for whom the *latter* augments the *former*" (30 December, 1909). Jammes thought Charles-Louis Philippe was a good writer because he "let himself go with inspiration," but Gide said he never learned more about the art of writing than from the manuscripts Philippe left, among which were half a dozen versions of one novel, "almost equally good and mutually exclusive" (1 January, 1910).

Yet Philippe became a prose-artist not only by advancing from a predilection for the poet, as Gide believed every great master of prose had done ("Lecture on Charles-Louis Philippe," given 5 November, 1910, *OC* VI, 145); but also by growing from tearful sentimentality to a passion for joy and justice, and the sense of belonging to a new race to be born of that passion. That his art de-

218

veloped through this feeling, more than through an increment of technical skill, and that he reached this feeling through culture, impressed Gide. The man had come across Dostoyevsky—*The Idiot*—and had called it the work of a barbarian: not a destructive barbarian but the kind Gide said culture should produce, quoting from Philippe: "The time of gentleness (*douceur*) and dilettantism is over. Now we need barbarians." It was exciting to see how "Dostoyevsky and then Nietzsche pushed Philippe toward *joy*." Reflecting on this, and comparing it with his own course, Gide observed: "it seems to me that it is through knowing the man that one arrives most surely at understanding the work." The esthetic of the library, of textual criticism with glasses averted from the author, might suit a gentle reader, but not a writer who knew how real writers worked; how they were influenced; and how some of them strove in a sick civilization toward a joy compatible with a "virile and severe sadness," toward Nietzschean joy exalting the "savage sanity of the suffering," toward the joy of Dostoyevsky in quest of justice (cf. *ibid.*, 147–157).

For Gide to care about his own phrasing after identifying style with the man, may appear inconsistent. But this view of style kept it quite as important for him as for the phrase-maker he would hate to be. He wrote Lady Rothmere, who wanted to translate some passages of *Prétextes:* "The principal difficulty comes from the fact that my style never ceases to suggest rather than affirm, and proceeds by insinuations—at which the English language, more direct than the French, balks a little. It has always

219

seemed to me that the thought (*la pensée*) in my writing counted less than the movement of my thinking (*ma pensée*). The *gait*" (7 January, 1918).

The thought which counted less was that which could be abstracted and translated without trouble, because it was substantival, slowed and settled to a structure relatively permanent and impersonal. The thinking he cared about and felt to be his (*ma pensée*) had the participial quality of still going on, of being a process of shifting adjustment to pressures too intimate and fluid to be met except by all the living coordination of the organism—the *gait*.

This was something difficult to put on for effect, because it was the moving interaction between the individual and his shifting situation. If a man could be sensitive enough to this interplay, his expression of it would easily be his own. So it distressed Gide to see Péguy, whom he admired, forcing himself. And it was disillusioning to realize that by the same token Flaubert, whose *Correspondance* had for five years replaced the Bible at his bedside, was not a great writer: "he does not so much write well as strain himself to write well." And Gide himself? He had confessed: "Nothing of mine pleases me except what I obtain at the price of the most modest, the most patient effort" (*OC* VIII, 228). Perhaps there might be a saving difference between strain and patience. But: "The real masters, Montaigne, Retz, Saint-Simon, Bossuet, did not take such pains" (*Incidences*, 1924 ed., p. 93). Again he was to remark that what was play for born writers like Montaigne, Voltaire and Cervantes, was painful effort for Flaubert. In this passage, however, he added that whereas the gifts of a brilliant wordman like

220

Barbey d'Aurevilly, which could not be acquired, might be wasted, the value of Flaubert was that anyone was sure to accomplish something by adopting his method and discipline (*Un Esprit Non Prévenu*, 50–52).

Gide could be disdainful of facility. He had once noted that perhaps Léon Blum was justified in dashing off his things, because: "The artist in him has no great worth and his style, like that of Stendhal, has nothing to hunt for but the very movement of his thought; which spouts out of his mouth or pen, at once abundant and clear—more clear, it is true, than abundant, without much *Schaudern*—but consequently easy to express right through; having head and tail, and appearing properly, always." (*Journal*, 5 January, 1907).

Yet one could hardly be more fluent than Flaubert in the midnight letters poured out when his formal effort was over, and honored above his day-work on Gide's night-table. Neither Gide nor anyone has said they were not well written. Their charm for him, however, was not in their being unlabored but in their account of the labor a sentence in *Madame Bovary* cost. This gave him courage for his own endeavor, and "proposed for my fervor a new kind of holiness" (*Incidences*, 93). What lowered his estimate of Flaubert was not simply the idea that writing he prided himself on was harder for him than it should have been, but rather that his dedication to art was unholy in its antipathy to life.

Gide's admiration for Molière did not abate when he found to his amazement that Molière had worked slowly, though not averse to having people think him facile (14 February, 1908). Gide continued to feel that the prose

221

of *Le Malade Imaginaire* and *Le Bourgeois Gentilhomme* was unsurpassed (1 July, 1941). And he believed that the calibre of the author as artist was that of the man, declaring that in his comedies the laughter was generosity (16 June, 1932); that what he mocked was not mankind nor the science that would help men, but the tradition and pseudo-science which held them back (29 May, 1935). Gide admired Dostoyevsky all the more for knowing his furious slaving to get his books right, although under pressure for money: "correcting, tearing up, recommencing tirelessly each of his stories. . . . And nothing shows better the distance between the work and the worker who produces it. Inspiration! oh flattering romantic invention! Facile muses! where are you?" (*Dostoïevsky d'Après sa Correspondance, OC* V, 38). But the difference between what Dostoyevsky took off from and what he achieved was that between a confusion of simultaneous ideas and their ordered sequence—never a divergence between his life and his art.

Gide's disappointment in Flaubert can be attributed more surely to his supposed blasphemy against life than to his laborious composition. The two things seem related. It is easy to say that only a renegade from life would labor so fussily—spending hours in search of a better word instead of trying to find expression for a terrific life-complexity. Actually, the author of *L'Éducation Sentimentale* was concerned about social and political as well as intimate matters, and about their interrelation. Gide found this a great book because "it holds in suspense an exciting problem: is the least private the most representative?" (3 April, 1925). Flaubert's scorn was for the distorted form of living he called bourgeois and could not avoid, rather than for human life as such. In one of his letters he recognized the misfortune it was for humanity and writers to be mutually cut off—especially for writers, in that they lacked a footing and a fulcrum. He saw them withdrawing to the ivory tower not from choice but because they were disowned (Letter to Louise Colet, 24 April, 1852).

How much writers and other artists of his time were to blame for being disowned and setting up art for art in self-defense is another question. It is unfair to hold against him that he did not participate in the issues of a later day, or do as much about his own as one might see the need of in retrospect. Enough that he expressed the tensions of his day. At least this is enough to let him stand as a great writer, if he did it exceptionally well, no matter how hard it was for him. He even reached ahead to seize upon hope in the rapprochement of science and the rest of culture that for Gide is focal in the 20th century, saying in the same letter: "The further it goes the more art will be scientific, just as science will become more artistic; the two will join at the summit after being separated at the base. No human thought can previse now what brilliant suns will dawn from the works of the future. Meanwhile we are in a passage full of shadows; we are groping in the dark."

One may wonder whether Gide would have concluded from Flaubert's novels alone that their composition was finical, their author misanthropic. Perhaps. The letters give this impression, though not without qualification. For Gide a man's work was to be properly understood by

223

understanding the person behind it. He knew that the best of a man could be put into his work, but did not think this was the case with Flaubert, unless the *Correspondance* was his real work. Gide thought it outweighed all Flaubert's novels taken together (*Un Esprit Non Prévenu*, 55). He explained, however, that he would have liked the letters less if they had not been those of the novelist and full of the problems of his craft (*Interviews Imaginaires*, 96).

He could not imagine putting any letters of Racine above "the pure joy" of reading his tragedies (*ibid.*, 97). That was because he turned to Racine when he had to turn away from the impact of life. Then his mood was: "only perfect art is safe from age" (*Un Esprit Non Prévenu*, 57). The same when he read La Fontaine, whose perfection he could think even more sublime. "Oh! with him how far we are from the war!" (*Journal*, 19 September, 1939). Even so, Gide would never have to say that any art he cherished was inhuman or anti-social. He simply recognized that in some situations a particular kind of art was requisite as answering to a legitimate need. The demand for refreshment and exaltation could be vital. "To oppose art to life is absurd, because one can make art only with life" (*Prétextes*, 120).

It was honest responsiveness to the needs, opportunities and pitfalls of the human lot, as felt in or through himself, that he sought to cultivate in his own art. He wanted it to be entirely flexible, showing only in self-effacing sensitiveness to the calls upon it. "The technique (*métier*) I want would have an originality so discreet, so mysterious, so hidden, that it could never be pointed out in its essence.

I wish that the sole thing noticeable about me might be the perfection of my writing and that, for this reason alone, no one could imitate it" (*OC* VII, 551).

He could not stick to his own style when he let a character take over his pen, as in *Geneviève*. "But I experience no satisfaction in writing femininely, full tilt, and everything I write this way displeases me" (31 March, 1930). Yet in *La Porte Étroite* what he liked were the journal and letters of Alissa, who was feminine enough. She was too meditative to write hurriedly. That book he felt could not be well written because it was in the first person of the weak Jérôme. On the rebound Gide said he could write for ten years without using such words as "love, heart, soul." Eager as he was to do something different, however, he thought the book upon the whole successful, on account of its faults. Jérôme had to be ineffectual to leave Alissa's development "pure." Qualities the author sought in other books had to be kept out of this one (*OC* V, 419–420; and *Journal*, 11 July and 7 November, 1909). The style needed to displease the author to be in Jérôme's character. But he would rather not take up such a character again. "Henceforth I do not want to entertain a subject which does not permit, which does not demand the most frank, easy and beautiful language." And he wanted to become less conscious of his procedure. He found it deplorable that he still waited for a sentence to be complete in his head before putting down the first word. Mistakes would be better. He must "dare to write without order" (*OC* VII, 564). He must recover on paper the readiness of the organism to veer and jump with the situation.

225

This would seem to have been in mind in the throes of writing *La Porte Étroite,* when he said the difficulty was the anachronism of it from the standpoint of "what we think, feel and wish today" (*OC* V, 388). It called for a change of pace that was almost too much for him. He was obliged to put himself under a saddle he had shaken off. Somehow he could not avoid writing the book, no matter how out of step with its problems he felt. Yet he often spoke as though essentially the same problems were always with him, so that, whereas his books had to appear chronologically, they were one work and ideally should all have been written at once. Allowing for exaggeration in this contention, the critic may see that *La Porte Étroite* is not antithetic to *L'Immoraliste.* In both Gide was carrying on *Paludes, Les Nourritures Terrestres,* and *Le Prométhée Mal Enchaîné,* trying to break from the commonplace of tradition and convention toward further realization of life's possibilities.

He interrupted the slow effort of *La Porte Étroite* to write *Le Retour de l'Enfant Prodigue.* This little thing which he took in his stride, which refreshed him and sent him back to the other task with power, was itself less a departure from what preceded and followed than a concentration of the long career. Here "for my secret joy" he expressed love of youth's venturing intelligence winning out over deep attachment to the past. He did it through dialogue which let him tread with the firmness and lightness of his gait. It was neither walking nor running to a goal but a sinuous going, more for its own sake than to go somewhere; frivolous at first but finding a direction.

It seemed frivolous to want to run away from home and

226

denounce families and religion as obstacles to progress, if progress was just getting away from them. But the only way to find what life offered was to escape things that kept one back from life. In this the young Gide was serious enough, no matter how irresponsible and irreverent his betters thought him. He needed to shy from all they deemed needful in order to find what he wanted. A negative stand was the only outlet in the beginning, for a puritan; and for those who refused to follow him, he remained simply the negation of everything right and proper. For holders of the answers it was impious to ask questions. To seek a new freedom made one a prodigal and reprobate.

As only the ethic of the old answers would be tolerated by the custodians of morals, only an esthetic for which there were no new questions would be considered by the guardians of art. Gide was provided with one and the same reason for becoming impatient with puritanism and art for art. He said long afterwards that he had not realized how much courage *La Porte Étroite* took when his literary friends "thought religious and moral questions were anti-artistic, and that occupation with them was disqualifying—like any consideration of the public" (*OC* XV, 518). The demand to live more freely, more consciously and honestly, characterized him equally as artist and man. He did not stop being himself to become an artist, nor think he was a different person in each book. "The author of *La Porte Étroite* is the same and remains the same as that of *L'Immoraliste*. . . . While it has taken me time and patience to write these books, I have carried them simultaneously; and I have no doubt that if you re-

227

read the *Immoraliste* some day, lighted by my subsequent books, instead of finding there an attitude of which I must have been the dupe from the first, you will be able to discover there a latent critique of anarchy, as people have come to see in my *Porte Étroite* a critique of Protestantism or Christian abnegation . . ." (*OC* VI, 469–470). He was quick to add that by critique he did not mean satire, but that he was using the word in the Kantian sense of a thorough study.

He was not ridiculing Michel or Alissa but analyzing their conduct. And, though never declared, it can be seen that their common quality lay in basing their behavior on the gratuitous act. The defect of this basis was shown in the frivolity of throwing away the obvious values of human love in the pursuit of something more. But there was a serious and virtuous factor involved—the egg of progress—the insight that what has been best should not stand in the way of what might be better. The idea that men need more than what once seemed necessary, and need it so much that in revulsion against the limits of their little past, a free mind may not hesitate to scorn the whole inherited notion of the useful and sensible: this is the glory of the gratuitous act. It is uncalled for by circumstances that should be discarded. It is free of the familiar demands. It can have no recompense in the old pay, no merit in the known scale. The only ground for it is yet to be laid. Meanwhile the gratuitous act is pleasing to the disinterested—to those who are not held by what has passed for interest. This act, disdaining what used to be useful, is to ethics what art for art is to esthetics, and for Gide there is no difference. If he gives

228

up the gratuitous act as the epitome of virtue, after showing in Michel, Alissa and Lafcadio, the evil of it, he finds a place for their restless energy in the nobly controlled though adventurous notion of progress in *Oedipe*. If he gives up art for art, it is never to uphold art for life as it was, but to announce art for the art of living with science.

Finally, if with science he keeps in his own writing the love of formal excellence, it is no longer for form's sake but because he wants his work to last. And he wants it to last so that it will have time to convey its message. "The notion of perfection and the notion of continuance (*durée*) are closely linked. . . . How could he not wish continuance who knows that the new truth he brings will not soon be understood, or even heard? He knows moreover that only the perfection of its form can permit and promise for the skiff a rather long crossing; and that it is important to preserve from rot provisions which are not for immediate consumption" (12 March, 1933).

6. SCIENCE FOR LIFE AND ART

GIDE'S NEW TRUTH, WHICH HE HAS WANTED HIS ART TO
keep and convey, can be found in most of his books,
but each is more or less enigmatic by itself. Their drift
becomes clear when they are taken together, and he has
said: "I hold that the best explanation of a work is to be
found in the following work." In the same passage he
said he did not think it fitting or adroit for an artist to
explain his performance: "because he thereby limits it,
whereas if his effort is profoundly sincere it overflows the
meaning the author himself can give it" (*Incidences*,
1924 ed., 68). It may be felt that Gide has not been
coy about explaining his writing. Yet he has not done
so in a fashion to narrow its significance. And one could
not confine his message to a formula without ignoring the
fountain-like quality of his upshot. It can be said in one
word that his secret is science, but it must be understood
that science for him amounts to more than for most people. It means not only the so-called natural but also the

social sciences. It means a creative and experimental procedure which unites science with religion and art, as well as with industrial technology. For Gide science at bottom is human life alert to its problems and prospects, facing them with hope and boundless resourcefulness.

Science cannot be identified, except in a crude mechanical notion of it, with the descriptive naturalism of Flaubert and the Goncourt brothers, against which Gide revolted. Accurate detailed description is one of the techniques of science, but when it is taken to be paramount it fosters the pessimistic attitude of the spectator who feels helpless to intervene in the course of events. He may not like the way they are going but they are not his responsibility. There is a tie between this conception of science and art for art. With reference to life the effect of both is "Hands off!" There is always so much a sensitive person would want changed that if he thinks nothing can be done he is bound to feel discouraged and irresponsible. Gide could attack this outlook because he was fortified by a newer and more valid idea of science as the activity of men in such interaction with the environment that they can change it, change their own conditioning, and leave the past behind. So he chides all who would cling to what they have known or what they merely imagine, and obstruct progress. For he believes in progress through science and denounces doubters, "regarding every pessimist as a personal enemy. . . . How shameful to prefer the dream to the reality, through weakness and refusal to render reality more beautiful!" It will not be easy, but: "Shame especially on the *soft ones!*" Science is not magic; it can offer a legitimate expectation but no guarantee.

231

The call is for the courage of high adventure. Life is worth risk, and the life men could have is worth staking the life they have. If they love it, let them live it fully by "giving it with exuberance." The first task is "to struggle against the contagion of sadness" (11 March, 1933).

In this fight he valued the laughter of Cervantes, Rabelais, Molière. But more was needed than the natural prophylactic of humor, as more was necessary than the lightheartedness of childhood resting on illusion. "My whole effort has been to achieve for myself a happiness which could do without the illusory" (*OC* XV, 396). A new orientation was necessary: "nothing interests me in a book but the revelation of a new attitude toward life" (*Prétextes*, 1903 ed., 75).

Certainly this is the interest in Gide's books. He is almost unique among literary men for recognizing that science in its modern development is something new under the sun, and that appreciation of it calls for much less wistfulness about the past, much more confidence in the future. So he could say that he would rather see almost anything built in place of any ruin. "On principle I want to have a horror of all ruins." To him the great perversion was "this fear of the new, this respect for the old." He could explain it only as a "terrible confession of weakness" (*ibid.*, 104). The trouble was that men had the psychology of weakness. Their strength had been so little, compared with the odds against them, that they could not realize how hardy they were to have survived, or believe what an access of power was theirs in their new knowledge and techniques. He would have them come out of the caves of their old ignorance into the light.

Himself imbued with the sentiments of tradition, and prone to flee from European civilization, he wondered why he should prefer the charms of ancient cities to the widening of streets and all the engineering operations in modern Paris, including preparation for the Exposition of 1900. That event, despite some ugly features, delighted him as a manifestation of optimism. True, what he liked best were Japanese actor-dancers in antique dramas (*ibid.*, 129–135). But they were a side-show in a celebration of progress, without which this gift of the past would not have been seen in Paris. Faith in life and its new power did not blind him to what had been achieved. That did not have to be depreciated because now it was reminiscent and incidental.

There were fine things that might be worth raising up again, but not as a tower of retirement from the movement of history. "It is no longer a matter of restoring ruins but of building anew on a soil that must first be tested. Everything must be put back into question, put back into doubt; nothing but the authentic should be accepted, from which all mysticism has been dislodged. I mean by mysticism all blind belief" (*OC* XV, 394). From the traditional standpoint the paradox of faith in science is this open-eyed questioning, investigating character, and rejection of any final knowledge or authority. The unexpected thing is that men can have more confidence when they learn to doubt systematically than when they tried to believe implicitly and were afraid of finding discrepancies between belief and fact. The scientific attitude begins with willingness to loosen up settled questions and fixed ideas.

233

Paludes expressed this mood of suspended judgment, of entertaining suggestions before espousing any. For one not disciplined to it this state of mind, open to all possibilities, can be exasperating. Yet it is not non-committal through indifference but through control of responses tugging at the leash of inhibition. Action is not condemned but postponed until the relevant data have been sufficiently considered. The celibate youth looking out on the marshes may be taken to symbolize the provisional aloofness and deliberation of the scientist, though the youth seems to be considering just a journey to see something of the world. It would be out of proportion for Gide to make as much of travel as he does, in this and other books, were it not that in his thought travel becomes a symbol for the adventure of science, and for the radical change of scene to be available through science even for stay-at-homes.

He also has in mind that "perception begins with change of sensation: hence the necessity of travel" (*Paludes*, 1926 ed., 82). Going to foreign parts opened his eyes not only to strange sights but to fresh ideas. Getting sick abroad, and having his senses quickened by convalescence, was the occasion of a rebirth that was intellectual as much as anything else. He has told more than once of the impasse he had reached in his thinking about morality and religion before going to Africa, and how his travels of 1893–95 verified a hunch he took along. He was guinea pig and observer in the experiment with living which he recorded in his notebooks of that period.

It may be said that in adolescence it is rather normal to be experimental and self-conscious; and that his thoroughness in both might be attributed to a methodical habit and temper without the supposition that he was trying to be scientific. But if an investigation is carried on in scientific fashion, it is relatively unimportant that the investigator does not declare this to be his purpose. And it would be hard to show that Gide was too untouched by science or unaware of his own course not to see the connection. His autobiography notes that before *Paludes* was finished he was reading "the enormous manual of zoology of Claus which I had just bought and which lifted for my amazement the mysterious curtain of a world much richer and less shadowy than that of thought" (*Si le Grain ne Meurt,* Part Two, Ch. I). An earlier passage remarks how profitable it would have been for him in his youth if, among his literary and musical friends, there had been a naturalist: "if I had met one at that time, my liking for the natural sciences was so strong that I would have plunged after him, giving up literature" (Part One, Ch. X).

One might have expected emulation of the law professor father or the political economist uncle. But friends did much to keep André Gide's interest less in the public aspects of life studied by social science than in the personal and introspective realm where even psychology has not been as penetrating as imaginative literature. And there was his musical ability. He said: "Certainly it would have been easier to make myself a naturalist, a physician or a (performing) pianist than it is to become a writer— but the decisive consideration is that I can bring to this career the most diverse qualities; the others would have been more exclusive. . . ." Puritan strenuousness figured

235

too, for he went on to say that writing would take more willpower, "because I am not as naturally gifted for it as for the others" (*OC* VI, 442). Aside from the fact that one could hardly imagine him not a writer now, he would seem picked out for work in which he could show that all the arts are bound up with the sciences in the idea of progress.

He found a background for this view not only in the myth of Prometheus but in the Gospel, where he imbibed faith in life and its opening promise. The tentative, exploratory character of science is consonant with "Judge not." Jesus called upon men to see for themselves the consequences of different kinds of attitude and behavior. "By their fruits ye shall know them." But although this method is not altogether new, clear appreciation of it has been rare and its systematic cultivation recent, with results that could not have been foreseen.

In general there has been another way of looking at things—traditional and conservative, often superstitious, rather than inquiring and experimental. Gide hit off the difference in observing poor Arabs whose outlook seemed not to have changed much from that of the Semites in Biblical times. Sidi M., who knew the desert from Morocco to Tripoli, was a savant: "that is to say that apropos of everything he cites a text; the older the text the more it is venerated. He believes in every Arab fable; he will not listen to anything from Christians." Gide generalized that all the wise men he had met in Algeria were like that. "And when Athman 'informs himself,' I know what that means: instead of establishing precisely the questions involved, he quickly brings up the whole tradition of answers. . . . That is what was called science in the middle ages" (*OC* IV, 312).

Granted that from the level of primitive men there has been considerable problem-solving in somewhat the manner of modern science, the fact remains that the field of value—of art, morality and religion—has been habitually fenced off as not amenable to the technique of investigation more and more successfully employed elsewhere. The effect has been a split which constitutes the main difficulty in achieving an integrated life today. That he faces this difficulty, and tries to overcome it, is the significance of Gide.

His works are research-projects in the value-field, each with broad implications which, so far as possible, he submits in turn to a technique which can be recognized as that of science. He has worked in a region generally thought inaccessible to science—the personal, private or subjective sphere—and has used introspection with confidence that the great imaginative writers have shown it to be an instrument worthy of the most serious use. He admits no bifurcation between art and science, or between the world of natural science and the human world which has seemed to elude even the social sciences. As any scientist uses instruments and methods to get at matters beyond the bare eye and hand, so Gide employs the skills of literary art to bring within the scope of scientific procedure things which had escaped it. In a real sense any good novelist, personal essayist or diarist, is something of a psychologist. Gide is more clearly and consciously one than is usual for a literary man. A reader who realizes the shortcomings of psychology may well feel that, unless new psychiatric methods change the situation, an imaginative writer has something more to offer. Gide puts that "more" of artistic insight and ability deliberately into the technique of research, as a refinement of it.

This means that he sees the anachronism of separating the "humanities" and the sciences. Life for him cannot be departmentalized according to a university catalogue, and even universities are at a loss to classify psychology. It belongs with physiology, but also with logic, ethics, esthetics, philosophy of religion, philosophy in general, and every social science. Gide has acted upon the working assumption that things of most intimate human concern might be investigated if, as in each branch of science, the appropriate specialization of tool and approach could be used. He found in "creative literature" what he needed, simply modifying it to serve his scientific bent. Or, since he has practically identified art and science, it is quite as well to say that he found in scientific method the way to sharpen his literary purpose.

The zoologist Jean Strohl, of the University of Zurich, in a paper on *Les Relations Entre l'Art et la Science* (in *Hommage à André Gide*, by Henry Bernstein et al., 267–278), testifies to Gide's knowledge and ability as a naturalist; and comments on the need of overcoming the sterilizing isolation of science from the ensemble of intellectual interests. He says we are used to expecting fresh expression from a writer, but should also demand the freshness of content which would result from the scientific method, since it "consists precisely in combating the dangerous laziness and indifference of the mind before terms and ideas accepted once for all." Strohl believes

238

that the striving "at each moment to put in delicately new and fitting language the very essence of a novel connection, glimpsed or established," is what distinguishes Gide. His literary creativeness was possible through scientific training of a natural capacity for critical observation. And with this cue much is understandable in Gide that is otherwise simply baffling or "demoniacal."

He discovered the convergence of art and science when he learned that science no less than art is focused upon the particular, although concerned with its relation to the universal. Then why not concentrate science-art upon the most particular events of human experience, instead of dividing them between psychology and "works of imagination?" If this is what Gide has done, and if it seems that he knew what he was doing, it is equally evident that he stated the import of his practice, and made the generalization part of it. With literary skill he has not only used scientific method on problems once thought inaccessible to it, but has expressed his enthusiasm for this undertaking, and tried to justify it intellectually. He finds it effective because it fits and confirms the basic character of life: experiment.

Thus he is not only a scientific worker but a philosopher of science; though people who associate philosophy with traditional belief in a fixed and final scheme of things might not think of him as a philosopher. They would object that he has no system, that he contradicts himself, and veers from one tack to another. But because he rejects anything like the static archetypes of Plato and Aristotle, as understood by the Schoolmen, it does not follow that he has no rationale, or company in the halls of philosophy. He would be hailed by Bacon, Bayle, Diderot, Hegel, Guyau, Nietzsche, Bergson, James, Dewey and Mead, if not by Marx.

Gide's philosophy is an affirmation of scientific method in quest of the exceptional, the novel, as the egg of progress. The great experience for him, and metaphor for the vital experiment in all experience, is travel. He said: "I have written a whole book, with a very deliberate madness, to exalt the beauty of travel," referring apparently to *Le Voyage d'Urien* (*Prétextes*, 1903 ed., 53). He quoted from Nordau a passage to the effect that the organism manifests originality only in unavoidably confronting a new situation, and went on to praise the challenge of the strange as the means of evoking virtues which otherwise would remain latent. Let the weak stay home in their habits and customs: "the education the strong man demands" will require a "gymnastic of adaptation . . . but there is no education short of instruction which makes over" (*ibid.*, 59).

Gide had a constitutional as well as intellectual aversion to being fixed. He was the least sessile of literary men. How he sat enough to do all his reading is a mystery. But he did much of it on trains, in waiting rooms and hotels—and not a little of his writing. For him the disvalues of being rooted in a region outweighed the dangers of leaving it, contrary to the thesis of *Les Déracinés* by Barrès. When Charles Maurras tried to support that book by demanding to know at what moment a poplar, however high it rises, will need to be uprooted, Gide's knowledge of botany stood him in good stead. He replied that the poplar Maurras had in mind, if well developed, probably came from a nursery; and quoted from a nursery catalogue: "Our trees have been TRANSPLANTED [the word is in capitals in the text] 2, 3, 4 times and more . . an operation which promotes their continued growth . . ." (*A Propos des Déracinés,* in *Prétextes;* first published in *Ermitage,* February, 1898). Throughout this "Quarrel of the Poplar" and its aftermath Gide had the advantage of pitting a scientific procedure against literary tricks. He admitted that only the strong could stand transplanting, but maintained that it fortified them; basing his assurance on his experience of travel, and upon his regular nine months out of twelve in the country: "where I give as much attention to my garden as to my books" (*La Querelle du Peuplier,* in *Morceaux Choisis,* 446).

As it is impossible to travel in every direction at once, so the most radical pursuit of novelty must concentrate and not to try to throw everything into question simultaneously. It is enough to be on the move, making discoveries. That none of them is final, and that much will always be left to explore. is not regrettable. For Gide, as for any true scientist, that is the breath of life. Choosing the field of moral phenomena as they impinge upon the individual and are felt from within, he went to work in research-fashion, to see what he could find. He was prepared to respect any fact actually observed, and to vouch for it with his signature, no matter how it contradicted authority or convention. If he wanted a precedent, he had that of Plato for carrying on his investigation in the mode of literary art, and largely in dialogue.

If he needed a safeguard against wasting time or endangering human values with irresponsible hypotheses, he had guide lines in his classical background and fondness for the New Testament. But, since he revolted upon principle from tradition, it would be apter to say that his taste for the classics and love of the Gospel stayed with him only because and as he continued to find confirmation there of ideas he trusted on the basis of his own experience. For a while he was so fascinated by emancipation from the past that he did not distinguish between the gratuitous act and progress, except to suggest that the former was the egg of the latter. But he showed, especially in the character of Lafcadio, how criminally irresponsible the mere impulse to act could be. The experimental attitude was full of promise but also of mischief. There had to be a love of human beings to arrest inhuman impulses or hypotheses. The old Oedipus, guided by Antigone, is Gide's symbol of the controlled and responsible idea of progress that should result when the gratuitous act has been trained and chastened.

It is not enough just to act. Nor is it enough just to have a hypothesis and be willing to test it, as if any hypothesis were worth testing, and as if to hypothesize and verify in a careful manner were a technique that could not be humanly harmful. The social scientist differs from other men of science in having no laboratory. A laboratory presupposes manipulable and expendable materials, the possibility of trying an alternative experiment if a first hypothesis is disappointing, and detachment of the investigator from untoward consequences. Spilt milk or soured cream is nothing to cry over in the laboratory. Still less does it matter on paper, one may think. Often it has seemed that what the writer did, cost only paper and ink and his perhaps not valuable time. But ideas do not stay on paper or in the laboratory. And while one may belittle the influence of mere ideas, they do seem to have considerable consequence by way of releasing or redirecting energies already afoot. The controversy over Gide himself indicates how a writer's words can jolt the unstable human situation. Since the crucial factor in that situation now is science—or rather science in relation to what men think about its effect on their values—a writer who helps to formulate what they think, and who will help them do more thinking about the role of science in culture, cannot be kept on paper. What he writes becomes a serious matter, especially at the close of a war which has left men more sensitive than before to the implications and tendencies of attitudes. Everyone is aware of the power and promise of science, but also of its threat. We know only too well how it can be perverted to inhuman uses. We know that a wrong hypothesis about how to preserve the peace cannot be followed out and then be followed by another hypothesis in the same circumstances. History will have moved on. Nor can anyone remain detached from the materials of social science, for everyone is involved in them in the oneness of a science-welded world. These materials are people. No line can be drawn between concern for people and the outcome of working with the stuff of their environment.

This means that no scientist is free to test just any hypothesis that occurs to him, no matter how tempting or in some ways fruitful it might be, without a careful prevision of the probable result in terms of human welfare. It can be said that, at least for all who have the democratic faith, it is forbidden to try out a hypothesis tending toward aggressive war or racial exclusiveness. But what hypothesis of this sort has not been tried out now to enough of its horrible consequences! Henceforth the range of permissible hypotheses must be narrowed to those that lie along the curve of human progress, as the direction if not the formula of that curve can be derived from the past, from history, from imagination, and from the expression of men struggling to be free of their disabilities. The call upon the imaginative writer is to learn from the past, be familiar with the striving of the present, and come to as full a notion as he can of progress. A clear definition of it might be desirable. More important as well as more attainable is a vivid feeling for what is involved in progress and the infectious communication of devotion to it. This is what Gide has to offer, though he has groped his way, with mistakes and lapses. He is a central figure in the contemporary scene because he has left an honest record of thought and feeling with regard to the enterprise of guiding life by a conception of scientific method that cannot be consistent without being humane.

His verbal gift has not only enabled him to make his ideas viable but also to offset the idolatry of the book within the camp of its worshipers. "For the true naturalist a bookish knowledge cannot suffice. He does not need interpreters but understands the language of nature when it is only half uttered, and puts questions directly to her" (*OC* XIV, 361). Gide would never dispense with books, but he would have people know when to toss them aside. He would hold that undue veneration of them fosters the illusion that the truth is all in print. "The 'everything has been said' of La Bruyère has long benumbed France" (in *Feuillets* of 1937, Pléiade ed. of *Journal*, 1277).

The moral difference between intellectual smugness and the teachable mind was brought home to Gide through an exchange with the Jesuit father Victor Poucel, who had attacked him in the Catholic magazine *Études*. In a letter of reply Gide spoke of "bad faith," and Poucel sent him a courteous protest. In the *Journal* Gide wrote: "But his whole letter leads me to think a little further: that *good faith* is an essentially lay virtue, for which 'the faith' is offered as a substitute" (*OC* XIV, 393). And in a letter to Poucel: "It seems quite natural to me that the flair and taste for truth should not be the same for him who seeks it and for him who thinks he has found it. The first is always afraid of being mistaken. The second walks full of assurance, 'so sure of himself that he does not hesitate to be rough, in good conscience, with the facts that get in his way.' These are your own words . . ." (*OC* XIV, 411).

In this vein Gide wrote again in the *Journal*: "The love of truth is not the same as the need of certitude and it is rather imprudent to confuse the one with the other. . . . One can love the truth all the more for not believing it possible ever to attain an absolute . . ." It may be observed parenthetically that Gide is not always free of the pre-scientific absolutism he opposes, for he adds here that "this fragmentary truth leads us" toward the unattainable absolute. But he goes on to note that belief in a superior Truth is likely to make one disvalue the limited knowledge at hand. It is not worth while to look for natural laws where divine intervention is believed to operate. "In the same way he who thinks himself in possession of a dogmatic truth will think all those are in error for whom dogma does not constitute a sufficient answer to their questions. All science has its point of departure in a skepticism against which the faith rises up" (*OC* XV, 222).

The effort of traditional faith has been to allay doubt. Cultivation of doubt is heresy for that position—at least beyond the point where authority and finality are flouted. Gide sees that man's natural insecurity has been not so much alleviated as aggravated by systematic inculcation of the contrast between the relativity of things and the idea of an absolute. "I have known someone who was plunged into deep melancholy just by the thought of having to replace soon and from time to time the shoes he wore on his feet; and the same with his suits, his hat, his linen, his tie. This should not be considered avarice, but a kind of distress over inability to rely on anything lasting, definitive, *absolute*" (*ibid.*, 222–223). Science assures men, not that there are things which never wear out but that they can learn to cooperate in providing reasonably well for their needs. Gide recognizes that the power of human providence derives from a method which makes constructive use of doubt, and was delighted to find this expression of that idea: "He (the good observer) knows the necessity and profit there is in readiness to doubt suitably, and knows how to doubt his own conclusions. . . His constant effort is to see the facts as they are and not as he would like to see them" (quoted by Gide from a paper by Maurice Tremblay, *ibid.*, 239).

Gide has realized that the shift from longing for an absolute to confidence in human capacity to build on the facts at hand entails respect for them in their particularity. He remarked that French literature had been "much more solicitous to know and paint man in general than men in particular. Oh! if Bacon instead of Descartes! But Cartesianism did not bother about *Every man in his humour;* no great desire for experience, and in short: insufficient curiosity. The sciences called 'pure' preferred to the sciences called 'natural.' Buffon himself is not a good observer. . . . The idea that one must take off from the simple to arrive at the complex, and that one can compose by deduction—this deceptive belief that the compound created by the mind will fit back with the complexity of nature, that the concrete can be derived from the abstract . . ." (*ibid.*, 278).

The empiricism of scientific work showed up the wisdom of the wordmen. Gide quotes this "astounding declaration of Montesquieu: 'I have laid down principles and seen particular cases bend into them as if by themselves. . . . When I discovered these principles everything I was looking for came to me. . . .'" Gide's comment is: "That means that he sought only what he had previously found. Terrible limitation! and how I admire, in comparison, Claude Bernard's saying: 'The investigator must pursue what he seeks, but also see what he was not seeking,' that which he was not expecting to see, though it should surprise him very much, annoy him. The Cartesian does not admit that he can ever be surprised. In sum he will not let himself be instructed by the unexpected" (*ibid.*, 279).

247

To admit the importance of the particular is to be alert to novelty, for it can be shut out only by abstraction and can always get back through an actual fact. It may be overlooked by the casual eye, but the scientific eye is trained to look sharp. "The most important scientific discoveries result from the patient observation of small subsidiary facts so particular, so slight, tipping the scales so imperceptibly, that no one consented until then to take account of them" (*ibid.*, 397); and noticed them only "because they deviated slightly from calculations . . ." (*OC* IX, 122).

Gide is emancipated from the old fear that science meant the reduction of variety and freshness to bloodless categories. For him neither science nor art is focused on universals or Platonic forms: at least not science the free research-worker is engaged in, and not art the artist is excited about. So, in writing, his point of view is: "that beside factitious and verbal preciosity there is a sincere preciseness due to the most exact and as it were scientific observation of minute facts, which owes its appearance of affectation only to this: that it is opposed to the conventional. . . . I think that which ages least in an author is what seemed in his time the most rare, exceptional, daring, if . . . the product of an observation direct and sincere" (*OC* XV, 398).

Finding science and art alike to be focused on the particular, and identifying respect for the particular with recognition of the importance of the novel, the exceptional, gave Gide a leverage on tradition, and made clear to him that progress depended on prying tradition loose (*ibid.*, 373). Observation of nature must supplant contemplation of the supernatural (*ibid.*, 390). All must be put back into question, everything reconstructed (*ibid.*, 394). And what made this not only possible but feasible was the stone which the builders of traditional philosophy and religion had rejected: the exception. There were quasi-exceptions in orthodoxy, but they were so tamed by it as to be parts of it. The unmitigated exception, which Gide believed to be always cropping up and holding out at the foci of art and science, would not subside into any pre-established universal, unless it were recast. From the traditional and conventional standpoint the unprecedented was, if not altogether unreal and unthinkable, something to be thrust out as unwanted, unholy, unspeakable. He quoted Mauriac as saying that what escaped the nets of the "moral law" was repugnant as well as unusual and strange. This attitude held over from the time when even science "refused to occupy itself with the unusual. . . . Confronted with abnormal cases the savants themselves would willingly have used Mauriac's word 'repugnant,'" said Gide's zoologist friend Professor Strohl (*ibid.*, 516).

Strohl spoke of how hard it was to learn that study of monstrosities might help to explain the norm: "Goethe alone seems to have glimpsed the clarification which natural laws can receive from that which appears to elude them, from what withdraws from the apparent rule. The latter is established only on habit and the dictation of the greatest number. Let us look out for exceptions: they imprison the secret of a natural law more general, consequently more important, which includes both the greatest number and the particular case that differs from this

249

'greatest number.' It is consideration of the abnormal, of what escapes the rule, that permits the discovery" (*ibid.*, 517).

This contrast between the traditional rejection of the exception and its becoming the head of the corner for science was seized upon by Gide, not only as an intellectual generalization of great value but as justification. Because he had felt himself to be out of step, he could realize in his own person the unfairness of dismissing the abnormal, whether in knowledge or morality. "To feel oneself an exceptional being: I sobbed with terror when I first made this discovery; but I had to stand up to it, and I had already accepted the exceptional enough not to be very astonished when it became necessary to admit the same thing in sexual matters. . . . No, my astonishment came rather, later on, from discovering that at least in this field the exceptional (I mean: what people gave out to me as such) was upon the whole pretty frequent. . . I experienced the sense of the exceptional while still quite young, in realizing that often I did not react like others; like most others. And in the sequel it was in vain to humiliate oneself, depreciate oneself, want to be just folks, refuse every distinction for oneself, seek to melt into the mass and be pleased there—one remains no less a being apart. This feeling of differentiation the child may experience while still very young, now with sadness, now with anguish even, and quite seldom with joy" (Pléiade ed. of *Journal*, 1264).

Gide's early sense of his own peculiarity may be attributed to his being an only child, being rich and favored, being brought up a puritan. He came by it naturally. The significant thing is that he made this sense a lens through which he could see the role of the exception in science and progress; and, by contrast, the lag of culture attached to verities once eternal. His suffering from awareness of his oddity, perhaps from exaggeration of it, was compensated by optimism founded upon watching the stride of evolution from one exception to another; and feeling that man could step into the shoes of evolution to go where he would. There was nothing to hold him back but backwardness, the fear of going forward.

This fear Gide has assigned especially to the Catholic Church. "The Church has, if not very well understood, at least had a strong presentiment of the redoubtable enemy science would become for her (and become more and more), and in particular the doctrines, however groping they may still be, of transformism and evolution. They are addressed not only to the future but equally to the past. What has already changed can change further, and, reciprocally: if man is susceptible of change in the future, one may be equally assured that he has not always been what he is. The idea of a profound modification of man and of society (the one being impossible without the other) sees erected against it, necessarily, religion, which quite justly realizes that there man escapes her, despite the virtuous effort of certain believers today to embrace the idea of evolution and, which is better, of revolution, within religion itself. . . . And he who thinks the social world should be changed, who proposes to help that change, who devotes himself to it, is not wrong, alas! in regarding religion as the most serious obstacle to progress. This 'alas!' comes from my heart, for it is always

251

ready to resist what reason alone proposes. But here, as everywhere else, reason should win; not through necessity, but through the will of man—of some men" (*ibid.*, 1287).

So the conflict shapes up for Gide: traditional culture and institutions against modern science. Fear of change is confronted with the demonstration and control of change, not merely in the trans-human environment but in man and society. The conception of a world planned for man, once and for all, is met by the idea that men can plan for themselves and go forward according to their own thinking and feeling. The notion of adventurous creative going into the future is thrown against that of submission to the dead hand of the past. A democratic faith in the ability of men to find their common good, to foster and share it, is rebelling against arbitrary authority which presumes to know best and do best without respecting the will of the people.

"Culture is not inherited; it is won," Gide quotes from Malraux (22 August, 1937). At least this is true of culture Gide thinks worth having. So he looks to youth which naturally looks forward, which always wants to go on its own, in spite of parental fears. He sees the struggle between the elders—who represent society as established, culture as inherited, with all that is threatened by any departure—and the young. He believes in the young too much to blacken them or their impulsiveness with original sin. He would fire them with confidence in their buoyancy. They are in his mind when he declares: "I cannot bear to hear it said that I have discouraged anyone. But

252

those whose good will wilts the moment it is no longer supported by lies and chimeras—it is not for them that I write" (Pléiade ed. of *Journal*, 1288). Yet he would be lying if he did not admit how hard it is to get rid of lies and chimeras. The handicaps honesty starts with, the old evils the young are exposed to from birth, the inadequacy and hypocrisy of education, all must be admitted and weighed against faith in youth and the future, even with science in the balance. Science is misused by man, as everything good is perverted or counterfeited by what seem to be powers of evil—to such an extent that it may be naive not to believe in the devil.

Geneviève touches on all this but without seriously going into it. The heroine wants knowledge and wants it for independence. Her father, the Robert who tried to subject her mother in *L'École des Femmes,* naturally would prefer that his daughter learn nothing but manners. Her endeavor is to cut under flowers and poetry to useful information, and she gets Dr. Marchant to teach her something of the sciences on the side. She opposes the nihilism upon which his social kindness seems to rest, while he ridicules the hope of social betterment that replaces for her the religion discredited by her father. She senses but does not try to think out the dedication of science to welfare. Catholics seem more certain of what they believe than other people are, but it occurs to her that "the real answer of the others is their life. One may remain groping when it is a question of words and resolute when it comes to action" (*Geneviève,* 26th ed., p. 110). She says she is through with theories. Obviously the

253

theories she is impatient with are those that depreciate human effort. She is eager to overcome intellectual inertia with action.

The suggestion is that if action can be launched it can be guided and corrected by the kind of intelligence which is developed in practice and in connection with it. Gide believes that this Promethean intelligence of science will take care of men if they can have the courage to act. So paralyzing is the spectator-tradition of knowledge, along with the religious tradition of man's helplessness, that it seemed to the young Gide superhuman to plunge into action. In *Le Prométhée Mal Enchaîné* it was from the gratuitous act of a god that progress sprang, but through men that it was promoted to modern science and technology. The moral advance from the Promethean act, and its technical development, to the responsible idea of social meliorism is made dramatic in *Oedipe*. In *Les Faux-Monnayeurs* full cognizance is taken of the fact that, while science provides an alternative to the outlook of traditional religion, it is still necessary to go beyond evidence, with faith in the place of guarantee—faith that scientific method can become the guide and means to human betterment. This novel faces the point that, whereas belief in a divine creator and ruler of the world involved the problem of evil, reliance on science makes a problem of good. Who will decide what is good? And how?

Leaving out of account the different mores and clashing ideologies in the world at large, Gide here confines himself to one class in one country. It might be asserted that in treating the French middle class he was bound to have discouraging material because here are people frustrated by their deteriorating position, trying to maintain an economic individualism that is obsolescent. They are not as far gone as the aristocrats and would-be aristocrats of Proust, but Gide's characters are losing their grip. The only one who is sure of himself, and justifiably so, is the stranger within the gates, Bernard the bastard of unknown origin, who can readily break with the inhibitions of the past, because he does not recognize the paternity thrust upon him. Here is a later Lafcadio, quite as self-reliant but more sensible. If Gide had chosen (and been able) to write of the working class, the virtues of Bernard might have been less exceptional. In a story allowing him to grow as old and other-regarding as Gide's Oedipus, with the cooperation of socially conscious comrades, the good might have appeared less confused and compromised than it does in *Les Faux-Monnayeurs.* But the novels of Silone and Malraux may be taken to indicate that a man of Gide's background could hardly espouse the proletarian cause in fiction without misgivings, any more than in life. And even if he could, the question would remain whether taking sides in class-conflict would settle the problem of good except from a partisan point of view. For one who can believe that the triumph of one class will be to the ultimate advantage of people in general, the die is cast. But as long as people have different value-beliefs, and one group seems perverse to another, the good must be a problem. To a degree it may be settled by discussion, by concessions, by forbearance. But so far as value-opponents cannot tolerate a difference there is no recourse but force. Yet force cannot establish which side is right—only which is stronger. And on each side of a value-conflict there will be doubts and questions, in private or in confidence, if people are normally reflective. A united front in public is possible only through a provisional suppression of all but a few points. So Gide's treatment of the problem of good is less limited than might be suggested by his location of it within the class he happens to be familiar with.

His novel makes vivid the difficulties of a thoughtful person or group in approaching values, apart from and in connection with the opposition of others who have a different standpoint. The focus is on the cleavage in any society between old and young; between those who feel that they know better because of what they have done and gone through, and those who feel that they will do better if they can go their own way. The elders have more power to begin with, but know that might alone scarcely makes right in the minds of the young—as their minds develop. The time comes soon when the young feel their strength in contrast to the growing weakness of age, and tend to identify their advantage with their right. The elders, becoming painfully aware of inadequacy, cover it up with authority and hypocrisy. The youngsters, quite as uncomfortable in their own sense of inferiority, try to compensate through bravado and reserve. The sincerity which Gide considers the basic requirement of good relationships becomes almost impossible.

For a man to believe in life and human nature and write *Les Faux-Monnayeurs* may seem paradoxical. The explanation of the author's attitude and procedure is that he seeks the truth, and relies upon scientific method for getting at it, even as a novelist. To believe in life intelligently is not to deny its evils, but to take note of them and know how to attack them. "You are well aware that the stumblingblock to my optimism is not in sorrow and adversity, but in the ugliness and malignity of men" (*OC* XV, 402). This is what he must face, because it is most discouraging to good will. He need not pretend he has the answer, and it might be well not to show it if he were sure of it. As he said in connection with *La Porte Étroite*, "It is better to make the reader think than to give him ready-made opinions" (*OC* VI, 360). Premature conclusions should be avoided especially in psychology, for there seem to be no "simple sentiments" and "many discoveries in the human heart are yet to be made" (*OC* IX, 122). A writer who turned from poetry to prose because he wanted to be not hallucinated but awake to reality was not going to simplify the facts to unify a story.

Whatever edge a novelist might have had over a psychologist in the way of insight, was no reason why a novel now should forfeit the recognized value of approaching problems in the spirit of experiment and hypothesis. Gide was impressed by the possibilities of this spirit even in poetry, as he commented on Valéry's many years of study for the production of a few poems which he regarded as experiments—much as Leonardo considered his paintings (essay on Valéry in *Incidences*). Leonardo's habit of notebooks, also found in Valéry, was no less characteristic of Gide. For him to present as a novel what appear to be the notes for writing a novel, about a group of persons and their problems, was in keeping with his experimental temper. This is what makes *Les Faux-Monnayeurs* hard to read—it is like a laboratory notebook. Some of the notes

257

overflowed into *Le Journal des Faux-Monnayeurs* and into Gide's regular *Journal*, though they might have been included in the novel but for overloading.

Should a novel be composed of notes? And how much should it include of all that could be noted in connection with it? The question of what a novel, particularly this one, should be, is taken up at length within it. But the author could explain briefly that he would have it "a crossroads—a rendezvous of problems" (*OC* XI, 380). And he said it would be up to the reader to work the book out. To disturb him was the author's business, though he knew people wanted to be reassured (*Le Journal des Faux-Monnayeurs,* 29 March, 1925). Put at ease they would not reflect, and the human lot needed reflection. The problems of life were essentially those of the novel. To ask how it should be written was the same as asking how life should be lived. But it would be ironical if the only answer was the advice to realize the presence of problems and become uneasy about them. Granted that complacency should be overcome, this would scarcely be a sufficient reply to Pauline, the worried mother of boys, who had been obliged to draw in her hopes and almost to wish she had never had children. She said to her half-brother Édouard, whose reflection upon the effort to write a novel is central in *Les Faux-Monnayeurs,* that the novelist should solve problems which in life were not resolved but simply continued (Part Three, Ch. X).

Although he is at a loss to satisfy her—and there is nothing he can say to change the fact that her husband's relation to her has been false, that her oldest boy Vincent went completely to the dogs, while Georges is in a

258

very bad way—Édouard has made her deeply grateful for his good influence on Olivier. The love between the uncle and this youth shines out as the saving thing amid the surrounding deception, frustration and self-destruction. That this love can flower occasionally in a stupid society, which condemns it without a hearing, is one point of the book. A reader might think it would have been much better, if not more natural, for Édouard to have married Laura, since he had loved her, she continued to love him, and Olivier is decidedly not superior to her as a person. Bernard would have been more worthy of Édouard's affection, but needed it less. Bernard himself was capable of devotion that did much for Laura in her trouble. She and her sacrificing sister Rachel had the generosity which would have made for happiness if reciprocated on a mutual basis. Such might have been the case in the relationship of Boris and Bronja—though marred by a nervousness that was aggravated rather than assuaged by her mother Sophroniska, the doctoress—if Édouard had not taken Boris away.

The pseudo-psychiatry of Sophroniska might seem a slur upon psychoanalysis, but is rather an attack upon abuse of it. So the Azaïs-Vedel *pension*, whose religious atmosphere has the opposite of a wholesome effect upon Boris and his companions, should in fairness be charged to aberration of religion. This place is a kind of "home" where youngsters return daily for supervised study and living, after their classes in a secondary school. That this institution happens to be run by Protestants does not seem significant except to show that, whereas Gide often attacks Catholicism for obstructing progress, Protestant

259

orthodoxy is almost as anachronistic in his eyes. Catholic
and Protestant children in the novel are in the same boat
as they come together under the Azaïs-Vedel care. Certainly Édouard's familiarity with that care made it inexcusable for him to entrust Boris to it in his neurotic state.

But the idea was not to help Boris so much as to write
a novel, and less to write one than to exhibit the problems
of writing a serious one, showing them to be the same as
those of life. For their gravity to be appreciated in a
limited space they should be shown at their worst. And,
with the corpus of Gide's work in mind, it is no exaggeration to say that for him the worst problem is the discrepancy between youth and age, when distorted by traditional
religion into a clash between insubordination and sheer
authority. Cast-off absolutes are too discredited to control the young who are left so ignorant of any other orientation that, unless they are lucky, they become victims
of impulse and unscrupulous leaders.

The subtle but powerful suggestion of this novel is that
despite bogus values, official and surreptitious, making
counterfeiters of young and old, genuine values are still
available, real appreciation of them is still possible. The
suggestion is further that, just as the young are thrown on
their own resources in the presence of elders they cannot
trust, so modern men in general must rely upon their
own wit and judgment instead of on the seniority of tradition. Gide's writing as a whole would indicate that, in
his view, tradition has not lost efficacy simply through
age but also through contrast with the growing power
and point of scientific method.

The fact that *Les Faux-Monnayeurs* is written in the
260

form of a research worker's notebook is most significant. Here, in the very technique of writing this novel, is the author's answer to the problems raised by the life it represents. If he believed in a final scheme of things, revealed by inherited religion and the rest of received culture, he and his counterfeit in Édouard would be stumped by Pauline's bitter outcry: "In life nothing is resolved; everything continues. One remains in uncertainty; and one will remain to the end without knowing what to hold to; waiting, while life continues, continues, exactly as if there were nothing. . . ." (*Les F-M*, Part Three, Ch. X). For Gide and Édouard there is no final answer in which the movement of life will come to rest. But they have an outlook enabling them to rejoice in that movement and to trust that it can be guided toward ever more worthwhile living. The idea of starting out with a fixed goal does not appeal to them even in writing a novel. Édouard is made to say: "As for me, who let mine develop without design, I hold that life never proposes anything which cannot be considered a new point of departure as well as an end. 'Could be continued' . . . it is with these words that I should like to terminate my *Faux-Monnayeurs*" (ibid., Part Three, Ch. XII). And that is practically the way Gide does end his and Édouard's novel. It reverts to Bernard's younger brother Caloub, who has not figured in the story, and the last line is Édouard's: "I am quite curious to know Caloub."

Eagerness about the young coming along is fundamental in Gide. "It has been said that I run after my youth. That is true. And not only my own. Even more than beauty, youth attracts me, with an irresistible attraction" (*Inci-*

dences, 1924 ed., 92). He adds that each generation has its message which it should be allowed to deliver. Thus his emotional responsiveness to the young is supported by the intellectual and moral conviction that wisdom will not die with the old. New directions unknown to them or closed for them are always opening for posterity. To doubt this would be to deny the theory of evolution which is indispensable to modern science. In turn science, with its method of observation, hypothesis and experimental verification, has been so irreversible in removing the limitations under which men have been obliged to live and think, as to be the main reason for Gide's faith in human progress. Here is the objective justification for his attitude which otherwise might be only subjective; and for his persisting in optimism despite the evil revealed in *Les Faux-Monnayeurs.*

It is science that gives the edge to Gide, that enables him to be sanguine though not hallucinated, to be serious without ceasing to be urbane and entertaining, to strike home with a light touch and oblique approach. The disturbing thing about him is that in a world largely governed by tradition and convention he investigates as if nothing were settled, and shows that nothing is. He delights in that. Yet his insight is surgical, not cynical. Among contemporary literary figures of his stature his hopefulness is almost alone. Though he has had moments of discouragement, as a sensitive intelligence must, he has never despaired for long, and has not fallen back for more than a mood upon a realm supposed to be above the battle, where what happens here is not important. He sees that inherited philosophy, religion, literature and social organization seem for the most part on the defensive against the advance of democracy. He sees that what gives power to democracy, and what makes it feared, is not only the success of science but its dependence upon free cooperation and discussion rather than upon authority and tradition. The implication is plain that appreciation of science calls for education quite different from the kind in *Les Faux-Monnayeurs*, which is obviously obsolete though not yet discredited. He realizes that values, and their inculcation, must be reconstructed in keeping with science or be dishonored.

Proust and Joyce knew this to their sorrow. Their contribution to the riches of modern consciousness need not be questioned, but they failed to see the promise of science and the social upsurge coming with it. Cherishing antiquated culture they had no idea that anything past was fecund for the future. Their misunderstanding of science killed their religion and they found nothing to replace it. Blind to the order of the signs their vast imagination was retrograde, whereas Gide has moved to meet the new day. In the light of it he sees art, religion, and culture in general becoming one with science in the endeavor to free and order the capacities of men for finer living.

Gide is a scientist in the guise of an artist. The assumption has been that these roles are contrary. That Leonardo and Goethe turned from one to the other has seemed superhuman. With Gide, however, it is not a question of versatility—now artistic pages, now scientific notes. He has assimilated the novel to the laboratory notebook. He does not pick some branch of science to make fiction of it, except in touching upon Sophroniska's psychiatry

263

and—in *Les Caves du Vatican*—having fun with the experiments of Anthime Armand-Dubois, who was trying to reduce all animal activity to the tropisms he observed in rats. The tone of this passage would not suggest respect for science. And Gide is never trying to popularize it as Sinclair Lewis did in familiarizing himself with medical practice and research to get material for *Arrowsmith*. Gide is not a writer imagining how it would feel to be a scientist, but a researcher in his own right. He does not mention science except incidentally. He is occupied with using its method as the tool of his own investigation.

Although this was not announced as his program he always seemed aware of what he was doing. And he was "particularly pleased" to have his turn of mind identified as scientific in *André Gide* by Ramon Fernandez. "In this I well know today that I am distinguished especially from those of my generation and from most of those who are younger" (31 May, 1931). To make sure of being understood, Gide patted Fernandez for being careful to point out that it is the procedure of the experimental or "natural" sciences which is in question here; not that of "sciences called 'pure' and deductive." The latter have their long-standing importance, and retain it at least as the phase of logically developing the hypothesis within the experimental technique. But what is exciting to Gide in science, and in his own use of its method, is the way it opens up the possibilities of life and throws off the authority of the past: lifting the exception from ignominy to the status of discovery; raising the gratuitous act from truantry and crime to the organized quest of progress.

He knows that for science the only resting place is on

the oars of progress. "No theory is good unless it permits not repose but the greatest work. No theory is good but on condition of being used for going ahead." Theory is for the release of living. One should not be intimidated: no single theory is final. "The greatness of Dostoyevsky comes from the fact that he . . . never let himself be reduced by *a* theory" (*OC* IX, 121–122).

Appreciation of scientific theory and practice as the means of increasing human freedom separates Gide from the "naturalists" who preceded him in assimilating science to literature. Balzac and the Goncourt brothers had relied heavily upon observation and documentation in the effort to record actual existence; believing in a tight relation between the environment and the quality of life. Yet they were romantic in thinking the writer himself should remain aloof in the attitude of art for art. To Zola a novel was an experiment exhibiting the determination of character by heredity and circumstance. The tendency of the naturalist school, despite its vaunted objectivity, was to seek out depressing situations and degraded figures, though this did not weaken Zola's faith in brotherhood and justice. Depicting the evils of industrialism was an important step toward their removal, but social idealism was logically inconsistent for writers accepting the 17th century interpretation of science as teaching lack of freedom in a reign of law.

But while Gide understood that science was the key to release men from pressures hemming them in, by giving them control of energies and connections which had been ungovernable, he was not naive enough to suppose men would realize over night, more than from Deuteronomy

265

30:15, that a new day had set life and good before them, along with death and evil, with the power and the responsibility of choice. He recognized that in men personally and institutionally there was obtuseness to improvement, amounting to perversity. This quality so impressed and distressed him as to make it sensible to believe in the devil, and have him be the chief character in *Les Faux-Monnayeurs*.

By preventing sincerity Gide's devil forestalls the honest facing of problems and the open cooperation basic to science. One may say that blaming the devil for the difficulty people have in getting together and dealing squarely with their lot is just a means of expressing how great the difficulty is. But this needs to be expressed. Human beings are so irrational, between impulse and habit within and social forces without, that they cannot easily change their ways or attitudes even when the advantage of doing so is evident. The reconstructive role of scientific intelligence comes into conflict with the inertia of ignorance and fear, laziness and selfishness, weighted by self-deception. It is not only convenient to call all this the devil, but a warning of the serious opposition to be met in the struggle for human decency.

Speaking of the devil, Gide explained in the *Journal:* "I am consciously using here, as before, words and images which imply a mythology that it is not absolutely important for me to believe. That it is the most eloquent for explaining an inner drama is enough for me. Psychology in turn may explain it, as meteorology has certain Greek myths . . . I do not mind!" (*OC* VIII, 220). Another time he said psychology could not discountenance the
266

devil any more than evolution could supplant God, and that his whole life would have been clearer if he could have *supposed* the demon. "It is completely indifferent to me, moreover, whether this name of demon is or is not the true name for what I want to say, and I grant that I name it thus for convenience. If someone comes along to show me that he does not inhabit hell but my blood, my loins or my insomnia, does he think to suppress him thus? When I say the Evil One, I know what this phrase designates, just as clearly as I know what the word God stands for. I outline his form by the absence of every virtue" (*ibid.*, 350–351).

Yet, just as Gide could not be satisfied that he knew what he wanted to mean by the idea of God until he had sifted from it much that was unacceptable to him and had worked over the remainder in terms of a humanistic philosophy, so his notion of the devil was not arrived at merely by imagining the opposite of God, or of every virtue. In the first place, virtue for Gide goes beyond the conventional contraries of good and evil to include something from each. In the second place, even the devil of tradition, far from being altogether bad, has had the engaging educational role of Goethe's Mephistopheles and the Promethean resistance to arbitrary power of Milton's Satan. Gide shifts from devil to demon—from the less equivocal term for the personification of evil to the word which has meant a good or bad genius and was ready to mean both in *Les Faux-Monnayeurs*. Bernard's demon at the beginning is an angel toward the end. And the angel too is equivocal: referred to by Bernard as "I know not what demon" when he comes to tell Édouard about his

267

experience with the angel (*Les F-M,* Part Three, Ch. XIV). In Blake's *Marriage of Heaven and Hell,* which Gide translated, there is a concluding *Note:* "This Angel, who is now become a Devil, is my particular friend."

Gide had said: "What kept me from believing in the devil was that I was not very sure of detesting him" (*OC* VIII, 137). He had also said: "Belief in angels is so disagreeable to me that I hasten to add that what we have here is only an image—though such as expresses my thought quite well" (*OC* VII, 566). Feeling the need of such an image in his novel he prepared for it from the first: by making the Luxembourg Garden, where the angel was to appear, seem as "mythical as the forest of Arden" (*Journal des F-M,* 27 December, 1923).

The devil or demon (except in becoming an angel) would need no particular setting because he "would circulate incognito through the whole book, while his reality would be affirmed the more, the less one believed in him" (*ibid.,* 13 January, 1921). Passavant, the popular novelist, whose literary taste and moral influence on young men irritate Édouard, is something of a devil, but too easily spotted and resisted to be very dangerous—except to the unresisting. Really to reckon with is the demon working on Bernard at the outset; on Vincent when he decides to gamble with the money he could have used to help Laura (*Les F-M,* Part One, Ch. IV); on Vincent and Lady Lilian when she gets the money he won; again when he comes back to find her alone (*ibid.,* Part One, Ch. V); and finally after they have gone off together (*ibid.,* Part Three, Ch. XI). It is this formidable devil who must be blamed for whispering to Édouard that it would be a good thing

SCIENCE FOR LIFE AND ART

to send Boris to the Azaïs-Vedel house (*ibid.*, Part Two, Ch. VII); and who must be suspected behind the mischief at several other points.

As Klaus Mann has observed, however, Bernard's demon is not simply evil; and is not just the reckless energy of Lafcadio; but also a reflective, searching, generous spirit like that of Gide's Prodigal Son (*André Gide: The Crisis of Modern Thought*, 188, ff.). Bernard is driven to run away from home, to rely on his own wit and will out in the world; yet also to sit down and study, to take examinations and get his degree at the Sorbonne. When the diploma is acquired his demonic urges, becoming highly conscious, appear in the form of an angel. Rather, some of his urges assume this aspect: those which constitute the tendency to conform, to fall in and follow along. This side of Bernard's nature, though it could turn up with the suddenness of his own impulse, really is a guise of restraint laid upon the individual by society, more subtle than external pressure—working through the social molding of the self, to become as intimate with its initiative as the "me" is with the "I."

In Mead's *Mind, Self and Society* the sessions between the "I" of the psychophysical organism and the "me" of the generalized other (which is developed in the private forum through taking over the responses and roles of other persons and groups) would provide the natural basis for Bernard's conversation and struggle with his angel—and for the fact that neither could down the other. Gide meant this drama when he said: "The only drama which really interests me, and which I would relate again, is the contest of each being with what keeps it from being

269

authentic, with what is opposed to its integrity, its integration. The obstacle is usually within the self. And all the rest is only accident" (*OC* XV, 307).

The angel came at the moment when the ocean of life, vast before Bernard, made him consider what course to take. The angel led him into a church where he could not pray, because he believed in no god: "but his heart was filled with a loving need to give, to sacrifice; he offered himself." The renewing spirit of religion was in him, though not in the old mode. He noticed a stupid student, who was lucky to pass the final examination, buying a candle. Bernard, going out to buy cigarettes, wondered why the angel had left him. Did they have "nothing to say to each other?" But the angel came back to say that if he was not to live at random he must serve something and find out what. Asked for guidance, the light-footed figure took him to a crowded hall where orators were urging loyalty to tradition, acceptance of regimentation, and distributing pledges. Bernard, looking round, saw the classmate who had bought a candle in gratitude for passing, and saw his own older brother who had never left the paternal roof. "Do you think I should sign?" The angel replied: "Yes, certainly, if you are not sure of yourself." Bernard tossed away the paper, saying, "I have no more doubts." The orator was telling how one could avoid ever being mistaken: "give up ever judging for oneself, and submit always to the judgment of one's superiors."

"These superiors, who are they?" Bernard demanded; and suddenly a great anger seized him, because he was divided. He rebelled, yet was tempted to sign for service in a cause which, he admitted later, "seemed to me beautiful and noble." He wanted the angel to go up and floor the speaker. But the angel smiled: "It is with you that I shall wrestle. Tonight, will you?" The struggle would take place in Bernard's room, in Bernard's self, between his independence and his reverence. But first the angel took him on a tour: showing him the self-centered anxious rich. Bernard asked if that was the image of happiness, "feeling his heart fill with tears." Then they visited the poor of the city: "disease, prostitution, shame, crime and hunger. It was only then that Bernard took the angel's hand, and the angel averted his face to weep" (*Les F-M*, Part Three, Ch. XIII).

Confronted with the evil of the world, Bernard felt the old need of comfort and support. The angel, seeing afresh how deep and instinctive that need was, yet how inadequate the ancient resignation he personified, was troubled to have Bernard turn to him in spite of himself, on the eve of struggling with the strength of tradition. The youth and the angel wrestled all night; or the youth's demon wrestled with his angel, as evenly matched as a man's own "I" and "me." Within the close quarters of a room which was the self, they had it out: the demon of release that spurred Bernard to break free for better things; and the angel who was the reflection, the smile, the anguish of a social but passionate intelligence in the effort to become wholly conscientious.

Though neither won, Bernard was glad to have held his own, as he had to against himself. But he was able to feel that on both sides of the inner struggle, the tendencies which were his "real" self, had come through. His

271

creative energy had stood up to inhibitions fed by social inertia. In that good sense the demon had won. On the other hand, the genuine needs and values of the human community had enabled the angel to overcome the selfishness that might have kept individual initiative from a progressive role in the reconstruction of society. In the sense of irresponsibility the demon had been defeated. So Bernard felt matured. A larger and more balanced self had been achieved. His audacity was not gone, but he would no longer be ready to pay for it with the happiness of others. Aware of his force, he wanted to put it to the best use. Feeling the need of guidance, and unwilling to accept it simply from others, he said he would have to find it in himself—in self-development. But how would he know what to develop in himself? That was the question he had been debating in the all-night tussle with the angel.

Toward morning he had got so tired he had thought of volunteering for military service before his class was called, he told Édouard when it was all over. "To avoid the question is not to settle it," Édouard replied. Bernard said he agreed—that was why he was coming for advice. Édouard said he had none to give: except to learn from living, and to follow one's bent, "provided it is upward."

All that had been gained in self-knowledge from the encounter with the angel might seem to have evaporated; else why seek advice now? But, while Édouard tactfully undervalued what he had to offer, he confirmed the upshot of the angel-episode: that a man should find his own way, if able to, and if careful to consider his social responsibility. To go without a fixed goal would not mean haphazard living, if one progressively projected a course ahead, Bernard thought. And Édouard said the same was true of literature: "only those count who launch themselves toward the unknown" (*Les F-M,* Part Three, Ch. XIV).

Gide said he wanted *Les Faux-Monnayeurs* to keep springing up afresh: "each chapter should pose a new problem, be an opening, a direction, a jetty ahead—of the reader's mind. But he should leave me as the slung stone leaves the sling." *Journal des F-M,* 10 April, 1924). Such a book could not be easy. "The extreme conciseness of my notations hardly gives the superficial reader time to enter into the game. This book demands a slowness of reading and a meditation which one is seldom ready to accord at first" (*OC* XV, 298). But Gide had faith that if his book was found worth coming back to, it would surprise people: because it undertook with uncommon seriousness to close the gap between literature and life, by showing the main problems of one to be essentially those of the other; and by suggesting that the path-finding of science, beyond the fixed and final, was right for both life and art.

That such a view is ultimately legitimate cannot be admitted by anyone committed to an established scheme of things. Thus René Schwob, though able to praise *Les Faux-Monnayeurs* for honesty, musical complexity and originality, considers that the refusal to discern a plan already laid down for life amounts to glorifying "the disorder of natural reality" as a mere "play of waves." (*Le Vrai Drame d'André Gide,* 324–325). He cannot see the difference between disorder and the advance of creative intelligence into the future.

273

The risk in approaching value-problems with the experimental attitude, when not guarded by the self-correcting and other-regarding caution of the scientist, is brought out in the novel. Rejection of religion does not constitute scientific training, or justify indulgence. One wonders what will become of Sarah Vedel when she announces, after Bernard has left her, that she will rejoin her emancipated English friend who "intended to live as she saw fit." (*Les F-M*, Part Three, Ch. XIV). Bernard's progressive thinking should not be considered more than incidental to Sarah's downfall: when waiting to meet him she had resolved "to accord herself every license, dare everything." She had her own demon. And she was instructed by the example of her sisters: "she regarded the pious resignation of Rachel as trickery; saw Laura's marriage only as a dismal bargain . . ." (*Les F-M*, Part Three, Ch. VIII).

Laura had no illusions about her marriage. It was just the best way out of her mistake, which was one that religious people often make without benefit of advanced ideas. And it was unkind to think Rachel not genuine in self-denial. If she deceived anyone it was herself, in letting others take advantage of her willing drudgery. But it may have been the author's intention to show that she was no more self-deceived or futile than those around her, though she never rebelled against futility.

A glimpse is given of the fate of Vincent and Lady Lilian when they went off to do as they pleased, and found themselves driven by the demon of boredom, then by that of sheer adventure. After apparently having killed her, Vincent was found thinking he was the devil. Yet he had kept his "scientific" interest in plants and insects (*Les F-M.*, Part Three, Ch. XVI). This was all that remained of his medical training and promise as a biologist. The only use he had made of science was to entertain himself and friends with its wonders. He did not let it light or lead him. His affair with Laura was perhaps understandable, but he did not consider its possibilities very carefully or face the outcome honestly. The counterfeit company of Passavant and Lady Lilian found him fatally devoid of caution that a scientific training would have made instinctive if it had been thorough. But thoroughness had been confused with intensive narrowness. The human scope of the scientific attitude had never dawned on Vincent. He did not give it a chance to help him. His science had been generalized enough to remove the old religious guidance, but not enough to replace it with the morality of science.

The diabolic Strouvilhou said it was a shame that science was not turned to improvement of the human race, as of domestic animals and grasses; and his idea was to eliminate the weak, for he made no secret of hating his fellow men. What he held against the arts and sciences was that fundamentally they "were working for human welfare." He would try to reverse this. That a man like him should see the kinship of art and science in their humanitarian tendency, and that it would be hard to reverse, is plausible support of Gide's scientific faith, from an unexpected quarter. Strouvilhou is clear that for literature to serve his man-hating animus, words would have to be used in a way to render them unintelligible (*Les F-M*, Part Three, Ch. XI). The implication is that if they retain their meaning they will tend to make the same sense

275

as science; and that science and art alike are characteristically devoted to clarification, truth, and the freedom that truth brings.

When science is thought of as systematic effort to find out what is good for men to cultivate, and what is bad for them to do, the moral of *Les Faux-Monnayeurs* is apparent: that the characters' troubles are due to their lack of clarity about themselves, their world, their relationships with one another. This confusion is kept up by the great difficulty of being sincere and open. What is most needed, and most conspicuously absent here, is primary in science: honest observation of a problematic situation to locate the crucial data, careful recording of what is found, free discussion of it, and communication for the benefit of all mankind. This is the ethical code of science. Without some approximation to it men are not in a position to collaborate in formulating a course of action or trying it out as a likely hypothesis. With a few exceptions, the characters in *Les Faux-Monnayeurs* do not ascertain and do not dare to face the facts in their case, much less communicate them clearly and early to people who might help. The relations between husbands and wives, parents and children, make it almost impossible to confide. The structure of a society based largely upon force and fraud is indicated as back of the trouble within the family. And, back of all in this novel, is the role of traditional religion and morality: substituting metaphysical for actual problems, and nursing the worst evils by cultivating the sense of inferiority and fear. Morbidity and hypocrisy flourish, instead of the sincerity that a scientific education would put first.

276

Armand Vedel, the minister's son, says he can be sincere only in joking; but is heartfelt in declaring "horror, hatred of all that is called Virtue." He tells Olivier: "Do not try to understand. You don't know what having a puritan education from the first can do to us" (*Les F-M*, Part Three, Ch. XVI). Olivier might be supposed to have an idea of this. Although raised a Catholic, he had spent some time in the atmosphere of Armand's family, and felt that release from moral confusion had come only through Édouard's understanding love. Olivier Molinier's younger brother Georges, presumably given the same training at home, was becoming corrupt; though perhaps not irretrievably like Vincent. Meanwhile Armand's older brother Alexandre, who had, in Rimbaud-fashion, escaped to Africa from official Christianity and the modern complexity it could not cope with, was squeezing money from his poor sister Rachel and apparently having a season in hell, when appropriately joined by Olivier's older brother Vincent in the role of the devil himself. It seemed to make little difference whether a family was Protestant or Catholic. The inability of parents to guide their children, the children's flouting of guidance, were the same.

Parental solicitude was justified by some knowledge of life's dangers, while filial rejection of restraint arose not only from a corresponding ignorance but more from the elders' ineptness. This is fully shown in the Azaïs-Vedel family, and in their educational establishment which is represented as better than average. Old Azaïs, who has the main responsibility, spreads hypocrisy through the inflexibility of his religious sincerity, for everyone is obliged to fit in with him. His daughter has lost touch with reality

277

so completely that little can be expected of her; while her husband, the pastor Vedel, is too busy outside the house to give attention to its problems, except with consoling phrases. He will never discuss anything; as if to pause and reflect would be disastrous for him. It would be indiscreet to pry into what he really thinks. His faith is not so much a matter of what he believes as what he has made it his business to preach. That is his role, his son explains. "He has stuffed his life with a pile of obligations which would lose all significance if his conviction faltered; so that this conviction turns out to be demanded and kept up by them. . . . He is no longer free not to believe." And the family livelihood depends upon "papa's faith," Armand says (*Les F-M*, Part Three, Ch. XVI).

Here is the extreme case, but in the novel it has the effect of a symbol with wide application. Pastor Vedel represents dependence upon tradition, through moral and intellectual failure to join the effort to understand current needs; and through economic interest in maintaining an outmoded structure of belief. The plight of his children is the price.

Another victim is La Pérouse, the broken music teacher who tries to earn his bread by supervising and tutoring youngsters in the *pension* who do not hesitate to make his life miserable. In a nightmare of insecurity his revulsion against traditional belief suggests how little comfort it may give when supposedly most wanted; and that society is as far from a scientific sympathy with the emotional requirements of the old as of the young. He and his grandson Boris are in the same lonely predicament, under the wings of the Vedel faith.

From the circumstance of being a bastard, Boris does not gain the self-reliance of Bernard. Frail and afraid, Boris turns to imaginary goods, away from the real ones that cost effort. He is shamed by Sophroniska into abandoning a crude escapism for the "puerile mysticism" he shares with her daughter Bronja. Inconsistently the doctor-mother thinks this a great improvement. Although she does not herself believe in the content of orthodox faith, "she believes in the efficaciousness of faith." She likes to have her daughter "see angels" and encourage Boris to hope that he will (*Les F-M*, Part Two, Ch. V). Édouard rashly supposed it would wean him from make-believe to put him in the Azaïs-Vedel house, and failed to foresee that having him there would be no comfort to La Pérouse.

When Bernard comes into the room he shares with Boris, to struggle with the angel, the unhappy lad seems to be asleep. He is in bed with a letter from Bronja, telling him she will not live. Unable to see Bernard's angel, Boris thinks the agitation of his room-mate is a way of praying; and prays himself to Bronja not to go from him with her angels (*Les F-M*, Part Three, Ch. XIII). The longed-for vision of them, through which Boris would like to compensate for lack of self-development, is pale beside the wrestling presence that makes a man of Bernard. A person's demons or angels appear to be no more effective for good or evil than he is. Learning a month later that Bronja is dead, Boris can no longer believe in the angels he wanted to see. Meanwhile Bernard, whom he was beginning to trust, has moved out of the house.

It is hinted more than once that Boris might have made friends with one or two of the boys he sits with in the

279

study hall—enough for protection (*Les F-M*, Part Three, Ch. IV, XVII). But the bit of friendship he has desperate need of is not forthcoming. There is nothing to stop the one boy who definitely has it in for him. That boy, exasperated by the very charm of Boris and his helpless isolation, takes advantage of his hunger for companionship to undo him. That boy, Ghéridanisol, is backed by the fiendish Strouvilhou who introduces from the outside the evil that the novel's guardians of education do not suspect until too late, although a modicum of intelligent interest in their charges would have saved the day.

The evil is not presented as inevitable but as allowed to enter by men who had the power and should have had the intelligence and will to head it off, in their position. The idea is clearly that the impulsive energy and ingenuity of the boys could have been turned to constructive, happy use, if scientific sympathy had been brought to bear upon children of whom Strouvilhou was one a few years before. He does not simply bring vice from a wicked world beyond the halls of education. It is poetic justice that he pays back his alma mater in her own coin, by exploiting the counterfeit guidance that had made him or let him go out what he was.

One may say that a Strouvilhou or Ghéridanisol might appear in the best regulated institution and be incorrigible—the devil would see to it—and that if the Vedel place was responsible for its alumni, it should have credit for the qualities of Édouard, if not also for the virtues of Rachel. Yet they were both warped by it: he less seriously, because he got out. Still he was so conditioned by his experience there that he failed to see how unwholesome it would be for Boris. No one could have predicted the climax of the mistake it was to put him there, but the tragedy of it would have been much the same even if he had lived to tell the tale.

The suffering of a sensitive boy and the degradation of hardier boys in such a situation was an old story when Gide wrote it. The poignancy of his version derives from consciousness of contrast between the educational inadequacy of tradition, with its authoritarian ignorance or indifference regarding the actual needs of children, and the promise of a democratic-scientific schooling that would focus on giving children a fuller fairer life, through guidance in more purposeful and sharable activity. Bad as matters are in *Les Faux-Monnayeurs*, they are presented as a problem that genuine interest and modern techniques could deal with—not as original sin out of reach of human effort. "There are forces in man considered bad, yet which can in their turn become elements of strength and progress," Gide was to say (at the 1935 meeting of *L'Union Pour la Vérité*, recorded in *André Gide et Notre Temps*, 30). So far as the story goes, only one member of the rising generation, Ghéridanisol, is really malignant. Even if he could not have been won over, his influence and that of his older cousin outside the walls, could have been offset—at least within the Azaïs-Vedel establishment—by some adult direction of the good will dormant in the other youngsters. But any genuine direction was lacking.

Something has been done toward making science the guide of life through education; and much is being done to make education a platform for authoritarian attempts to discredit science as having no bearing on the question of value. That *Les Faux-Monnayeurs* bears upon this question is easy to see. That it does so in the scientific spirit, and with the democratic faith, may strike one at first as being read between the lines rather than in the text. But Gide said he wrote this novel to be re-read, and that he did not expect to win his case except by appeal (*Journal des F-M*, 7 December, 1921). Only so can the case for science be won—only when its implications have been appreciated, and those of the alternative.

How a novel could help in such a case, depends upon what a novel is. It is interesting that, although Gide had called *L'Immoraliste* and *La Porte Étroite* novels (*OC* IV, 595), he came to consider *Les Faux-Monnayeurs* his first novel, and them merely stories (*récits*). "The novel, as I recognize or imagine it, brings together a diversity of viewpoints, according to the diversity of characters which it puts on the stage; it is essentially a de-concentrated work." And he remarked that "the romantics tried to distinguish themselves from the world—I to merge with it" (*OC* VI, 361–362). He could do this best in the novel because of its capacity to include something like the many-sidedness of real existence without forcing upon it a too artificial unity. Thus the novel is for Gide a way of presenting human life in the thick of its difficulties, with imagination to see trees and forest. He does not expect a novel to get men out of the woods, but has used his to reveal how the ways fork; and to compare them as in a Platonic dialogue wherein ideas are more important than persons; because, however fictitious the characters may be, the ideas are real. They are what real people

282

think about when they really think, as they must when confronted with basic issues.

In the notes he kept about the writing of *Les Faux-Monnayeurs,* Gide was thinking of what it would mean to write a pure novel, from which would be eliminated "all the elements that do not belong specifically to the novel" (*Journal des F-M,* 1 November, 1922). One wonders what should be excluded from the novel when realizing how much Gide put in. His answer would be that by omitting the obvious he could save room for the important, and for him the important thing is: the discrepancy between what is and his idea of it, which is also his idea of what should be.

His novelist, Édouard, says the subject of the book he is working on will be "the rivalry between the real world and the representation of it that we fashion" (*Les F-M,* Part Two, Ch. V). How to squeeze the world into a perspective, is the problem. Édouard has said that he wants to get in everything. The attempt to get in the whole is part of the whole, and the most interesting part. He cannot get in much without stylizing it. How will he stylize without distorting? The question is how to plan the book. A plan laid down in the beginning would falsify the subject, if this is to be "the struggle between what reality offers and what he tries to make of it" (*Les F-M,* Part Two, Ch. III). If the struggle is genuine the course of it can be written down only as the progress of a research project can be recorded in a notebook. This is what Édouard realizes. He thinks of a work of art as being, like a piece of scientific work, "the sum or the

283

product of the solutions for a succession of many minute difficulties." And he says of his own procedure: "instead of contenting myself with resolving each difficulty as it comes up, I spread out each of these difficulties; I study it" (*Les F-M*, Part Two, Ch. III).

Édouard does not arrive at the idea of including his working notes in the finished work. It is Gide who puts them into *Les Faux-Monnayeurs*. Yet much notation of his own on this novel is to be found not in it but in the *Journal des Faux-Monnayeurs* and the regular *Journal*. His novel itself, though largely made up of Édouard's reflection upon the problems of writing such a novel, with Gide's very title, is controlled for effect upon the reader, with respect to introduction of characters, fugue-like movement of dropping and picking up the revelation of relationships, gathering suspense and climax. It is unlikely that this effect could have been achieved without considerable rearrangement and pruning of the material as it was originally gathered. The ostensibly casual nature of the result must be calculated. There is only the semblance of working notes in *Les Faux-Monnayeurs,* as there is only the suggestion of living persons. A novel is a counterfeit after all, and Gide has said: "what an admirable novel that would be which would make us understand that it is false!" (*OC* XV, 195).

The idea would seem to be that truth can be approached only indirectly, only by a process of qualification wherein a one-sided stand would have to be modified. Thus a novel that would make clear its failure to corral the full truth would be most truthful, especially for one who believes the truth to be relative and developing in a dialectic of

284

discovery and revision. So Gide said of his effort to be autobiographical: "I am a being of dialogue; everything in me conflicts and contradicts itself. Memoirs are never more than half sincere: everything is always more com· plicated than one says. It may even be that one comes closer to the truth in the novel" (*Si le Grain ne Meurt,* note at end of Part One). In contrast to a simple narrative, the diversity of viewpoints which can be comprised in a novel enables it to grapple more effectively with truth, by turning up many aspects of reality, as hypotheses give science a multiple leverage on fact.

By casting his novel in the form of a laboratory note-book, Gide has made obvious the kinship which is always there between the most serious literature and science. The letters, diaries, and notebooks of many writers have revealed the tentative, exploratory, empirical character of their imagination; regardless of how much revision they did on particular pieces. The correction of a previous writing might appear in a later one; though refusal to alter anything, as in the case of Francis Jammes, struck Gide as inability to think. The way thinking writers work has been overlooked in awed admiration of their finished work. The same thing tends to happen when the results of scientific labor are presented as if they had appeared in their final form to certain men. In any field, the flash of inspiration fades out if not worked out with patience. Perhaps because, in comparison with the popular notion of the artist, the scientist has been more modest and honest, while his admirers have been more eager to learn than to be impressed, the painstaking of science is better known than that of art. But Gide's purpose is not just to bring out

285

that writing a serious novel is, like a scientific project, first of all a matter of taking notes on a problematic situation. His further aim is affirmation, through his art, of the idea that probing problems in the manner of science is the method of creative intelligence in general, over against adherence to authority and tradition.

So when Bernard comes to Édouard for advice on how to direct his energy, how to know his goal, Édouard applies to living the answer he has found for writing: to push off toward the unknown, following one's bent, "provided it is upward." This formula is so simple that Bernard wonders for a moment, but it is significant that he accepts it without much hesitation. To his youthful self-confidence no explanation is necessary. He will put his mind on the practical matter of earning a living, letting self-development take care of itself. Since he cannot support himself without entering into social organization, the implication is: when men together go about the natural business of life, with something like his buoyancy and decency, with the best education they can get, and after wrestling in dead earnest with opposing possibilities, they must trust themselves to go on their own. There is no advice beyond that, except for those who lose their nerve. For them convention is ready, and orators with formulas of obedience.

To see what Gide means by going upward or forward, it is necessary to review his humanistic morality and religion, his faith in sympathy and intelligence, in democracy and science. This is what enables him to go on believing that life is good, and will be better, despite all the wrong and suffering. If one cannot see the goodness

286

of life to begin with, the idea of improving it with science is absurd. But he is not afraid to assume the natural value of life. His Laura says in her trouble that her mistake was to stop expecting anything more of life (*Les F-M*, Part Two, Ch. IV). He suggests that losing the sense that life is worth while constitutes in every case a problem, to be met with the method of science.

It would seem that in his own case the saving sense of life-value came from taking the Gospel seriously. One might ask what authority or validity the Gospel could have for him, beyond the fact that it appealed to him, once he gave up belief in its supernatural origin. It would be easy to answer that his biography accounted for his value-feeling, and say that Protestant upbringing implanted it in him so that it stuck when he became a humanist. The question would remain: whether one could justify believing in the rightness of social reform on a wholly naturalistic basis. It would not be enough to say that humanists happen to be social meliorists and that from their point of view this is a natural and normal position to take. Holding a position, finding it widely shared, and feeling that all good men would share it if they understood it, is different from saying that all men ought to share it. If they have another outlook, how can they be persuaded to give it up? They may be forced to, but a humanist does not want his social idealism reduced to might is right.

He would like to show that his ideals are reasonable, and he would like to say they are reasonable in the sense of being scientific rather than rational. For he rejects the old belief in a faculty of reason, innate and necessarily

287

the same in all men. The humanist believes that intellectual equipment varies with training and environment. And for him the problem-solving intelligence does not work purely by thinking, but with the help of operation and experiment. Men who challenge the cultural conclusions of that intelligence, and wonder about its theoretical foundation, feel they have not received a satisfactory answer from philosophers. It may be unfair to expect a literary man, though philosophical, to succeed if professional philosophers have failed to give a systematic and intellectually tight argument. Yet the imagination of Gide, if not his philosophy, hit upon something often overlooked by professorial minds.

Whether he fully justified it or not, there grew on him a faith in human dignity, a conviction that all men were basically entitled to the same consideration, whether they had the same endowment or not—and much as many of them pained him. "The stupid remarks of my neighbors last night at the movies in Nice! Though rich and 'distinguished.' But it is for those people that the films are turned out. Success depends on them. They are numbers. They are humanity. . . . Where Flaubert laughed I feel only an immense sadness" (*OC* XV, 334).

Though this sadness has been offset by an enormous hope in science, Gide's diabolism keeps his optimism from being the easy kind that often weakens humanist thinkers, with their confidence that changing the outer conditions of life will be enough to make it wholesome. His dealings with the devil show the need of psychiatric techniques for controlling the irrationality and insincerity that vitiate

288

intelligence and good intentions. The ambiguity of his devil is suggestive: symbol of impulsiveness that might be channeled constructively, as promises to happen with Olivier and does happen with Bernard; symbol also of deceit and cruelty that defy all decency in several characters. The unhappy Boris, as a victim not only of other boys but of blundering psychotherapy, shows what problems await the coming science of human nature. But so many problems have been solved by science that its known limitations are all provisional.

Faith that life is good, that its evils can steadily be removed or softened, is justified by the results—if the justifying ones are trusted and the others can be treated as problems. From this standpoint the worst evils thrive upon reluctance to use the resources of science for human benefit, and upon effort to restrict benefit to a few people only. The use of science to kill and torture may be considered evidence that science is just a tool, equally serviceable for good or ill, hence needing to be guided from higher ground. But when science is taken in the broad sense of free inquiry into any problem, and the will to cope with it through joint application of men's experimental intelligence, interacting with the natural environment, in the systematic and self-corrective effort to improve the human situation, there is no higher ground for Gide. Belief that there is something higher, and the role it plays in holding up progress, is the target of his art.

He would have men lower their eyes to their lot, and look with the light of science upon the false relations between parents and children, upon the counterfeit education

289

they receive, and realize that from such roots misunderstanding and violence will grow in the future of individuals and of nations.

It will be objected that doom lurks in too much, not too little science in education. A specialized technical training may fail quite as badly as traditional schooling to bring about a scientific attitude toward life-problems outside the laboratory. A novel like *Les Faux-Monnayeurs* should be written about that. What is needed may seem to be not more science but a philosophy of science and its role in civilization. A philosophy in keeping with scientific method, however, is just its generalization: a realization that freedom in every sphere comes with free inquiry and discussion, with the equipment and the encouragement for a full pursuit of truth. Genuine education will lead out from the injustice of the past toward a fairer, more sharable world, made possible by the development and exercise of scientific techniques for the guidance of life, in every reach of fact and value. "Education is deliverance," said Gide (*OC* IX, 407).

This is his faith: that science will enable men to get at the roots of any problem. His hope is for a culture permeated by the honesty and patience, the cooperation and progress of science. Then art would be one with science, or at least co-scientific, like his own art which conveys the promise of achieving through science the conditions for undreamed levels of life and art.

BIBLIOGRAPHY

·I. ANDRÉ GIDE

The date and place are those of first publication. The author wishes to acknowledge his indebtedness to the bibliographies in Gide's *Interviews Imaginaires* (Jacques Schiffrin & Co., New York, 1943) and Klaus Mann's *André Gide: The Crisis of Modern Thought* (Creative Age Press, New York, 1943).

1. Books

Les Cahiers d'André Walter. (Anonymous.) Librairie Académique Didier-Perrin & Cie., Paris, 1891.

Le Traité du Narcisse. Librairie de l'Art Indépendant, Paris, 1891.

Les Poésies d'André Walter. (Anonymous.) Librairie de l'Art Indépendant, Paris, 1892.

La Tentative Amoureuse. (As above.) 1893.

Le Voyage d'Urien. (As above.) 1893.

Paludes. (As above.) 1895.

Les Nourritures Terrestres. Mercure de France, Paris, 1897.

Réflexions sur Quelques Points de Littérature et de Morale. (Anonymous.) Mercure de France, Paris, 1897.

291

ANDRÉ GIDE

Philoctète, Le Traité du Narcisse, La Tentative Amoureuse, El Hadj. [First edition of *Philoctète* and *El Hadj*.] Mercure de France, Paris, 1899.

Feuilles de Route, 1895–1896. Imprimerie N. Vandersypen, Brussels, 1899.

Le Prométhée Mal Enchaîné. Mercure de France, Paris, 1899.

Lettres à Angèle, 1898–1899. Mercure de France, Paris, 1900.

De l'Influence en Littérature. Petite Collection de l'Ermitage, Paris, 1900.

L'Immoraliste. Mercure de France, Paris, 1902.

Saül. Mercure de France, Paris, 1903.

De l'Importance du Public. Petite Collection de l'Ermitage, Paris, 1903.

Prétextes. Mercure de France, Paris, 1903.

Amyntas; Mopsus; Feuilles de Route; De Biskra à Touggourt; Le Renoncement au Voyage. Mercure de France, Paris, 1906.

Le Retour de l'Enfant Prodigue. "Vers et Prose," Paris, 1907.

Dostoïevsky d'après sa Correspondance. Jean et Berger, Paris, 1908.

Bethsabée. "Vers et Prose," Paris, 1908.

La Porte Étroite. Mercure de France, Paris, 1909.

Oscar Wilde. Mercure de France, Paris, 1910.

Nouveaux Prétextes. Mercure de France, Paris, 1911.

Charles-Louis Philippe. Figuière & Cie., Paris, 1911.

C.R.D.N. [*Corydon.* Anonymous. Imprimerie Sainte-Catherine, Bruges.] 1911.

Isabelle. N.R.F., Paris, 1911.

Souvenirs de la Cour d'Assises. N.R.F., Paris, 1914.

Les Caves du Vatican. (Anonymous.) N.R.F., Paris, 1914.

La Symphonie Pastorale. N.R.F., Paris, 1919.

Si le Grain ne Meurt. Imprimerie Sainte-Catherine, Bruges, 1920.

Morceaux Choisis. N.R.F., Paris, 1921.

Numquid et Tu . . . ? (Anonymous.) Imprimerie Sainte-Catherine, Bruges, 1922.

Dostoïevsky. Articles et Causeries. Plon-Nourrit & Cie., Paris, 1923.

Incidences. N.R.F., Paris, 1924.

Caractères. A l'Enseigne de la Porte Étroite, Paris, 1925.

Les Faux-Monnayeurs. Éditions Éos, Paris, 1925.

292

BIBLIOGRAPHY

Le Journal des Faux-Monnayeurs. Éditions Éos, Paris, 1926.
Dindiki. Éditions de la Lampe d'Aladin, Liège, 1927.
Voyage au Congo. N.R.F., Paris, 1927.
Le Retour du Tchad. N.R.F., Paris, 1927.
L'École des Femmes. N.R.F., Paris, 1929.
Essai sur Montaigne. J. Schiffrin, Éditions de la Pléiade, Paris, 1929.
Un Esprit non Prévenu. Kra, Paris, 1929.
Robert. N.R.F., Paris, 1929.
La Séquestrée de Poitiers. "Ne Jugez Pas!" collection, N.R.F., Paris, 1930.
L'Affaire Redureau. "Ne Jugez Pas!" collection, N.R.F., Paris, 1930.
Oedipe. J. Schiffrin, Éditions de la Pléiade, Paris, 1931.
Divers. N.R.F., Paris, 1931.
Pages de Journal, 1929–1932. N.R.F., Paris, 1934.
Perséphone. N.R.F., Paris, 1934.
Les Nouvelles Nourritures. N.R.F., Paris, 1935.
Nouvelles Pages de Journal, 1932–1935. N.R.F., Paris, 1936.
Geneviève. N.R.F., Paris, 1936.
Retour de l'U.R.S.S. N.R.F., Paris, 1936.
Retouches à Mon Retour de l'U.R.S.S. N.R.F., Paris, 1937.
Journal, 1899–1939. Bibliothèque de la Pléiade, N.R.F., Paris, 1939.
Oeuvres Complètes. [15 volumes, to be continued.] N.R.F., Paris, 1932–1939.
Interviews Imaginaires. Jacques Schiffrin & Co., New York, 1943.
Pages de Journal, 1939–1942. J. Schiffrin, Pantheon Books Inc., 1944. (Appended is *Dieu, Fils de l'Homme.*)
Thésée. Pantheon Books, New York, 1946.

2. Translations by Gide

L'Offrande Lyrique, by Rabindranath Tagore. N.R.F., Paris, 1913.
Typhon, by Joseph Conrad. N.R.F., Paris, 1918.
Oeuvres Choisies, by Walt Whitman. N.R.F., Paris, 1918.
Amal et la Lettre au Roi, by Rabindranath Tagore. Lucien Vogel, Paris, 1922.
La Dame de Pique, by A. Pouchkine. (With B. de Schloezer and J. Schiffrin.) J. Schiffrin, Éditions de la Pléiade, Paris, 1923.

293

Le Mariage du Ciel et de l'Enfer, by William Blake. Claude Aveline, Paris, 1923.

Antoine et Cléopâtre, by Shakespeare. Lucien Vogel, Paris, 1926.

Nouvelles, by A. Pouchkine. (With J. Schiffrin.) J. Schiffrin, Éditions de la Pléiade, Paris, 1928.

Hamlet, Ier Acte, by Shakespeare. Échanges, Paris, 1929.

Récits, by A. Pouchkine. (With J. Schiffrin.) N.R.F., Paris, 1935.

Antoine et Cléopâtre, by Shakespeare. (Translation revised and completed in 1938.) Bibliothèque de la Pléiade, N.R.F., Paris, 1938.

Hamlet, by Shakespeare. (Translation completed in 1944, edited by Jacques Schiffrin.) Pantheon Books, New York, 1945.

3. Translations of Gide into English

Prometheus Illbound (*Le Prométhée Mal Enchaîné*). Chatto & Windus, London, 1919.

Strait Is the Gate (*La Porte Étroite*). A. A. Knopf, New York, 1924.

The Vatican Swindle (*Les Caves du Vatican*) [later called *Lafcadio's Adventures*]. A. A. Knopf, New York, 1925.

Dostoievsky, with an Introduction by Arnold Bennett. A. A. Knopf, New York, 1926.

The Counterfeiters (*Les Faux-Monnayeurs*). A. A. Knopf, New York, 1927. Taken over in 1931 by The Modern Library. Reissued by A. A. Knopf, 1947.

The School of Wives (*L'École des Femmes*). A. A. Knopf, New York, 1929.

Travels in the Congo (*Voyage au Congo* and *Le Retour du Tchad*). A. A. Knopf, New York, 1929.

The Immoralist (*L'Immoraliste*). A. A. Knopf, New York, 1930.

Two Symphonies (*Isabelle* and *La Symphonie Pastorale*). A. A. Knopf, New York, 1931.

If It Die (*Si le Grain ne Meurt*). [Limited edition.] Random House, New York, 1935.

Return from the U.S.S.R. (*Retour de l'U.R.S.S.*). A. A. Knopf, New York, 1937.

Afterthoughts on the U.S.S.R. (*Retouches à mon Retour de l'U.R.S.S.*). The Dial Press, New York, 1938.

294

BIBLIOGRAPHY

The Living Thoughts of Montaigne: Presented by André Gide. Longmans, Green & Co., New York, 1939.

II. SECONDARY STUDIES

Bernstein, Henry, et al., *Hommage à André Gide,* Paris, 1928.

Braak, Sybrandi, *André Gide et l'Ame Moderne,* Amsterdam, 1921.

Drain, Henri, *Nietzsche et Gide,* Paris, 1932.

Du Bos, Charles, *Le Dialogue avec Gide,* Paris, 1929.

Fayer, Mischa Harry, *Gide, Freedom and Dostoyevsky,* Burlington, Vt., 1946. (This excellent book came to hand too late to be used.)

Fernandez, Ramon, *André Gide,* Paris, 1931. (One of the best.)

Fernandez, Gide, et al., *André Gide et Notre Temps,* Paris, 1935. (An important discussion by Gide's critics, with his replies.)

Gouiran, Emile, *André Gide: Essai de Psychologie Littéraire,* Paris, 1934.

Hytier, Jean, *André Gide,* Paris, 1946. (This expert analysis was received too late to be used.)

Lalou, René, *André Gide,* Strasbourg, 1928.

Mann, Klaus, *André Gide: The Crisis of Modern Thought,* New York, 1943.

Martinet, Edouard, *André Gide: l'Amour et la Divinité,* Paris, 1931. (Brings out the significance of Gide's Protestantism in his work.)

Naville, Claude, *André Gide et le Communisme,* Paris, 1936.

Pierre-Quint, Léon, *André Gide: Sa Vie, Son Oeuvre,* Paris, 1933.

Rouveyre, André, *Le Reclus et le Retors: Gourmont et Gide,* Paris, 1927.

Schreiber, Lotte, *Leben und Denken im Werk von André Gide* (doctoral dissertation at the University of Berlin), Berlin, 1933.

Schwob, René, *Le Vrai Drame d'André Gide,* Paris, 1932.

Souday, Paul, *André Gide,* Paris, 1927.

Wittrock, Willy, *Der Gottesbegriff im Werk André Gides,* Marburg-Lahn, 1936.

INDEX

INDEX

INDEX